GW00578159

Sir John Hawkwood

Sir John Hawkwood
An English Mercenary Commander of the
14th Century

John Temple Leader

Translated by

Leader Scott (Lucy Baxter)

LEONAUR

Sir John Hawkwood
An English Mercenary Commander of the 14th Century
by John Temple Leader
Translated by Leader Scott (Lucy Baxter)

First published under the title
Sir John Hawkwood (L'Acuto)

Leonaur is an imprint of Oakpast Ltd

Copyright in this form © 2020 Oakpast Ltd

ISBN: 978-1-78282-896-9 (hardcover)
ISBN: 978-1-78282-897-6 (softcover)

http://www.leonaur.com

Publisher's Notes

Contents

Preface

The history of the mercenary companies in Italy no longer remains to be told; it having been published in 1844 by Ercole Ricotti; however, several successive monographs on the same subject have produced such a wealth of information from new sources that Ricotti's work, estimable as it is, almost requires to be rewritten. The *Archivio Storico Italiano* has already recognised this by dedicating an entire volume to *Documents for the History of Italian Warfare, from the 13th to the 16th Centuries* collected by Giuseppe Canestrini.

These are of great importance; but even taking into account all we owe to them, and to all that later historical researches have brought to light, the theme is not yet exhausted: truth is like happiness, and though as we approach we see it shining more intensely, and becoming clearer in outline, yet we can never feel, that we have obtained full possession of it.

One of the most celebrated *condottieri* was the Englishman John Hawkwood, or as contemporary Italian chroniclists put it "Giovanni Acuto;" whom Filippo Villani proclaims as "grand master of war." Giovio with elegant laconism defines him *acerrimus bellator et cunctator egregius*, (fierce and outstanding warrior), while Muratori recognises him as a "brave and wary captain," qualifying his praise however by adding "a brigand of the first rank;" and Ammirato says "by many proofs he showed himself valiant and courageous in his own person, astute in reaping advantages, and a man who could wait the results of action without hurrying to obtain fame."

As for popular tradition, we have the testimony of Franco Sacchetti, who (in his 181st Novella) tells the story of certain monks who gave Hawkwood the greeting of "Peace" on which he replied: "May the Lord take away your alms." The alarmed monks excused themselves, by saying they "meant only to be kind," and he explained: "Do you not know that I live by war, and that peace would be my undoing?" And the story-teller adds:

It certainly is true that Hawkwood fought in Italy longer than any other man ever fought, and nearly every part of it became tributary to him: so well did he manage his affairs that there was little peace in Italy in his days.

Warrior by trade, in peace his occupation was gone.

It was said that if he had wished, he might easily have cut a principality out of Tuscany for himself, or perhaps have become Lord of the whole province—a new Castruccio or Uguccione della Faggiuola;—but either he lacked the ambition, or else he knew the place and the times well enough to realise how impossible it would have been to found a lasting dynasty.

In any way he was for more than thirty years one of the most effective dominators of Italian affairs, and in her history—military, political, and social—he figures as a personage whose character and actions have an importance more than sufficient to justify the simple curiosity of biographical erudition.

It is now evident that there is more than a little to add and to rectify in his history: and—taking into account several unedited documents corroborating that which has, it is true, been already narrated, though neither clearly nor precisely—it would seem that, a new monograph of John Hawkwood may well be attempted.

Paolo Giovio gave a place to the English *condottiere* in the *Elogia virorum bellica virtute illustrium*; but it is a short record with more rhetoric than biography in it—more romance than history; it is a sketch in fine Latin prose with an ugly woodcut, and two unhappy verses by Giulio Feroldo; and as to truth, the famous bishop of Como always had (since Benedetto Varchi shewed up Paolo Giovio's errors in history) the most justifiable reputation of giving it quite a secondary importance.

Domenico Maria Manni collected many valuable facts edited and unedited, and formed a praiseworthy biography (published in 1760, in Vol. II of the appendix to *Rerum Italicarum Scriptores*), but it was incomplete and not always exact.

From the literary correspondence in 1640-1641 between Sir William Boswell English ambassador to the Hague, and J. de Laet of Leiden (British Museum, *additional* MSS. 6395) it results that Mr. John Maurice had compiled, and written in English, a life of Sir John Hawkwood, profiting by the Italian authors existing in the ambassador's library, and by Sir William Boswell's own observations. It is possible that this is the MS. biography of Hawkwood, which is preserved in the *Ashmolean Collection* of Oxford (N 749). It consists of 100 pages folio, and diverges from the subject in long digressions on general contemporary history, complacently quoting Tacitus and other Latin writers. The author thus metaphorically announces his subject:

> I nowe applie my selfe to my intended theme, the life of the valiant and famed Sir John Hawkwood, or rather some few discourses, considerations, and observations on several passages of his life, and acts, for these we have growing at, our own home, and the other must chiefly be imported from forraine parts where they grow too thinne.

In any case the book would only have a very limited biographical value were it not for the documents which were furnished by the Italian archives.

Thus, if our subject is not without, precedent, neither is it yet exhausted.

For the rest, in narrating and documenting the life of this soldier of fortune, it is enough merely to indicate, and not reproduce entire, those general facts of the time which are well known, or easily found in accredited histories. Our labours refer to the career of the classical *condottiere* in the midst of his soldiers, and to his relations with the princes and republics to whom he sold his sword; and it will suffice for this, if we throw some of the modern lights on the social and military conditions of Italy, during the second half of the 14th century.

To simplify chronology, we have indicated the dates by marginal numbers. Dates of the old Florentine and Pisan styles have been reduced to modern style.

CHAPTER 1

The Hawkwood Family

On the left bank of the little River Colne in Essex, in the parish of Sible Hedingham not far from the ancient city of Colchester, there still exists an old house and estate named Hawkwood Manor—once a feudal dependance on the Castle of Hedingham belonging to the Earls of Oxford, and which was in the possession of the Hawkwoods as far back as the reigns of John Lack-Land and Edward III.

Tradition says that our John Hawkwood was born here, and we have no reason to doubt it.

The epoch of his birth is not proved: we only know that he died very old in 1394, and that in 1360 he was already a captain of assured reputation; we may therefore conclude that he came into the world in the beginning of Edward the Third's reign, about the year 1320.

John's father was named Gilbert and he was by trade a tanner; a fact perfectly compatible with his well-to-do condition as a landowner.

There are not wanting fabricators of marvellous genealogies, which make Hawkwood's ancestry originate with Memprecius, King of the Frisians. On the other hand, Filippo Villani and Ammirato believe Hawkwood to be a personal cognomen, rather than a family surname, recounting that "the mother being about to give birth to a child, had herself carried into a forest, and here the boy was born," hence the name *hawk* and *wood*.

The Florentine historians were better informed in saying that his parents "were well born although not of grand lineage (*gentil' huomini mercatanti e antichi borghesi*)." The fact that they used the aristocratic particle "de," and that they possessed lands, goods, and money, is proved by some English documents, among which is the will of Gilbert de Hawkwood himself. (Tommaseo, in his *Comments on the Letters of St. Catherine of Siena*, has romanced too much in attributing to "Acuto" the title of Count.)

In this his last testament, (1340), Gilbert de Hawkwood declares his wish to be buried in the church of Sible Hedingham; then in the first place he leaves 2 *solidi* to the building fund of St. Paul's in London; then 17 *marks* 10 *solidi* for his obsequies on the day of the funeral, and on the seventh and thirtieth days after it.

He had three sons: John the elder, John the younger, and Nicholas. The elder no doubt inherited, by right of seniority, the Manor of Hedingham Sible, of which the will makes no mention, it being only a series of legacies in money, goods or furniture:

> to John senior 10 pounds, the cart and six horses, two oxen, 10 quarters of wheat and 10 of oats;
>
> to John junior 20 pounds and 100 *solidi*;
> to Nicholas 10 *marks*;
>
> to each 5 quarters of wheat, 5 of oats, with bed and maintenance for a year.

There were besides four daughters: Agnes and Jane, married; Alice and Margaret still spinsters, to each of them Gilbert left 100 *solidi* and to the two spinsters 10 pounds besides, with bed and maintenance for a year.

Then follows a long list of petty legacies to priests, menservants, and maidservants, abbesses, and nuns; with a general legacy of "all the remainder" to his executors to be employed in charity and prayers for his soul.

The executors were his sons, the two Johns, and the Vicar of Gosfield: this indicates that those two sons were both at home in 1340; in fact, they obtained, after Gilbert's death in that same year, the official documents giving them legal possession and power of administration of the property mentioned in the will.

Of the three sons, the least favoured, Nicholas, embraced the ecclesiastical career, with such success that in 1363 we find him in holy orders, and holding a territorial benefice of such value that it placed him on an equal rank with John senior, who as head of the family was Squire of Sible Hedingham.

The other cadet John junior, being provided with his 20 pounds and 100 *solidi* (in those times a considerable sum), lived for a year at his brother's expense, as legally enjoined—he might even have prolonged the visit in fraternal fashion—but after that he began to think, as cadets must do, of making a career for himself.

Now at that time there was war in France, and thither went many Englishmen to seek their fortunes, and gain money, lands, and titles, while King Edward III on his part appropriated whole provinces—and these temptations induced our hero to become a soldier.

This seems the most probable version of his story; nevertheless, the tradition was generally accepted in England that John's first weapons were needle and scissors, and that they were wielded during an apprenticeship to a London tailor. Fuller gives this as a fact adding:

Now that mean men bred in manual and mechanick trades, may arrive at great skill in martiall performances, that Hawkwood, though an eminent, is not the only instance of our English nation.

On this account a popular modern writer, Smiles, registered Hawkwood among the illustrious men of the working classes in his *Life and Labour*.

It is also noteworthy that some French authors give John Hawkwood the cognomen of Jean de L'Aiguille. But all this is not at all authentic, and accords ill with the condition of the family de Hawkwood. As to the real Jean de L'Aiguille, Matteo Villani is our best informant; he says that:

After having shewn himself a brave man of great spirit in feats of arms, Gianni della Guglia, English tailor, in the summer of 1359, got together a company of English plunderers and swordsmen; and either pillaging open lands or protecting them for money, he made a great fortune in a few months, and returning to his allegiance to the King of England placed a great part of the wealth he had accumulated at his sovereign's disposal.

When in later times Hawkwood appeared as hero of the Tuscan wars, Filippo Villani, who continued Matteo's history, while trying to throw light on the origin of the *condottiere*, does not even dream of identifying Giovanni Acuto with Gianni della Guglia: and Froissart, on his side, assures us that in 1360, Giovanni Hacoude was still "a poor knight, having gained nothing but his spurs."

Skippon, an English writer, on reading in Florence the name of Johannes Acutus, translated it literally into English as "John Sharp," without even suspecting that it referred to Hawkwood.

★★★★★★

The numberless variations in the spelling of this name in ancient documents, contemporaneous chronicles, and later historians is incredible. Every possible combination of the letters which do or do not compose it, as long as they approximated to the sound of *Hacoud*, were experimented upon by secretaries, and authors, learned or popular. Even his own amanuensis signing for him (as we see in several letters in the Archives of Mantua) indulged in the most fantastic aberrations of orthography. It would be useless to give a long list, suffice it to state that we can ring all the changes between *Aguto* and *Kauchicole* and that S. Antonino constantly calls him *Agostino*.

★★★★★★

Some mistake of this sort may have given rise to the metamorphose of "Acuto" into Giovanni dell' Ago, and thence to the legend of his exploits in a tailor's shop.

It has been frequently asserted that Hawkwood was enrolled by a press-gang, but it has also been said that he made his own choice of the career of arms, and that he was educated for it by his uncle who was an expert warrior. Some declare that his first campaign in France in 1343 was made as a vassal of John de Vere, 7th earl of Oxford; and it is probable that he fought in the famous battles of Cressy and Poitiers, (1346 and 1356), for it is an accepted tradition, that he so distinguished himself in those actions, as to win the favour of the Black

Prince, and receive from the king the honour of knighthood.

All considered however, there is much less documentary proof for the story of his early career than even that of his origin; while the history of his vocation as Captain of Mercenaries is on the contrary sufficiently recounted by the French chronicles.

During the war, many companies of mercenary adventurers had multiplied on the disputed soil of France, some fighting on their own account, others for belligerent potentates.

The peace of Bretigny being concluded, (1360), a great number of the troops were dismissed and returned to their homes across the sea. Many of the Englishmen however were too much accustomed to the excitement of fighting and setting ransoms in an enemy's country, to willingly return to peaceful occupations in their own; they preferred following up the career, and finding numerous adherents, Germans, men of Brabant, Flemings, Gascons, and French, they formed into companies both great and small, known by the common name of *Tards-venus*, to distinguish them from other troops which had preceded them, or to express that they gleaned the little that was left in France, which had already been devastated by so many years of war.

English captains of the higher rank being laden with spoil and full of honours, after victorious campaigns fought for the right; obeyed the proclamation of peace, and declined to mix themselves up with the *Tards-venus*, who therefore elected new leaders, "choosing," says Froissart, "the worst among them."

★★★★★★

Perrens would give us to understand that the nucleus of these companies was composed of Gascons and Normans, who had served England and hence the name of English. But from their own documents in Italy we find that the element of real English blood existed, especially in the knights and constables.

★★★★★★

John Hawkwood may have been "a poor knight," but he must have won reputation as a man of war, because one of these companies placed him at their head.

CHAPTER 2
The English in Piedmont

The *Tards-venus* under Bernardo de la Sale, after having desolated Champagne and Burgundy, and made a rendezvous at Lyons, descend the Rhone by long nocturnal marches, (December 28, 1360), surprise the bridge and fort of Saint Esprit, and take it by assault, thereby gaining both women and spoil; establishing themselves there they command the whole river, and menace Avignon itself; John Hawkwood gives great assistance in this enterprise.

Pope Innocent VI to defend himself has recourse to arms temporal, spiritual and moral: he fortifies Avignon, proclaims a crusade with liberal indulgences, writes to Conte Verde, (Lord of Savoy and ancestor of the royal family of Italy), and other transalpine princes, that they may oppose the companies, and prevent their passage; for already a troop got together by the Countess of Harcourt to avenge the murder of her husband by the King of France, and another large company of Englishmen are hastening to new prey in Provence. (January and February, 1361.)

The Cardinal of Ostia succeeds in collecting a few men; but they do not remain staunch, on the contrary several go over to the enemy.

Not being able to brave the storm, the Pope carefully takes the opportunity of turning it aside, by putting his hand in his purse. He comes to an understanding with the Marquis of Montferrat who requires soldiers to fight against the Visconti: so counselled by Conte Verde, and backed up by the money of the Church, the marquis takes into his pay the larger part of the great company of *Tards-venus* as well as the *brigand-paladins* of the countess—in all 6000 horse.

How much did this financial operation cost the Pope, besides the plenary indulgence?

Froissart says that he advanced 60,000 *francs* in gold, of which 10,000 were paid to Hawkwood's brigade.

★★★★★★

It must be specified that in ancient times two kinds of *francs* were used in France: the silver one of twenty *soldi*, and the golden one of six Florentine *lire*. The Florentine florin of that epoch had an intrinsic value of about eleven of the modern *francs*.

★★★★★★

Baluzio talks of 30,000, Matteo Villani of 100,000 florins: but Martene's document proves only one of the payments—that of 14,600 florins to be consigned to the marquis. (June 6.)

Here then we behold the great English band marching towards the sea; attempting in vain to take Marseilles, they set fire to her suburbs, and pass by the Riviera to Nice; cross the Maritime Alps by the feudal estates of Malaspina, favoured by Simon Boccanegra *doge* of Genoa, and enemy to the Visconti; and thus descend into the valley of the Po.

And did Hawkwood go with them? It seems that he did like the Countess of Harcourt, who after conducting her brigade into Piedmont, returned directly into France, for Froissart assures us that our *condottiere* was one of the chiefs in command of the English bands, who under Jacques de Bourbon at Brignais vanquished the troops of the French king.

The Battle of Brignais, which was a pitched battle, took place on April 6, 1362. (Froissart, it is true, gives the date April 12, 1361, but Simeon Luce, the learned editor of the famous French chronicler, has shown this to be a chronological error.)

The English, superior in number, had the extra advantage of prudence. They, dissimulated the real extent of their forces so as to mislead Bourbon's spies, and they also occupied the best positions.

The French troops attempted an assault by an open march, but they were first thrown into confusion by a storm of large stones aimed with singular vigour and precision (the English were expert slingsmen as well as archers), then they were shaken in the flank by a compact mass, bristling with lances six feet long, and finally, routed and disbanded with great loss, they left many important prisoners on the field. Bourbon, mortally wounded, hardly succeeded in flying to Lyons to die, consoled as well as may be, by the tears of the Lyonese dames and maidens.

In fact, we perceive by this combat that the French had learned little from the terrible lessons of Cressy and Poitiers, and that the English were possessed of very ripened tactics for those times; even in brigandage they were artists of war.

After this signal victory the companies diffused themselves without obstacles,—some stayed in France, some turned towards the Rhenish provinces, to such effect that Rudolph of Hapsburg had to league eleven imperial cities, to oppose the damages and devices of "those villains vulgarly called English;" a good many more passed or repassed into Italy and among these John Hawkwood.

Va; raccogli ove arato non hai,
Spiega l'ugne: l'Italia ti do.
(*Go, reap where thou hast not sowed,*
Spread thy claws: Italy I give thee.)

The maritime Alps passed, the English left behind them in France their name of *Tards-venus*. It is not certain, however, that they formed immediately, as is generally believed, that single "White Company," or *Compagnia Bianca*, as Matteo Villani calls the largest of the English bands in 1360.

The ancient *Chronique de Savoie* speaks of *aucunes compagnies d'Anglois* (no English companies) which had for leaders Robert Canolle, John Auguth, and Anuechin de Bongarden.

As to the last name it is equivocal: Bongarden came with Count Conrad Lando (or Landau) bringing from Apulia two troops of Hungarians and Germans, who were first in the pay of the Marquis of Montferrat, and then hired by the Conte Verde: finally they passed into the service of the Visconti, Lando first, and Bongarden after a new expedition into Apulia.

On the other hand, Azario, a most valuable contemporaneous eye and ear witness, certifies that the English companies took as general leader a German, Albert Sterz, a man so valorous in the field, as to inspire others with courage. It was necessary to have a captain, who knew the country, which was new to themselves, and Sterz suited them, not only for his military qualities, but especially because he spoke English.

The fact remains that Piedmont was devastated by the Hungarians, the Germans, and lastly by the newly arrived English, and it is difficult to say which were the worst, the cruel horrors of the slaughter at Savigliano by the first, or the equal horrors perpetrated by the others, in proof of which Azario gives the names of many witnesses.

It is not true that the English brought from beyond the Alps the plague, of which 77,000 people died in Milan alone (?); the pest was already in Piedmont, as it was in Provence, but they brought violation, burning, extortion, rapine, murder, and torture, ill-using women in the presence of their husbands, and fathers, and then demanding ransom; putting men into irons, and drowning those who were not prompt to pay the money demanded.

The only thing in which the English were less brutal than the Hungarians and Germans was in not roasting or mutilating their victims. Azario, however, does not omit to call them *perfidi* and *scelleratissimi* (perfidious and villainous), and from their entrance into Italy they justified the old proverb *Inglese italianato è un diavolo incarnato.* (An Englishman Italianised is an incarnate devil.)

★★★★★★

The origin of this proverb is not known, it dates from before the 16th century when Serdonati registers it in his MS. collection with a note "English Proverb." It has some analogy with another saying *Inglesi hanno coda di serpe* (The English have serpent's tails), referred to by Landino in his commentary on *canto XXVII* of Dante's *Paradise*. Strange contrast between this proverb and Gregory the Great's *Non angli sed angeli si christiani forent.* Which play on words it is curious to find some centuries later in a Turkish poet-Fazilbeg, who speaking of the English in his book of women, says: "Not anglica, but an angelic creature." But in the 16th century they were anything but angels! The Italians of that age could no more say *Gesta Dei per Francos* (Actions of God through Franks) but *Gesta diaboli per Anglos* (Devil directed by the English.)

★★★★★★

The *Chronique de Savoie* says coldly almost excusing them, that being many they could not live in Piedmont, without spoiling the country, so that Conte Verde, who had imprudently counselled the Marquis of Montferrat to employ the English, repented, and took arms to defend himself.

They could indeed boast of an illustrious adversary, but nevertheless under Robert Canolles they held their own against him, and after having taken, with other places, the town of Lanzo, obliged him to shut himself up in the castle, which they held in siege, till he was reduced to such extremities that he had to make terms through the mediation of Sir William de Grandson, knight of "the *Annunziata*," and agreed to pay an indemnity.

★★★★★★

This Roberto Canolles or Knolles, a German of low origin, knight and leader of brigands, had as his motto:
Qui Robert Canolle prendra
Cent mille moutons gagnera.
(Who Robert Canolle will lose
One hundred thousand sheep will win.)

★★★★★★

By forfeiting the sum of 180,000 florins, Conte Verde obtained the restitution of his lands, and the English passed on to fight the Milanese, under the Marquis of Montferrat, making their headquarters at Sicciano near Novara. Count Landau was then serving Galeazzo Visconti, who being weak in the field tried to defend himself by fire. He burnt twelve castles and villages, thinking thus to cut off the enemy's provisions; but the English answered by fire, burning fifty-two places, destroying hundreds of others, and sacking all the territory as far as the Rivers Ticino and Trebbia.

In fact, the English preliminaries in Italy were terrible, and that first campaign was enough to give them the reputation of being invincible.

They easily occupied Castelnuovo at Scrivia for the marquis, and then Galeazzo Visconti sent the counts Landan and Nicholas, to Tortona against them with several Germans, and 500 Hungarians, and eventually dispatched Giovanni de' Pepoli to treat with the English. They remained faithful to the marquis, and the enemy not daring, even with double their forces, to emerge from Tortona, they devastated the surrounding country up to Pavia. Only Luchino dal Verme opposed them with five hundred *barbute*, (German name for "lances," *barbuta* was 2 men, a lance of three), and obliged them to return to the Novara district, where they occupied Romagnano, and five hundred of them died of the plague. (September 1362.)

It appears that they were wanting in cross-bow men, a weapon very important in those days, because when the Doge of Genoa placed 30 bands at their disposal, they again took the offensive, and were able to attack with success several places on the right of the Po.

December 26, Conte Verde proposed an alliance with Galeazzo Visconti, with the object of driving out the English from their states, and dividing Montferrat, between them, but it must be admitted that the undertaking to rout the English seemed very difficult to Visconti, for he was at the same time attempting to make a treaty of peace with them.

Albert Sterz feigned to consent, by which means the English succeeded in making a fierce incursion, passing the Ticino, and pushing on to within six miles of Milan. (January 4, 1363.) It was night, and people in the castles and villages were keeping the New Year's festivities; while the Milanese nobles were having a merry time, playing at *tabulas et scaccos* (draughts and chess) unsuspecting and undefended, so that they were unable to prevent the robbers from taking anything and everything they chose. Luckily for the ladies and maidens they were in a hurry, and contented themselves with goods and chattels, abstaining from their usual incendiary proceedings.

They made prisoners of over 600 nobles, and would have taken more if ropes and time had not failed them. Some of the gang dragged behind them as many as ten nobles, together with their cattle; they could not save them all because they were attacked by Visconti's boats in recrossing the Ticino, but it is said that with the money paid for ransoms, they pocketed about 100,000 florins.

Having returned to their nest in Romagnano they made fresh efforts to treat with Count Landau, but after their having sacked Briona, the count lost patience, and met them at the bridge at Canturino, where leaving their horses they came to a hand to hand encounter (April 22.) It appears that the Hungarians having quarrelled with their German comrades deserted the field, and the count, mingling in the *mêlée*, had the nose-piece of his helmet broken, and then with a lance-thrust in his face and another under the arm-pit, he was taken prisoner in a dying state.

His death was deplored even by the English leaders who hoped by his means to come to terms with the Visconti, when their contract with Montferrat should be fulfilled, but they made good the occasion by crossing the Apennines and carrying their arms into Tuscany.

There were already Pisan Ambassadors at Novara offering to hire the English Company, which was certainly called at that time *Compagnia, Bianca* on account of their white flags, white vests, and shining arms. They numbered 3500 horse and 2000 foot, and were still commanded by Sterz.

CHAPTER 3
Entry into Tuscany

The city of Pisa was engaged in one of her usual wars with Florence. The Pisans had formerly availed themselves of English adventurers, as in 1314 when they took "Messer Folco" of England into their pay, with his 1500 knights; and now wishing to come to some decisive result, they had recourse to the White Company, in which Galeazzo Visconti, who was only too willing to be rid of the scourge, willingly aided them. They therefore hired them for six months at the stipend of 40,000 florins, and to this end a forced loan of 30,000 florins was imposed on the Pisans in June 1363, which was reimbursed in September.

★★★★★★

The treasury had other expenses for the Company besides the stipends; for example in September 1363 the council of the *Anziani* absolved the Municipality of Sarzana from a debt of 10 florins, their part of a second tax of 8500 florins levied on the Pisan territories, to compensate the damages suffered by many private persons in the coming of the English Company.

★★★★★★

Florence too had former experiences of the English mercenaries (as we find in the *Consulte e pratiche* of 1353), and again at this time might easily have had them on her own side. Friendly commercial and banking relations had existed for some centuries between Florence and England, and the traffic in English wool—indeed, almost the monopoly—had survived after the famous bank failure of the Bardi and Peruzzi. Giovanni Boglietti, a Florentine, had been taken as guide to the White Company, who knew as yet very little of Italian geography, and the Company willing to conclude the suspended treaty with Florence, would have been contented to take from her 30,000 florins.

Galeazzo Visconti favoured, and would have facilitated these negotiations: and Piero Farnese, the Florentine captain of war, and an expert soldier, insisted on having the assistance of the English whom he considered spirited, brave and clever.

But the policy of economy, suggested by the Gonfaloniere Ridolfi, prevailed.

Or vi dirò; siccome è di ragione,
Seppe la volpe qui più del leone.
(Now I will tell you how as it might be expected,
the fox in this case was wiser than the lion.)

Thus, sang Antonio Pucci, a Florentine of that period, when he put into verse the story of the war between the Florentines and the Pisans, which the two Villani recount in prose. And the chronicler Velluti writes:

To save the evil of present expenses we to our shame and loss spent in the end six times as much, while if we had only engaged the Englishmen for our side, we Florentines would have been lords and victors in the war.

Touching at Arona, to which place they were escorted by Giovanni de' Pepoli, on Galeazzo Visconti's account, the English stopped at Pontenure in the vicinity of Piacenza, to supply themselves with arms and horses and then pushed on to Pisa.

Up to this time the war had been going badly with the Pisan "fox"—the Florentine "lion" was hitherto triumphant, but the arrival of the English sufficed to secure to Pisa a decided superiority.

They even enjoyed the fame in anticipation by a ruse, for they secretly despatched a company of their own soldiers from Pisa by night, and causing them to enter next morning covered with dust as from a long march, gave them a grand reception as though they were the Englishmen, which so intimidated the Florentines that they forthwith raised the siege of Montecalvoli (a neighbouring fort), and retreated.

The real English having reached Lucca (July) by way of Lunigiana, rode at once through the Florentine territory by the Pistoia road: and with them was the "Pisan host," making altogether a force of 6000 horse, besides infantry and archers. There were also about a hundred itinerant salesmen, provided with tinder and *acciaiuolo* (flint and steel) to set fire to the houses, as municipal enmity in those days demanded.

The captain general of the Pisans was a Florentine exile, Ghisello Ubaldini; but on his death a few weeks later Manetti da Jesi succeeded to the command. The general of the English Company was the German Albert Sterz. Some contemporary chroniclers do not mention this, nor does the name of Acuto (Hawkwood) appear in that year, but they all accord in saying that the very backbone of the war was the English contingent.

It was only an heroi-comic skirmish after all.

In the first incursion, lasting a fortnight, the English assembled under Pistoia, and threw into it lances, arrows, and *bombarde*; "they ran races according to their custom" (a far off prelude to the modern prevalence of English sport in Italy) and then they advanced on Florence. When hearing the bells and trumpets ring out for war, and believing that the people were about to make a sally, they retired, but the Florentines remained secure within their walls. Albert Sterz dubbed General Ubaldini and others knights; the Pisans might have boasted of flinging into the city arrows with the tickets "Pisa sends you this" and of striking Pisan and Florentine money; of hanging a donkey and a dog, while as to burning:

> If the English had not forbidden them (perhaps they wished by clemency to keep open a way to future contracts with Florence) there would not have remained a house unconsumed, nor a palace which they would not have set fire to.

The "host" having returned to Pisa, the English were sent to the Chianti to reconnoitre. The Florentine poet chronicler thus characterises the rapidity and caution of their nocturnal marches:

> *E prima a Poggibonizi venuti*
> *Fûr, che di lor si sentisse niente*
> *E poichè i passi tutti ebber veduti*
> *Di notte si partir subitamente.*
> (*They reached Poggibonsi before anyone*
> *had heard of them, and after having*

21

reconnoitred the country, they
went away quickly by night.)

Exploring the roads and finding the right one, they reached the upper part of Val d' Arno where they took Figline. (September 16 1363.)

Pandolfo Malatesta, the accepted friend and counsellor of war to the Florentines, placed the captain general Ranuccio Farnese at Incisa, for its defence, with some peasant bands and 2000 German men at arms under his command. They were brave but youthful and badly armed, besides which he so enlarged his lines of battle, that 500 of the best horsemen were lost sight of and returned to Florence. The English, under pretext of sending unarmed witnesses to a duel between one of their knights and a Florentine, obtained exact information about the enemy, and the following day gave the assault, in two or three places at once, thus gaining possession of the field. (October 3.)

Ranuccio was taken and Messer Luca di Totto de' Firidolfi da Panzano, knight, succeeded him as lieutenant; he gives the following account of the action:

> In the morning after the *mezza-terza* (half-*tierce*, a canonical hour) Incisa was assaulted and conquered—all day the people were flying without striking a blow, and I was attacked, wounded in the face and taken, being dragged by the neck, and bound head and foot. On the day that I was taken—I lost my horses, arms, silver belts, and gold rings.

The general flight continued as far as Florence.

The barbarous treatment of the prisoners must not however be laid to the English. "The Commune of Pisa," he says, "spoiled me to dishonour and disgrace our Republic."

Having given out that they intended to attack Florence at the Porta S. Niccolo, they got the Florentines to shut themselves up in the city to wait for them, and in that way secured a free march along the Arno, encountering no opposition except a heavy rain, which rendered the road so bad that the horses lost their shoes. At night (October 22) they dispersed to sack and pillage in the plain of Ripoli, taking, as prisoners, some four hundred people warm from their beds, and nearly a thousand heads of cattle, fresh from their stalls; then raising their standard on the parish church they saluted it with a grand blowing of trumpets and the flames of incendiarism.

Malatesta, the new captain general, shut himself up within the walls, allowing the enemy to return, joyful and gorged with prey to Figline, where they kept in their quarters undisturbed for two months, since the Sienese had themselves undertaken to fight the Company of the "*Cappelletto*," just then hired by the Florentines in the Maremma.

There were altogether (so Messer Luca di Totto says) 600 horse, and 3000 infantry who formed the garrison at Figline, whence they made sallies as far as the Casentino.

Several castles fell, into their hands more or less easily; but they fought two days in vain, against the fortress of Tre Vigne, "leaving several killed and wounded by stones and other missiles, while the moat was full of ladders, and the ground strewn with bows and arrows."

Having amassed an enormous quantity of spoil, they thought it time to return to winter quarters in Pisa. They spread the report however that on November 11, they would pass under the walls of Florence to consecrate a priest at San Salvi, and in fact that morning almost as if they would fulfil the impudent menace, they raised their camp and feigned to take the road to Florence.

The Florentine spies fled at once to the city with the terrifying news, but the English halted directly, and burning field and town passed on by the Chianti and Val di Pesa, arriving safely at Pisa, while the Florentines ringing their bells to call their men to arms, put themselves on the defensive at San Salvi and waited to see the enemy descend the heights of Rovezzano.

There was certainly work to be done in the service of Pisa; the town of Barga for some time past blockaded, rather than besieged, by the Pisans, still obstinately resisted, but the English considered that they were brought there to fight in Florentine territory and would not undertake the enterprise to Barga, except perhaps a few who had as yet got little prey. The greater part well provided for, preferred to winter in Pisa and amuse themselves to "the harm and discomfort of the citizens whom they outraged so much, that many sent their women to Genoa and other places for safety."

So says Filippo Villani, and Sozomeno emphasises it still more strongly in Latin; indeed, so strongly we refrain from quoting: it is however possible that Villani, a Florentine, and Sozomeno, a Pistoiese, painted in vivid colours, so as to vituperate the hated Pisans through their wives. It is certain that the part of the city assigned as quarters to the soldiers did not suffice them, nor did they respect the barriers beyond which the Pisans had prohibited them from penetrating or molesting the inhabitants.

They had no fear of cold, "in the middle of the winter, those hardy men did not desist from running about and plundering," but this they did at their own will, without heeding the wishes of the Pisans, who endeavoured to send the bands out under pretext of defending them from imaginary incursions of the enemy.

The Pisans were obliged to tolerate every exorbitance of the English, who were so necessary to them in the field, that with their aid they were certain of victory; so, they made a new treaty (January 1364) for six months at the price of. 150,000 florins, with the compact that all other stipendiaries were to be dismissed (perhaps this was because the English desired all the spoil for themselves), and that they should have the faculty of marching wherever they chose outside the territories allied to, or protected by Pisa.

The company also obliged the Pisans to accept as captain general the man of their choice—John Hawkwood—whose name the Pisan chroniclers Italianise as *Giovanni Auti*, which choice proves that he had distinguished himself as much during the last year's campaign, as he had previously done in Piedmont and France. From this time forth till his death, we almost always see him as general in chief, in which character he takes a prominent part in the annals of Italy.

This superior rank must have been conferred before December 1363, for a document of that date determines the monthly pay of the foot soldiers "lately received into the service of the Pisan Republic, and forming the guard of Signor Giovanni Acuto, captain general of war for Pisa."

The pay consisted of 20 *lire* in Pisan money, to the two constables Simone de' Gangalandi and Lodovico di Bernardo da Micciano: 10 *lire* to the constables' two pages and to 38 foot soldiers and their 6 boys (all Italian). In fact, a sufficient and honourable bodyguard.

The highest in command of the White Company under Hawkwood were the German Albert Sterz, and an Englishman named Andrew De Belmonte (styled *Dubramonte* in Italian); some chroniclers say the latter was of royal race, and that he was distinguished from the other *cruel and ferocious* English by his gentle manners. (It is often difficult to guess the authentic ultramontane names, so curiously are they travestied in the Italian documents of the time.) He fell in love at Figline, with Monna Tancia wife of Guido lord of the Forest, and served her with such knightly devotion that he managed to make even his enterprising comrades respect her castle.

The important office of treasurer was filled by Guglielmo Toreton

(William Turton?).

******

The Pisan archives contain the order of the *"Anziani"* to the chamberlain Pellario Griffo, dated October 1364, to pay Guglielmo Toreton, treasurer of the Grand English Company, 5000 gold florins of 3 *lire* 10 *soldi* in Pisan money, and 6000 of 3 *lire* 15 *soldi*, on account of the sum which the company is entitled to receive from the Republic of Pisa.

The accounts of the chamberlain with the company were complicated by frequent anticipatory payments to this and that official; for instance, in the same month we find "100 florins to John Onselos (Onslow?) and Conrad Schonechen *ultramontani*, who are now entering the English Company on the Florentine territory and will remain with it as long as the said company is in the Pisan service"—with promise to repay it within two months (here follow signatures of witnesses).

Another entry has 150 florins to Robert, 100 to Dughino (Duggan?), 10 to William Prestim Englishmen—small sums between 20 and 2 florins to 108 men, English and Teutons—and 2 florins to Marcuccio and Marco trumpeters, and to Antonio *naccarino* (kettle drummer).

******

CHAPTER 4

Hawkwood Faithful to the Pisans

In February 1364, the English, in spite of heavy snows, made a sally from Pisa attempting several places, but they found unexpected resistance from the peasants in every part, and the Pistoiese at Seravalle even attacked them with some success.

Many of their men died of the intense cold, so they retired with decided losses, and certainly no gains.

Soon after this a considerable reinforcement arrived at Pisa. Annechin Bongarden, who had gone to Lombardy in the service of Galeazzo Visconti, with the permission March, of that prince conducted his 3000 German *barbute* to Pisa to share the pay of that Republic—the Pisan Army thus amounted to about 6500 horse, besides a great number of pioneers and native infantry. (The English introduced the manner of reckoning their forces by "lances" instead of the older name *"barbute"*. A lance consisted of three men, a *barbuta* of two.) In the spring the campaign was resumed in earnest.

In three marches the Pisan soldiers reached Prato, where they had the temerity to occupy the drawbridge. They passed close to Florence, so near that three or four of the boldest rode on and knocked at the Port' a Prato, but the body of the forces pressed on at once to the Mugello.

Here however they encountered the German bands which were in the Florentine pay, led by Pandolfo Malatesta and Count Henri de Montfort, and in a skirmish of the vanguards forty Florentines defeated a hundred Pisans, (1364); one good strong German named Heinrich Paer, with his own lance unhorsed ten Englishmen, killing two of them.

Hawkwood and Bongarden finding some backbone of resistance here, pretended to pass on, but retiring instead, reapproached Florence by the slopes of Monte Morello, where they penetrated into the woody folds of the mountain, leading their horses by the most difficult passes, and sacking and burning. . . . But from this time forth we may spare ourselves the mention of plunder and incendiarism: they were the rule, and are understood as part of the business in a march of the mercenaries, being always practised in an enemy's country, and often in that of their friends.

There was nothing more terrible than to hear even the name of the English.

It should be noted that the spirited Brunelleschi family victoriously defended their castle at Petraia against three assaults.

Meanwhile Malatesta finding he was not so much master of the situation in Florence, as he had flattered himself, he would be, retired, and the sword of command of the German legion was given to the brave Montfort. Hawkwood and Bongarden occupied the hills of Fiesole, (April 30) while Montfort fortified the suburbs of Florence outside Porta San Gallo, with hastily erected barricades and fences.

A fierce battle was fought on the 1st of May, a day which Florence usually gave to popular merry making, and auguries of love. The priors who had to enter office that very day, did so without any of the usual solemnities, they did not appear on the *ringhiera* (balcony) outside the palace, no bells were rung, or trumpets blown, because there was fighting at San Gallo.

Hawkwood's Englishmen and Bongarden's Germans made a fierce attack on the barricades and breaking them, penetrated as far as the city gates, where the fray became bloody. Grimaldi's Genoese cross-bow men on the walls made a great noise and did a little damage; while the English archers, from the houses in the suburb, did a great deal of damage with very little noise; the Count of Montfort paid dearly in his own person, fighting hand to hand with Averard the German. (Count of Landau, son of Count Conrad who was killed two years before in Lombardy, and brother of Count Lucius, all three dauntless soldiers, and perfect brigands.)

In the heat of combat amid smoke, fires, and the ruins of falling houses, Bongarden was created knight and then he conferred the spurs on Averard, and an Englishman named Cook, besides others who distinguished themselves for their valour.

But the brilliant action had little result, the assailants ended by retreating to the hills; and when night came, they celebrated the new-made knights with processions of coloured lamps, with games, song and music on the *piazza* of Fiesole. Then they took a fancy to send some drummers and trumpeters down to the Port' alia Croce at Florence, who made such a warlike noise that the city was in a tumult, so that the screeching women put lights in the windows, and got heaps of stones ready on the towers as if the enemies had already entered.

The mercenaries employed three days in burning houses on the Fiesole hills, and on the plain to the right of the Arno, and then crossed the river at a place still called "*la Sardigna*." (An empty space on the left of the river opposite the Cascine.)

★★★★★★

Tradition says that among the castles ruined by the English one was Vincigliata, which belonged successively to the Bisdomini, and to the Albizi, who took the name of Alessandri; it now (1889) belongs to John Temple-Leader Esq., who has completely restored the ruins in the style of the 14th century. Cav. Gaetano Bianchi's *frescoes* in the *loggia* of the cloister at Vincigliata are entirely in artistic accordance with the medieval style of the castle. The inscriptions in old Italian beneath them would run thus: "John Hawkwood with his company of Englishmen and the Pisan marauders, moves to the injury of the Florentines.—The English with John Hawkwood having taken the hill of Fiesole, disperse over the surrounding country and after having destroyed Vincigliata, depart in May 1364."

★★★★★★

For three more days they occupied the hills of Arcetri and Bellosguardo, destroying the orange trees, trampling down the green wheat

27

and barley, robbing farmyards, and renewing daring and useless attacks on the barricades of the suburbs of Legnaia and Verzaia. In this last place the English descended the hill in such a mass that they looked like ants, and discharged a shower of arrows over the walls into the city. (May 10.) The scuffle might have been fierce, if a heavy rain had not separated the combatants.

Thus, skirmishing they retreated, and ascended the banks of the Arno to Incisa.

The city of Florence was, or rather had been well defended, but she could not tolerate seeing her enemies masters of all her territories, and not having forces enough to subdue them, she resorted to that *"ultima ratio"* of Philip of Macedon:—corruption.

The poet-chronicler Pucci, though Florentine himself, clearly confesses it.

Allora i Fiorentin tennon trattato
Con gli Inghilesi e col detto Aunichino,
E que' che fanno fare ogni mercato,
Concordia fêr tra loro e 'l Fiorentino.
(*Then did the Florentines propose a treaty with the English*
and with the said Annechin (Bongarden), and some people
who would get a profit out of everything,
made a peace between them and the Florentines.)

Ammirato gives a name to one of these mercenary agents, he writes:

Lapo di Fornaino de Rossi, was made Podesta of Prato in consideration of his services in making terms with Bongarden's Company.

Some historians have it that the golden florins were infused into certain flasks of wine, which were sent to those leaders whom they wanted to corrupt. This must have been a small payment on account, for the affair cost Florence more than 100,000 florins: *i.e.* 9000 to Bongarden, 35,000 to his Germans, and 70,000 to the English, of which 5000 were for Belmonte. It appears that Bongarden deserted the field outright, with his Germans, while Albert Sterz with Belmonte (in spite of his royal blood), Ugo della Zecca (?—perhaps Hugh Mortimer) and the other English leaders limited themselves to agreeing to a truce of five months with Florence.

All were traitors, except John Hawkwood, who tried with bitter reproofs to keep Bongarden to his duty. The fact is certain that when Sterz and Belmonte returned to Pisa with the sanction of Florence to provoke a revolution in favour of Gambacorti who aspired to the tyranny of the city, our hero hastened to warn the *"Anziani"* of the treachery by a letter. It is true, that with his troops disordered by infidelity, he could no longer continue his tactics on the offensive, the English contingent therefore marched through the territories of Arezzo, Cortona, Siena, Valdinievole, and Lucca, finally halting at San Piero in Campo near Pisa, where they inspected the troops and realized a loss of 600 men.

None were allowed to enter the city except those whom Hawkwood recommended as faithful.

Tornaudo a Pisa, e non possendo entrare,
Di fuor la gente d' intorno s'attenda
E cominciauo a Pisa a domandare
Molta pecunia di paga e di menda,
Di che i Pisan gli tenieno in pastura
 Ed e' guastavan d' intorno alle mura.
(To Pisa come, but not allowed within,
The men wait round about the city gate
And to demand imperiously begin
Large sums for pay, and wrongs to compensate,
So that the Pisans send them off in haste,
And all around they lay the lands to waste.)

Thus, perfidiously June was passed, the last month of their engagement, when they ought to have been opposing the Count of Montfort who without let or hindrance was domineering the Pisan territories.

Hawkwood with only 800 men remained in the Pisau service, while the greater part of the English, being again free and their compact ended, openly treated with Florence, and took Albert Sterz as their captain.

A solemn act was signed in the Palazzo Vecchio (July 28), between the *"Signoria"* and the representatives of the captain, the constables, and marshals (Belmonte was one of the representatives). These agreed to serve the Republic of Florence faithfully (?) for six months, fighting against Pisa and Lucca; they besides swore that after the six months were over, they would observe the peace for six years, towards Florence and all her dependent Communes;—the Florentines on their side promised to treat them "as dear brothers and friends." Albert Sterz reserved to himself the personal faculty of leaving the company at his pleasure, provided that none of the troops followed him, and that the company should elect a new captain in his stead. The witnesses on the English side were the Scotsmen Walter and Norman Leslie.

Thus the "great White Company" was divided. An anonymous Pisan chronicler observes:

> It is certain that if they had not split among themselves, they would have become masters of all Tuscany and all Italy, so brave and powerful were they.

As to Sterz and his men, they might have had the goodwill to serve their new masters better than the old—but in any case, they came too late—for in those very days the final fate of war was decided near Pisa.

CHAPTER 5

The Defeat at Cascina

Before stretching itself across the wide and fruitful plain of Pisa, the winding Arno bathes the feet of that high and steep mountain which bears the very descriptive name of "Verruca" or "Verrucola" (a wart). This rises straight up on the right bank of the river, and was from ancient times crowned by a strong fortress—no place could be better adapted to survey the whole of the lower Val d'Arno as far as the sea.

There was no passage then between the river and the cliffs of the Verruca—in modern times a road has been cut in the mountain—but on the left side of the Arno, a pleasant stretch of land lay between it and the first undulations of the distant hills, and here was the borough of Cascina, a strategic point, predestined to be the scene of several Tuscan battles.

At the end of July, Galeotto Malatesta, the new Florentine captain general, was encamped there with Count Montfort's Germans, and many civic volunteers, besides the Genoese crossbow, in fact with all the force Florence had at her disposal: 11,000 foot and 4000 horse. They encamped in disorder, and lived negligently, but this was supplemented by the zeal and vigilance of Manno Donati who took care to fortify the front of the town, towards Pisa with entrenchments, and to place Grimaldi's skilful Genoese cross-bow in the houses.

Pisa only had in her pay Hawkwood's 800 Englishmen and a few *ultramontane* brigades, but the approach of the Florentine Army inflamed the warlike ardour of all the citizens; everybody took arms who knew how to wield them, and Hawkwood was commissioned to attack the enemy's camp forthwith. He tried to make up for the inferiority of his forces by prudence, and leaving Pisa he encamped at the abbey of San Savino, four miles from Cascina. Here he waited for midday, so that the enemy might have the sun and the dust in their eyes (in the afternoon, a sea wind generally blows from the west across the plain of Pisa), and to deceive them, he preluded the action by three feigned attacks, so that Malatesta believed he did not mean to fight at all.

Then he made a move in earnest, sending part of his English troops to the van, and keeping the others with him in the rear. He left his cavalry behind, so that the advance might be less noticeable, and to stir up the energies of his Englishmen he told them that in the Florentine camp they might make prisoners of three or four hundred young nobles, worth from one to two thousand florins of ransom, and besides, in the name of the Republic of Pisa, he promised double pay for a month if they were victorious.

This alluring prospect so fired the courage of the mercenary vanguard, that although they were fatigued by a march of four miles in a suffocating heat, and weighed down by their arms and armour, they did not wait a second command, nor even the reinforcement of the Pisan militia, but rushed to the assault of the trenches.

The horses were unsaddled and the men in the Florentine camp unarmed; Malatesta was asleep, and had told the bell-ringer of the *carroccio*, or war chariot, that he was not to ring the bell under any pretence or he would kick him.

There was tremendous confusion, and the English could not be prevented from breaking the trenches, but Grimaldi was watching, and from the temporary loopholes in the houses, commenced a very tempest of arrows; Count Montfort was on guard and he bore that day the standard of the *feditori*, the most willing of the Florentine volunteers; Manno Donati was also vigilant and with a corps of chosen men of Florence, and Arezzo, with some mountaineers from Casentiuo, he sallied unobserved from Cascina, made a circuit and fell on the flank of the assailants, who fought desperately to get out of the trap, but being poorly seconded by the other mercenaries, they were broken and destroyed leaving 30 dead, and 300 wounded men, who had to wait the Pisan doctors before they could get the darts of the Genoese archers out of their flesh. (They had indeed splendid doctors in Pisa, under the care of whom a great many perished in a few days!)

The defeat of the advance troops put the Pisan militia into such disorder that the Florentines, now victorious, captured the waggons of wine sent from Pisa to her army.

Seeing the day irretrievably lost, Hawkwood, leaving the citizens in the midst, withdrew with his English rear-guard to San Savino where he gathered together his wounded and followed up the retreat to Pisa in good order.

Malatesta took no trouble to molest him, for he gave his mind to collecting trophies of victory, but though he took 2000 prisoners he merely disarmed the foreigners among them, and set them free. He carried the Pisans (a thousand) back to Florence together with an eagle which had flown from Pisa to the camp where it probably scented prey.

Florence long retained a memento of those Pisan prisoners in the *Loggia dei Pisani* on the Piazza della Signoria, which was constructed by their forced labour. There is too an altar dedicated to S. Victor in the Duomo, and the feast of that Saint, the patron of the Guelphs, was for many years celebrated with the *palio* (races) in honour of this victory.

The victorious army did not neglect to celebrate the occasion by passing under the walls of Pisa, where they made reprisals, by returning the insults they had received at the gates of Florence the year before, with even greater spirit and opprobrium than the Pisans had done, after which they marched home. It was not long before peace was concluded between these two cities which were starved out to fatten the Germans and English.

But before peace was concluded, Giovanni Agnello, profiting by the misfortunes of his country, and the ensuing confusion of events, usurped the Lordship of Pisa and took the title of *Doge* (August 28); Hawkwood in his character of captain being his principal assistant.

It is probable that he consented to aid Agnello's arrogant ambition, because he, being a rich merchant, guaranteed the payment of the 30,000 florins required for the stipend of the martial company. To the soldier of fortune everything gave way to the question of pay.

It is certain that Agnello, as the chronicler tells us, had "tuned the lyre" (*temprato la cetera*) with Hawkwood, for having lulled the vigilance of the citizens to sleep, by means of the most absurd dissimulations, he bravely struck his blow by night, while the English soldiers occupied the palace and *piazza* for him; and as universal suffrage was unnecessary in those days he declared that the Blessed Virgin had revealed to him in a dream that he must assume the *dogeship* of Pisa for a year. As soon as the 30,000 florins were paid to the English, and peace concluded with the Florentines, he got himself elected *doge* for life; moreover in the following year he nominated his sons as his successors, Francesco the second was named Auti or Aukud after his godfather, the English *condottiere*, so intimate was the friendship between him and the usurper.

Florence was meanwhile suffering from an *embarras de richesses* in the way of stipendiaries, having engaged a multitude just as the need of them ceased. She sent them into the Lucchese territory where the English White Company, and the German "Company of the Flower" encamped separately. For the good luck of the Florentines, there was an old hostility between these two bands, who were in their ill humour constantly menacing each other.

The Florentines had the wit to keep them on such terms, with each other, that they had neither long truce nor time to quarrel, and when things became serious between English and Germans, Malatesta interfered to pacify them.

Peace assured, the great object was to get them out of the way—the English were sent to encamp on the Cecina, (September) but they would not stay there. Belmonte and his leaders (Sterz according to his clause in the compact had resigned) complained that their horses suffered in the cold nights of the coming autumn, and they wanted covered quarters.

For the rest they protested their devotion and willingness to fight, saying they would rather take 100,000 florins in war than 300,000 in peace. But it was just peace that was being stipulated.

Nothing could prevent them from coming to encamp near San Miniato. Here they behaved courteously, paying their way and doing no damage; very likely they were afraid of Florence favouring the Germans, and setting them upon them, and so they respected the Florentine territory, and unfurled her standard together with that of their own captain.

But as to departing, they put it off as long as possible, waiting "their people and things" (*lor gente e cose*) probably the women and spoil they left behind when they went away in the spring.—At the end of September they were still on the lower Val d'Elsa, not without some struggles with the peasants of San Miniato, nor losses on each side; it seems in fact that the populace knew so well how to return blow for blow, that the Florentine authorities had to interfere and make them return the horses and other things taken from the mercenaries.

To complicate the situation Belmonte, the captain, was absent.

Florence at last managed to send Bongarden southward with his Germans. Albert Sterz united with him and they formed a strong band called the "Star Company," which turned towards the Reame (Kingdom of Naples). As to the White Company, just at that moment Cardinal Albornoz received the commission to engage 6000 men for 200,000 florins to fight for the League against Bernabo Visconti, but the project was not carried out; the Florentines had great difficulty in inducing them to go to the Maremma, and to smooth matters with Siena, but all their efforts could not prevent the English from sacking the land. It was of this that Antonio Pucci sang:

(Which may be thus rendered into English rhyme):
A fine brigade they had, the which a scourge
For ensign bore, and wrought about its way
More damage in the three first hours of dawn
Than other armies worked the live-long day.
Now when the Sienese perceived their freaks
The Florentines for love of God they pray
To draw them off, to offer terms or pact
To procure peace at any price in fact.
The men of Florence straightway did forget
Old injuries which Siena them had wrought
And sent ambassadors who soon did meet
And parley with the English host they sought.
A treaty they arranged, so prompt, that soon
Siena courteously her peace had bought.
Twenty-six thousand florins did she pay
And to Perugia rode the bands away.
No more do I intend to follow up
These Englishmen, nor where they went that day.
But please the Lord where'er they go or stop
They'll go and never more return, I pray.

CHAPTER 6

The Organism Of Mercenary Companies

We beg the reader to excuse us if we refer at this point to some particulars, which if not directly connected with Hawkwood, are necessary to show with what kind of soldiery he had to deal, and what was the general aspect of war in his days.

The White Company, like other bands of freebooters, consisted of both horse and foot soldiers. The infantry were chiefly archers armed with long and strong bows made of yew, which they carried on their backs when marching, and rested the point on the ground when taking aim; they had long arrows and were besides armed with swords and knives. For defence these famous bowmen, who had subdued the French Army, wore an iron helmet, a *cuirass*, or rather breast piece, and iron gloves. The "lances" were mounted soldiers; the name lance was imported by the English, for the hired cavalry used to be called *barbute*, from the shape of their helmets. Each "lance" consisted of three men, the *caporale* (knight), the *piatta* (squire) and the *ragazzo* (page). The two first rode chargers, and the page had a pony or nag. Five lances usually made a *posta* (post), and five posts made a *bandiera* (standard); there was generally a *decurial* leader for every ten lances.

★★★★★★

It is rather difficult to translate the word *caporale* by a just equivalent in English. The nearest approach to it is "knight" or "cavalier." He was a gentleman of independent means who gave or sold his services, together with those of his followers or servants; sometimes one leader furnished several lances, in which case all the *caporali* may not have been knights, until they had distinguished themselves. Sometimes, as Chaucer has represented it, the squire was the son of the knight, and became knight in his turn when he had won his spurs by any great deed of valour. Froissart and other old chroniclers speak of five or six hundred knights fighting in Edward the Black Prince's army at Cressy and Poitiers, where Hawkwood himself was a squire and probably won his spurs. The general name for the whole troop was "men-at-arms."

★★★★★★

With the exception of the Hungarian cavalry—which were rather archers on horseback, being only armed with bow and arrows—the English cavalry was lighter than that of other nations. The German, Burgundian, and Italian lances armed their squires lightly, with only sword and knife (*coltello*), but their knights were much more heavily accoutred than the English. As a rule, they carried helmet, breastplate with iron framework, *cuirass* and *pancerone*, greaves, armlets, gauntlets, iron gloves, sword, knife and lance. The English had no *pancerone*, and wore a *cuirass*, instead of a breastplate, with sleeves of mail and a gorget.

The English horses were also more lightly caparisoned than the others; in fact, the "Codex of the stipendiaries of the Florentine service" which was modified in 1369, conceded permission for men of other nationalities to wear armour in the English style, but not so for the horses.

The English cavaliers generally fought on foot, their horses served more to expedite and facilitate their marches; in fact, they corresponded more to the modern dragoons, who were originally mounted infantry, and in most countries only became exclusively cavalry about the latter half of the last century. In Russia they still retain their mixed character. The Hungarians were a fair representative of modern light cavalry, and the German and Italian lances of the *cuirassiers*.

Filippo Villani and Azario minutely describe the tactics of the White Company and explicitly tell us they almost always fought on foot, leaving their horses in charge of their pages, who retired to ambush during action in some wood or fold of a hill. When fighting, the knights and squires formed themselves into a circular mass, with their long and tough lances lowered closely and compactly, each lance being held by both knight and squire. The attack was made by slow steps, and with fierce shouts. It is true, they had not the advantage of a sudden rush or onslaught, but they gained that of solidity, and were formidable in thus opposing great difficulty to the enemy who should attempt to disorder this species of porcupine.

These tactics, analogous to those of the Swiss in the 16th century—being more defensive than offensive even in an attack—explain the relative incolumity of the White Company even in a defeat, as well as its indecisive victories. It was a convenient method to those who made warfare a mere trade, for they had every reason to prolong hostilities without uselessly exposing themselves.

In consequence of this style of fighting, they carried neither shields nor bucklers, they had no firearms (except now and then a *bombarda* (mortar?) and were very well disciplined in file and duty, but they were disorderly in quarters, and the difficulty of finding provision and forage obliged them to frequently change their camp.

As to their appearance, they were a splendid troop, were it only for the diligence of the squires, who polished the arms till they shone like mirrors.

★★★★★★

Here is a recipe of the year 1402 to prevent arms from ever getting rusty: "Cut off all the legs of a goat from the knee downwards, let them stay in the smoke for a day, then keep them 15 or 25 days. When you require them, break the legs and take out the marrow from the bones, and grease the arms with it and they will always keep bright even when wet."

★★★★★★

That which made them formidable was their custom of nocturnal and still more the cowardice of the Italians, who were unused to arms. They were insuperable in a "sacking", for plunder was their ordinary method of provisioning—and in the constant menaces with which they obtained heavy ransoms and large stipends from the Italian cities. For purposes of plunder they carried a great many scaling ladders made of separate pieces fitting into each other, that is to say, to take exposed or ill defended places. Where they found vigilance or valid resistance, they did not attempt to attack a fortress.

In the 14th century, when artillery had scarcely begun to be known, a castle or walled town presented almost an impregnable obstacle, because the besiegers had usually exhausted the resources of the country before the besieged had consumed the provisions stored in the city; hence in wars of that time, there was always great devastation of the country, while the occupation of the cities by the enemy was rare, and as the towns sheltered the inhabitants and their wealth, the battles were very inconclusive.

The funds of the mercenary company then chiefly depended on depredation and extortion, and the squires who made a business of it, were not at all accustomed to save their earnings: play, women, luxury, in short a gay life, consumed quickly, often in anticipation, such ill gained money, which often passed, together with arms and horses, into the hands of usurers.

This was a serious inconvenience to the republics that hired the companies. Their equipage lost, the soldiers could no longer serve, and reduced to their last shifts, they had more temptation to break their agreements, to sell themselves elsewhere, or to demand more than was in the compact.

To relieve them from the risks of usury was sometimes a wise provision, and consequently, in 1362, Florence opened a bank for Loans to the stipendiaries which was reformed on a very simple basis in 1367.

★★★★★★

Matteo Villani XI, c. 38: "The greedy and dishonest usurers, under cover of lending help to the soldiers of their republic, took away their money, arms, and horses, so that they could no longer be of use to their employers, for this the commune was moved to form a bank which will the public money should assist the soldiers. In the month of February 1362, it was organised with all its officials, and the republic placed 15,000 florins at the disposal of the bank with which to commence operations."

★★★★★★

They opened operations by allowing a credit up to 1000 *lire* to each company of 25 lances; a constable might borrow as much as 600 *lire*, an ordinary knight up to 100, and it remained with the officials to determine what sums they should allow to the subordinates. No interest was extorted, but every loan must be backed by the security of two *conestabili* (superior officers, of very high grade). This last condition and the incurable improvidence of the adventurers left still a large field to the usurers, so that at the same time severe laws were promulgated against procurators and money lenders, prohibiting exchanges, or the negotiation of credits with the stipendiaries: laws which implicated even the loss of political rights, and remained in force till 1431.

In the banking books numberless names of constables and knights of every nation are to be found, dating from 1367 to the end of the 15th century and even later. There are however few English names after the end of the 14th century.

The mode of living of the mercenary militia in Italy during that century, their internal relations, and those with the States employing them, are completely explained by Ricotti and Canestrini, who quote from undeniable documents, such as contracts stipulating their stipends, and the special laws of some Tuscan Republics. The numerous contracts with English Constables up to 1395 which exist in the Florentine Archives of the *Riformagioni* and correspond with those already published, are all made on the same scheme. They frequently contain a clause "not to fight against the King of England" and another "that the leaders of companies are responsible for the crimes committed by the soldiers in camp, while the Commune shall judge those committed in the city, or to the damage of subjects of the Republic."

That important, curious, and complete codex of the Florentine militia in 1337 with its fifty-three chapters, containing the rules, and various conditions for the troops, are referred to and illustrated by the aforesaid authors (Ricotti and Canestrini). On his side Gregorovius has given what we might almost call the philosophy of mercenaries. He considers the system as an organic social disease, like the degeneracy of chivalry, or the rising of the lower classes, massing themselves together against the higher; it would perhaps be easier and more exact to define them as "military brigands under command."

On the other hand his observation is true that the condition especially favourable to mercenaries in Italy was, that the republics, with their democratic mania for exiling their nobles, had lost their military virtue; but he is silent as to the chief reason, which was that there was much more to plunder in Italy than in other lands, and the hunter chooses the ground that most abounds in sport.

Their organisation favoured by circumstances was so complete, that they might almost be qualified as "Nomad Military States": they elected their captain or freely accepted him if entering a company already formed; the captain had great power, but it was limited by the council of constables and marshals, while in the most important decisions the cavaliers or *caporali* were called into the deliberations.

The decisions were not enrolled until they had been accurately debated, and the conditions fixed by the captains: they often demanded pay in anticipation, and security against preceding enmities with soldiers of other nationalities whom they might find in the company. In treaties they required a written reply, or if it were a case of parley, they demanded a safe-conduct for themselves and their embassy. This is evident from a curious letter from Constable Swiler to our John Hawkwood.

They had a numerous following of women (even nuns carried off by force) and of voluntary courtesans, and when the soldiers thought it wiser to keep on friendly terms with a district, they honestly purchased their provisions.

★★★★★★

In the Battle of Brentelle, June 25, 1386, the Paduans took 211 of them, and crowning them with flowers and putting bouquets in their hands, they conducted them in triumph to Padua, where they were invited to breakfast in the palace of the ruling Lord Francesco Carrara.

★★★★★★

They employed usurers and bankers in every city to lend them money or to keep it for them: they had able ambassadors and eloquent orators to conduct their diplomatic treaties: treasurers to regulate their financial affairs, and attorneys for their private ones, secretaries, notaries and registrars for their correspondence and the due preparations of legal acts and documents.

Gregorovius observes:

The sole reason they did not establish lordship in Italy, is because the leaders lacked the political idea, and the adventurers the bonds of nationality.

It is a fact that natives of so many different countries were enrolled in every company that they were called from the majority of the men composing them, English, German, Burgundian, or Breton, Hungarian or lastly Italians.

As to the leaders, if ever there was one who for talent, constancy, valour, prudence, and resolution might have aspired to the highest aims, but who had the wisdom to moderate his ambition, and practically remain at his post, it was Hawkwood, as we shall see in following the history of himself and his men.

CHAPTER 7

The Perugian War

What between contemporaneous chronicles, posterior historians, and modern commentators, together with the equivocal dates, and doubtful names which one hears without knowing to whom they belong, the history of the mercenary companies just after the Pisan war is so complicated that much of it is undecipherable. Let us see if we can find our bearings in this sea of difficulty.

Both the English White Company and Annechin Bongarden's German band of "the Star" marched southwards, the latter against the Kingdom of Naples and the former towards Perugia. (November 1364.) But on the way they were set against each other as foes, for the Perugians opposed the English invaders by hiring Bongarden's troops armed with long axes and with hand grenades.

This was enough for the English, who, driven also by hunger, were soon brought to terms, stipulating peace and friendship to Perugia, promising not to injure Annechin Bongarden for a year, and to withdraw within ten days. On this compact provisions were conceded them by purchase. The treaty was celebrated by a banquet to which the courteous priors of Perugia invited the leaders and knights of both companies.

Then the tables were turned, for Bongarden, who advanced towards Naples, devastated the Roman *campagna* by the way, so much that Cardinal Albornoz for the Church, and Queen Joanna of Naples made a contract with the White Company, (January 14,1365), which bound the latter for the price of 160,000 florins, to keep the peace towards the kingdom for five years, and expressly to fight for it against

Bongarden. This act was stipulated by Hugh de Mortimer, Captain General, by the Captain Nicholas Count of Thod (Hungarian) and Andrew Belmonte; George Brise *conestabile*, Eugene Ecton (Acton?) and many of the knights.

The White Company, reinforced by the Hungarians, had evidently elected a new captain to succeed Sterz, Hawkwood, and Belmont.

Hawkwood remaining in Pisa for the winter made a trip to Lombardy, perhaps sent there by the Doge Agnello, who had an understanding with Bernabo Visconti: and from this time may be dated the relations of Hawkwood with this exemplary tyrant and head of the Ghibellines, who sent the English *condottiere*, in his pay, into Tuscany to assist the Ghibellines. In other words, Hawkwood on Bernabo's account reassumed the command of the White Company which had now returned to menace Florence, and in spite of their treaty attacking the Perugians. He had besides the disposal of a Pisan contingent and was receiving Pisan pay.

★★★★★★

In June 1365 in the name of the magnificent and potent Lord Giovanni de' Conti by the grace of God, Doge of Pisa, and of the *Anziani*, 100 florins on account were assigned to Hawkwood who authorised Janni (Johnny), an English sergeant, to receive them for him, and again in July (500 florins were decreed as provision for a year from August 1st by the great general Council of the Church and that of the Senate and Credenza, ratified by the Council of the people of Pisa.

★★★★★★

As soon as the English reappeared on the Perugian territory, (July 22, 1365), that city recalled Bongarden from the Campagna of Rome and united the city militia with his Germans. Three thousand cavalry and infantry commanded for the Church party by the Bolognese Tommaso Obizzoni, and sent by Cardinal Albornoz also arrived in time to assist.

The old animosity between the Germans and English, by this time had become bitter and bloody, and rendered the battle decisive. Hawkwood with the Pisan supplement had 6000 horse, but still his forces were very inferior and consequently the English were overcome.

There have been many exaggerations about this defeat especially regarding Hawkwood. Machiavelli says he was taken prisoner; Ghirardacci describes the battle as taking place between Arezzo and Cortona, and says that for four hours it was indecisive, and that finally

41

Tommaso Obizzoni becoming victorious took Haucud the English captain. Even Bonincontri in his Caesaresque *Annals* attributes the merit of victory to Obizzoni, and adds that "the English were all taken with their leader Giovanni Acuto and put into prison." We find elsewhere that the Pope liberated Hawkwood from prison.

These authors evidently romance. Machiavelli is inexact enough to attribute the action to the time of Pope Innocent VI who had then been dead three years. Ghirardacci compiled his *History of Bologna* from chroniclers who were inclined to exaggerate Bolognese achievements.

★★★★★★

In his preface Ghirardacci boasts of diligent fidelity in having followed the most serious authors, and collated both public and private MSS., and in the dedication to Pope Clement VIII he says he has consulted "the public documents of the Vatican Library, authentic MSS. in many archives, as well as personal deeds, especially those of the Bologna Archives." And in fact, we shall frequently have occasion to refer to him as an authority; for, generally speaking, he seems trustworthy; but in this case the facts and dates weaken his testimony, and so we must refute it.

★★★★★★

He besides imagines Hawkwood fighting against the Florentines, while the Signory of Florence was in fact making offers for his services, and though he would not concede, was sending these instructions (July 16) to its ambassadors near him:

By the reverence of God. . . . and out of regard to him whom we esteem our dear friend we intend to use towards him and his brigade that courtesy which should satisfy him, though by reason of wars and great expenses we are much less wealthy and powerful than he esteems us, etc., etc.

This imprisonment of Hawkwood then becomes very problematical, and we had better turn to chroniclers nearer to the place and the deed. Now the Sienese chronicle relates that having suffered some loss in crossing the Sienese territory, Hawkwood arrived near Perugia in July, and here he had to combat the "Stella (Star) Company of Germans under Bongarden,"—which battle was a great and bitter strife (*aspra e grande*);—the Germans won the day, killing many of the English, and Andrew Belmonte and fifty knights were put in prison at Perugia. Hawkwood fled and got away towards Siena with many others.

The Perugians sent to tell Siena that John Hawkwood and his English Company were defeated, and the Commune of Siena presented the messenger with a scarlet vest lined with silk which cost 26 florins.

Graziani, the Perugian chronicler, does not even name Hawkwood. He only says that Bongarden and the Perugian militia, after two sanguinary but victorious combats, constrained the remnant of the English to retreat to the castle of San Mariano, where after two days, weak with thirst, and faint with heat, being deprived of water or other liquid, they were obliged to surrender.

Sixteen hundred were taken to Perugia as prisoners to await ransom, while of the *canaglia* some were killed and others set free. Among the prisoners were four knights with their respective standards, the only one of them named being the most distinguished;—Andrew Belmonte, "of royal race," the four banners are however heraldically described as,

1. Gules, *sémé* of *bezants*, or;
2. *Argent, a chevron gules*, starred of the field at point;
3. Quartered, *dexter argent*, charged with griffon, gules, and sinister *gules* with lion *argent*;
4. Gules, a bend or, charged with a crescent of the field.

This last must have belonged to the bastard Belmonte. Neither of them corresponds to that of John Hawkwood, which may be seen to this day in Paolo Uccello's *fresco*, in the Duomo at Florence, and which has for its blazon, "*Argent a chevron* sable, charged with three *escallop* shells of the field," nor is there the motto "*al falco*" which we find on his seal as allusive to his name.

Andrew Belmonte easily regained his liberty on swearing to respect the Perugian territory for five years, and leaving as hostages three captains, *viz* Hugh Mortimer, John di Breccia (Brise) and Thod the Count of Hungary, who were most probably the proprietors of the three other standards. From all this it appears that Hawkwood was defeated but saved himself with part of his men, while the rest were shut up with Belmonte in San Mariano; and that he was still in a condition to keep the field, for, on August 3rd , the Commune of Perugia sent part of the German forces to help Siena *contro Messer Giovanni Aguto inghilese.*

Thus says the Perugian chronicler and he of Siena confirms it, even saying that the Sienese did not think it superfluous to send both the German leaders, Bongarden and Sterz, against Hawkwood; and that it was only then that Hawkwood had to beat a retreat, and fighting his way through the Maremma, he passed thence, along the sea shore to Liguria, the Genoese territory.

CHAPTER 8

A Hawkwood, a Visconti, and a Hapsburg in the Company of St. George

The mercenary companies, as we see, were a hydra of a hundred heads, and their captains each like "Antaeus," who, defeated and overthrown, rose up from the earth more enterprising than before. Matteo Villani, in one of his eloquent outbursts, tells us how the Italian people suffered under them; astrologers tried to explain the scourge by the movement of the heavens, and conjunction of planets; other folks attributed it to the anger of God. Urban V gave ecclesiastical subsidies to princes, (1364) and indulgences to the people who would take arms against:

> That multitude of villains of divers nations, associated in arms by avidity in appropriating to themselves the fruit of the labours of innocent and defenceless people; unbridled in every kind of cruelty, extorting money; methodically devastating the country, and the open towns, burning houses and barns, destroying trees and vines, obliging poor peasants to fly; assaulting, besieging, invading, spoiling, and ruining even fortresses and walled cities; torturing and maiming those from whom they expected to obtain ransom, without regard to ecclesiastical dignity, or sex or age; violating wives, virgins, and nuns, and constraining even gentlewomen to follow their camp, to do their pleasure and carry arms and baggage. (February 17.)

Soon after this, (May 15) it entered the Pope's head to persuade the English to take up the cross like Christ, and to follow the King of Cyprus to fight the Turks—so he wrote to the captain and leaders—but Hawkwood who was not a "Conte Verde" remained unconvinced.

Seeing they were not to be persuaded, the Pope again began to thunder out excommunications against them, and to publish indulgences to those who would fight them. Seeing that neither excommunications nor indulgences had any effect, he thought to entice all the bands on both sides of the Alps, to pass into the East by land or by sea; and for this he formed an alliance with the Emperor Charles IV, the Pope promising money and benedictions, and the emperor undertaking to pay the expenses of the journey—he who never had a penny to call his own!

Cardinal Albornoz was commissioned to attempt the metamorphosis of brigands into crusaders, but the captains naturally laughed him to scorn. The cardinal was then set to form a league against Hawkwood, who was the most formidable of the lot. He treated with Florence, (August 1365) but nothing was concluded, for to destroy the companies it would be necessary to hire more foreigners and thus increase the evil.

In the meantime, the English and Germans being left without pay, wandered about Tuscany sacking wherever they went. Florence could do nothing but send ambassadors to one, and then to the other, to smooth them down, and keep them to their word, to find out their intentions and possibly also to edge them on to fight with each other. The Pope, as we find from his secret correspondence, followed the same tactics.

Bongarden was in the Lucchese, (Autumn) and intended to pass into Lombardy, but Hawkwood prevented him. The latter had become the effective leader of a new Anglo-Italian Company (one of several which bore the name of St. George) which had been hastily formed in Lunigiana, and was commanded by Ambrogio Visconti bastard son of Bernabo Visconti;—he acting Telemachus, and Hawkwood doing Mentor.

The Florentines sent out six ambassadors to the different belligerents: there were Lapo de' Rossi and Giorgio Scali who went to grant Bongarden free and friendly passage across their territory; Piero Canigiani and Niccolo Rimbaldeschi to congratulate Bernabo on the promotion of his son to the generalship; and Doffo de' Bardi and Giovanni Cambi, to treat with the Company of St. George, which was already on Pisan ground.

The compact was soon concluded and signed at Florence, on October 12, 1365, the company binding itself for the sum of 6000 florins, not to injure Florence or her allies for five years, even though it should change captains. They were besides granted passes, guides, and provisions, (by payment) with permission to hire 300 horsemen from either Siena or Perugia.

The relative document is mutilated. In the heading, figure the names of Ambrogio Visconti, captain general; Giovanni Ubaldini, Italian; Aymond de Rundell, and William Boson, Englishmen; Luca di Valco, Hungarian; Lodovico delle Spade of Parma, counsellors; Hugh

Ethon, English constable; Thomas Merezal (Marshal?), marshal of the English; Bartolommeo da Gaggio, marshal of the Italians. In the context frequent mention is made of a certain Signer Giovanni (Sir John) who can be no other than Hawkwood, for at the end we read:

> For the observation of the which things, all and single. . . . in the name of the above, do oblige and pledge themselves, to the above-named Signer Ambrogio Captain, and Signor Giovanni Acud. . . .

Among the signatures are the names and seals of Visconti, Ubaldini, Hawkwood, and forty-two others, amongst captains and constables.

Having pocketed the florins, the company lost not a day: "time is money!" so they immediately (on October 15) encamped at the Abbey of Isola near Siena. The Sienese sent a few fruitless embassies to offer terms, while they were seeking soldiers to fight them, and kept two sentinels night and day on their tower called del Mangia. They found eleven companies (*bandiere*) of Germans at Orvieto, and finally having got together a good many troops sallied forth to battle.

But the Company of St. George did not stop to fight! riding rapidly night and day, they halted only at Sarzana and then went on to the vicinity of Genoa. (November 28.) The terror they spread everywhere is expressed in a document in the Pisan Archives where a certain Francesco Bellebuono explains to the *Anziani* "that he cannot bring the goods to Pisa, for fear of John Hawkwood."

The speed of transport of those adventurers is incredible, as in a search for spoil, or pay, they rushed continually over the length and breadth of the peninsula.

Among the *condottieri* then 1364 and 1365) living at the expense of Italy, were a Count Johann of the illustrious and imperial house of Hapsburg, and his brother Rudolph.

On the other side of the Alps Johann had sustained evil fortunes, and had let himself be captured by the *burghers* of Zurich, and kept prisoner for three years in the little island (now so lovely in its cool and pleasant shades) where the limpid waters of the Limmat leave the Lake to flow through the city; and where at that time there rose on a rock a dark fortress tower called the Wellemberg. While in prison here he composed an elegiac song to the forget-me-not, which began

So, di un piccolo fiore azzurro.
(*I know a tiny blue flower.*)

He found brighter fortunes in Italy, where he and his brother at first followed the banner of Florence. Rudolf, being an effeminate looking man, was called by the Florentines *il Conte Menno* (the beardless Count); he belied his face however at the Battle of Cascina, where he performed incredible prodigies of valour—as Filippo Villani has it. Johann finally allied himself with Hawkwood and Visconti, (March 1366), who had returned from Liguria, to the misfortune of Siena.

The Sienese tried to conciliate them by presents of poultry and sweets, providing victuals, and sending to treat with them, but finding the two captains intractable, they tried the tactics of the soldiery, and set fire to the hay all over the country, so that the enemy could not lodge there. At the same time, they had recourse to Hawkwood's old friend the Doge of Pisa, to beg him at least to mediate with the English brigade.

But the company held out, and at length, (March 30), the Sienese were persuaded to put their hands in their purses, they made a forced loan, and stipulated on April 20 the "conventions and accords" between the Commune of Siena on the one part; and Ambrogio Visconti captain, Hawkwood, the Count of Hapsburg and Giovanni da Buda, constables of the Company of St. George, on the other. The price paid by the Sienese was 10,500 florins, of which the first instalment of 4000 was to be paid within fifteen days, besides which the company was to be allowed to pass over the Sienese territory once a year for five years, provided they did no damage nor annoyed the inhabitants. The contract was stipulated by the representatives and attorneys of the two parts, all knights or marshals in the respective brigades. John Quartery, Englishman, sealed it with Hawkwood's arms, a *chevron* and three shells, legend indecipherable.

The compact made, it was not easy to get it kept: many of the company's soldiers entered Siena to celebrate the occasion, and Visconti's men behaved so badly that the city rose against them, and several were killed or wounded.

Having taken the money, Hawkwood and his good scholar Ambrogio took the road to Pisa, greatly damaging Florentine lands by the way. Florence sent ambassadors to accompany them and keep them in order, one of whom, Doffo de' Bardi got Hawkwood to promise to move on in an amicable manner.

This probably meant only a day's march which cost Florence 350 florins paid to Hawkwood, and 55 more for indemnity to Bardi for horses lost (*perduti*) on the occasion. Then there was always the fear of worse things, so much so that (July 1st) Giovanni di Porcellino was sent to the company as a spy under pretext of finding certain boys who were said to have run away from Florence, and when Visconti wanted to return to the Florentine states, he (Porcellino) persuaded Hawkwood to pass wide of the city, sending warnings to all the places on the chosen route.

These particulars are necessary to comprehend what a terrible scourge these adventurers were, and why Italian potentates, both great and small, were impatient to find a remedy against them.

Pope Urban V had hurled a bull (formal papal document) from Avignon, (April 15), and ended with a highly coloured description of the brigandish achievements of the companies, and invocations to Heaven for their extermination; then he excommunicated the captains who did not disband their armies, and restore the lands they occupied; the princes and republics, who hired them, and the lords and people who served them; he stained with infamy everyone who should take their part, and then with the attraction of plenary absolution invited everybody to fight against them.

After this thundering prelude, the Pope returned to his favourite nostrum, of forming a general league against the companies to expel them from Italy, and oblige them to take up the cross against the Turks. The Emperor Charles IV and nearly all the Italian princes and republics adhered to it. Florence sent to Avignon, as ambassadors for the treaty, personages no less than Francesco Bruni and Giovanni Boccaccio, thus beginning to absolve herself from the censure of having wished to employ the Company of St. George.

Even Bernabo Visconti seemed disposed to withdraw his son Ambrogio from that career, and received the approval of the Pope, who offered to annul all the compacts made by different republics with the *condottieri*. But it was very difficult to come to any practical conclusion, for at that same time Florence was sending to make excuses to Ambrogio, who had asked a loan of money, and was also excusing herself to the Pope for her inability to enter the league against the existing companies.

They had then to limit themselves to the more modest wee. object of preventing new bands from descending into Italy or staying there, and they perforce resigned themselves to the ones already existing, almost recognising that they had acquired a right to, or even monopoly of the military stipendiary.

This admitted, the act of the league stipulated in Florence on September 19, 1366 added:

> The Companies which are at present in Italy are the under-mentioned and no others:
>
> The Company of Signor Ambrogio (Visconti);
>
> The Company of Signor Giovanni Acuto (Hawkwood);
>
> The Company of Signor Annechino (Bongarden);
>
> The Company of Signor Conte Giovanni (Johann of Hapsburg).

But even with this limited scope the league did not last long. It was dissolved in December of the following year, because Florence would have nothing to do with the emperor.

The Company of St. George lasted even less than the league. It was completely defeated in the Kingdom of Naples, and Ambrogio Visconti taken and kept as prisoner by Queen Joanna, (1367 to 1376): while the remains of his band went to reinforce Hawkwood, who had reappeared before Siena. For eight days (January 1367) he had been amicably furnished with provisions, and was then obliged to take the usual refuge at Pisa, the base of his operations.

Here he was joined (February) by his. old comrade the royal bastard Belmonte, who on his liberation from prison in Perugia had got together a great troop and refurnished them with arms. Thus strengthened, the two Englishmen marched against the Perugians with whom they had to settle an old account, the defeat they suffered two years before.

At Montalcinello they encountered the Sienese who were reinforced by the Perugians, and provided with Hungarian and many other soldiers. The Sienese were completely routed, (March 6, 1367) and their captain, the *comervadore* Ugolino, was taken prisoner and obliged to pay ten thousand florins of ransom. Then (March 29), the Perugians and Sienese were wholly defeated at Ponte San Giovanni, where 1500 of their men were killed, besides a great many horses. Their captain (that German Paer who had signalised himself in the Florentine service, fighting against the English in the Mugello) and the Podesta of Perugia remained prisoners.

Hawkwood and Belmonte were revenged to the full; so much so that the hall in which the Perugian magistrates had decided to give Belmonte his liberty, was called the Hall of Bad Counsel (*del mal consiglio*).

CHAPTER 9

Victory at Cascina

The successes of the English caused great apprehension to the Florentines, who had already sent the usual Doffo di Bardi to hear whether Hawkwood would enter their service, and to the captain himself they wrote (April 5):

> Although we have urgent need of soldiers, we are disposed to wait even a month for you.

He refused, pledging himself instead to an agreement with Cardinal Albornoz, the Pope's legate, on which the *Signoria* wrote to the cardinal and sent instructions to Bardi, and to their ambassadors at Perugia, for they were afraid that the English after having drained the territory of Perugia should turn their attention to the Val d'Arno; they feared also "the annoyances which such people occasion even against the will of their captain." For these reasons they were unwilling to grant them a passage, even when they promised to make good the damages. The instructions so run:

> Manage, that they shall not pass over our territory as M. Giovanni has more than once promised to do, to show the great love which he says he bears us. . . . At least get them to pass by the route which will do us the least harm, and at every place where they encamp send us a messenger, that we may know their movements.

After all, as soon as the Pisan War was finished, rather friendly relations were maintained, between Hawkwood and Florence; we have seen that the Florentines addressed themselves especially to him in treating with the Company of St. George; it would seem as though he foresaw that someday or other it would be to his interest to serve Florence.

On the other hand, (April 28) the Sienese perceiving that the affair was dragging on, decided to offer him money provided he would quit the country, and as their treasury was empty, they contracted a loan on the wine duties.

In fact, he returned peacefully to Pisa where he was accustomed to live at the "Inn of Martino" at Camperonesi, an honourable house, apparently, as the daughter of the Emperor Charles IV also lodged there, in 1369.

Here they were preparing great things in 1367, in honour of Pope

Urban V, who was coming to Italy by sea from Avignon. Pisa being Catholic wished to pay its respects to the Pope but being also Ghibelline, she took precautions against the head of the Guelph faction, who was to touch at the port of Pisa and land at Leghorn. The *doge* Agnello therefore went to Leghorn with more than a thousand cavaliers, led by Hawkwood; and the Pope, who had persecuted the *condottieri* with excommunications and treaties, was so afraid, that he would not disembark.

A little while after he had stopped the Pope, it fell to Hawkwood's lot to stop the emperor.

In 1368 he had returned to the pay of Bernabo Visconti together with William Boson, conducting four thousand Englishmen. His passage into Lombardy was probably connected with the arrival there of Lionel Duke of Clarence, son of Edward III, of England; who came to celebrate his marriage with Violante, daughter of Galeazzo Visconti and niece of Bernabo and it is very likely that he went to pay homage at the court of his own Royal Prince; for we already know that all the English adventurers in Italy stipulated a clause in all their contracts affirming their loyalty to the King of England.

★★★★★★

The Milanese annals say in general terms that Lionel was accompanied by about 2000 English, amongst whom were many archers. Giovio and Litta positively affirm that Hawkwood was in the duke's party, and the heraldic book of Sampson Lennard Bluemantle confirms the fact.

★★★★★★

The ceremonials of this marriage, and the rich gifts to the guests, with all other particulars, are amply described by the Milanese chroniclers.

It was a splendid wedding—Petrarch and the Conte Verde were there—but to the Duke of Clarence it was an ill-omened day, for by reason of a malady contracted by the change of climate, or intemperance in the too sumptuous nuptial banquets, or by other excesses, within three months he had passed into the other world.

Then arose a contest between the English nobles of the Duke's suite and Galeazzo Visconti, who demanded the restitution of the marriage portion (Alba, Mondovi, Cherasco, Cuneo, and Demonte). There is no sign (1368) that Hawkwood was mixed up in this, indeed such a thing would have been both imprudent and useless.

Besides he was otherwise employed on Bernabo's account. This prince had erected a new bastion at Borgoforte on the Po and stationed an Italian garrison, there, which by reason of old rancours, had disagreed with the German mercenaries in Visconti's pay, and was reduced to evil case, so that Bernabo had to ride in great haste to the place, where—order being restored—he placed the bastion under the charge of Hawkwood's Englishmen.

Then the Emperor Charles IV came down from the Alps (May 1368) and made common cause with the d' Estes and other Italian princes against the Visconti, persuading them to attack Borgoforte. It must be noted that what between the Imperials (Bohemians, Sclavonians, Poles, Grisons and Swiss) d' Este's Italians, those of Malatesta, and of Queen Joanna; and the Church party which consisted of Bretons, Gascons, and Provençals; as many as twenty thousand combatants presented themselves before that fortress.

In the army of Visconti were Germans, English, Italians, Burgundians, all with the firm determination to defend the bulwarks; in those days a small place, well provisioned and manned with a spirited garrison, might defy even "an army sufficient to subjugate Italy." To intercept succour, the d' Este party had launched on the Po a fleet of galleys and other boats, and the river being much swollen by the melting of the snows, the Imperialists bethought themselves of breaking the banks above Borgoforte, but the garrison knew how to save itself from the inundation, and returned it by breaking the banks towards the valley by night, thus flooding the plains of Mantua, and the entrenchments of the Imperial camp. Charles IV was obliged to raise his camp, and shut himself up in Mantua, after which, on account of the damage he had suffered, and of the scarcity of provisions, he hastened to agree to Bernabo's terms.

This brilliant operation completed, Hawkwood was commissioned to conduct a large force in aid of the Perugians, who had obtained the alliance of the Visconti in a war with Arezzo and the Pope. He crossed the Bolognese territory and the Romagna, without difficulty, giving it out that he was a captain on his adventures; and pretending that he was dismissed by Visconti and desirous of hiring himself to the Church, he comported himself "honestly, modestly, and quietly." Guided by a certain Monaldi, the Perugian ambassador, he arrived under Arezzo, but there he was completely defeated.

Ser Gorello of Arezzo celebrated this rout in hendecasyllabic triplets, but it will be better for us to hear the official report which the commune of Arezzo sent (June 15) to the Pope, from which it results:

That the English were encamped in the plain near the city, about a mile from the *Porta Buja,* that they were attacked by all the Aretian Army both foot and horse, by the soldiers of the Church commanded by Simone di Spoleto, and by two German bands, led by Flaxen von Riesach and Johann von Rieten. The combat was long and fierce, the deaths many, even among the higher grades, and finally the English were defeated and almost all taken prisoners including their captain "Signer Giovanni Haud" (Hawkwood), and many cavaliers, together with the unfortunate Dinolo di Bindo Monaldi, the Perugian ambassador.

The honours of the day, according to the popular poet, were given to the saints Vito and Modesto, whose feast it chanced to be; but, according to the official relation, they were principally rendered to the German "Rieten" who was knighted, "as was proper to his most excellent valour."

The poet Ser Gorello says that "Messer Giovanni Agudo" (Hawkwood)

Sconfitto fu, e tutta sua brigata
Con grande mio onor allor fu presa.
(*Was defeated, and all his brigade*
To my great honour was then taken.)

This would leave the imprisonment of Hawkwood doubtful, but the aforesaid official report is too explicit not to be admitted as truth.

★★★★★★

Ghirardacci, Buonincontri and others refer the pretended imprisonment of Hawkwood to his battle against the Perugians in 1365; they were probably drawn into error by this real captivity following the defeat in 1368 when he marched to the succour of Perugia.

★★★★★★

In fact, for some time the chronicles and histories are silent about him. Had he been free, he would not have been so long with his hands in his waist-belt.

We do not find him mounted again till a year afterwards; without doubt he was ransomed, and in the meantime had been reconstructing his company. English mercenaries were everywhere, the Pope had some troops of them, and the republic of Pisa had a great many lances.

★★★★★★

In fact, in March 1369 a "Ser Piero notary and public writer to the administration of the cavalry of the Commune of Pisa" was, by order of the *Anziani*, paid the fees and salary due to him from the English mercenary horse troops for his fees on the occasion of the *"mostre"* (show) at Cascina. He was reimbursed 30 *lire* and 8 *soldi*, at the rate of one *soldo* a month for every *"posta"* (five lances) and the payments were made for two months. They therefore amounted to 15 *lire* and 4 *soldi* a month, which would mean a considerable number of *"poste"* and brigades. In another Pisan document of the same year, for the usual anticipation of pay on account, there are many English names among the 46 leaders of brigades specified.

★★★★★★

And here it must be told how the Patriarch of Aquileja, who had come to Pisa as the vicar of the emperor, demanded the oath of fealty from the horse troops, and how all gave it except the English, from whom the Patriarch had to content himself with a simple promise of obedience. Italians and *ultramontanes* recognised the direct or indirect sovereignty of the emperor, the English on the other hand kept their insular independent nationality, loyal only to their own king.

Hawkwood's faithful sponsor the Doge Agnello had been exiled from Pisa, and so our hero had to seek elsewhere the elements to reconstitute his band.

When the troops were in order, by the commission of Bernabo Visconti, whose pay he pretended to accept, he actually moved again to aid the Perugians who rebelled against the Pope, and rode into the Papal States. (June 1869.)

The emperor, on hearing this news, wrote bitterly to Galeazzo Visconti, complaining that he was opposing the Church and he wrote desiring Bernabo to recall the company. Fruitless words.

The Pope after having been blockaded for some time in Montefiascone, where the English arrows reached him even in the palace, was able to retire to Viterbo publishing solemn condemnations against the Perugians; who under the guidance of Hawkwood responded by encamping at Viterbo, (August 8) where they occupied Montalto, and burned the vines of the surrounding country under the very eyes of the Pope.

The Pontiff promised indulgences to whoever would fight for him, and gave the Byzantine Emperor John Palaeologus the faculty to call the company into the East, absolving them from the oaths which bound them to their employers in the West.

Hawkwood preferred to follow his career in Italy and remained faithful to Bernabo who recalled him into Tuscany (end of November) to assist San Miniato which was besieged by the Florentines.

The plan of Bernabo was on a vast scale (1369): he intended to take Leghorn, to attempt Pisa, to make war against the Ubaldini in the Casentino, so as to cut off the Florentines from all their commercial roads by mountain, and by sea, and thus to starve her out, while they scoured the country. This scheme was discovered by means of an intercepted letter. For the rest, Bernabo would have scrupulously respected the Sienese territory. The war was thus restricted to the neighbourhood of San Miniato.

San Miniato "*al Tedesco*," the usual seat of the Imperial vicars in Tuscany, was a place as important to the Ghibellines as it was to the Guelphs. To put himself within range of it and await an occasion to provide provisions, Hawkwood took up his position at Cascina on the Arno. Here he had been beaten by the Florentines in 1364, and here he now had a chance of obtaining a brilliant revenge.

Although reinforced by Flaxen and by Messer Anisi di Natene or Rieten (the two German conquerors at Arezzo), up to two thousand horse, he only had at his own disposal five hundred men-at-arms. These were however the "finest and the best-armed men that ever existed and they would fight against a thousand men." The Florentines also had a very fine army under San Miniato—three thousand in all, between cavalry and infantry, and four hundred cross-bowmen.

They flattered themselves that they would win a second victory at Cascina, and their commissary at the camp, a certain Cavicciuli, constrained the captain Giovanni Malatacca of Reggio, reluctantly to attack Hawkwood;—the priors at Florence talked of sending to Malatacca the heart of an ox (*bue*) "as a reproof for so much prudence." (The word "*bue*" is used for "ox" and "dunce".)

The English had got up a great many boats from Pisa, (December 1st) to forage on the other side of the Arno, and they were tranquilly preparing their rations, when the alarm was given by the bells of Pontedera ringing *a stormo* to signify the passage of troops. They were scarcely in time to barricade the trench and place themselves on foot with lances in hand, when the Florentine vanguard of four hundred horse was upon them. They too dismounted and began to use their hands. More than five hundred lances having been broken and about five and twenty men killed, Hawkwood had recourse to one of his favourite stratagems to decide the affair. He made believe to retreat and appeared to be fording the Arno at any cost, while he had placed his best troops in ambush with orders not to move till the Florentines had crossed.

The pages of the English "lances" went down to the river with the horses as if to seek the ford; this being observed by some cavaliers, was reported to the Florentines, who were thereby persuaded that the enemy were flying as vanquished. The unlucky Cavicciuli obliged Malatacca to "follow up the victory," that is, to fall into the trap; eight hundred horse which were sent along the river to take the English in the flank, sank in the soft earth; and to make the story short, the Florentines overzealous, over tired, and disordered, attacked on both sides, remained in the claws of the pincers. Their captain was wounded, and Cavicciuli with many knights of rank, two thousand horses and two thousand men were all taken prisoners. It was said that to give himself courage Malatacca had drunk too much wine at the beginning of the fray and then went through the battle intoxicated, wherefore he vowed an oath and kept it, never to drink another drop—but this was Florentine gossip.

The state banner of Florence was sent as a trophy to Bernabo who had gone to Sarzana, and who from thence reinforced his troops encamped on the Arno, with a thousand men commanded by Federigo Gonzaga, sending also the pay due to the troops in action. In spite of the victory and reinforcements, the Visconti obtained no conclusive results. They sold their spoil at Pisa and then having equipped themselves anew, indulged in their favourite occupations of sacking the land, stealing fodder and cattle, and putting the peasants to flight, destroying, cutting, and burning. The old chronicler Sardi sighs:

> At my place, they pulled the portico at Oratoio down to the ground, set fire to the woodwork and cut the poles; they burned a great deal of my stores, with beams, benches, and cupboards, bedsteads, stools, and wardrobes, which were worth altogether more than two hundred *lire*. The Lord destroy them all.

It was the end of December, the English were making fires to warm themselves!

Chapter 10
Campaign in Lombardy for and against Bernabo Visconti

The victory of Cascina had been no doubt a great achievement for Hawkwood: he had terrified the Pope and other enemies of Bernabo, but the principal object of the campaign had failed: the English managed to get two convoys of provisions into San Miniato, but nevertheless they could not prevent Roberto dei Conti Guidi (the new Florentine captain) from reinforcing the camp which surrounded the town; this inaction was attributed by some to a lack of forage, by a few to want of money, and by others to bad weather and worse roads; the fact remains that the Florentines, coming to an understanding with the inhabitants, regained San Miniato, town and castle. (1370.)

Hence Franco Sacchetti, storyteller and popular poet, sang in one of his sonnets:

L' alto rimedio di Fiorenza magna
Ognor si vede quando è poi perduto:
Biscia, nè serpe, nè Giovanni Aguto
Per suo oprar non gli darà magagna.
(*Grand remedies has Florence! for more great*
Does she become, the more that all seems lost:
No viper, snake, (ensign of the Visconti)
nor e'en great Hawkwood's host
Can, by their deeds, work ruin to her high state.)

Nothing remained to Hawkwood except the satisfaction of riding on under the walls of Florence as far as the banks of the Mugnone, and the pleasure of running races and creating knights, one of whom, a Milanese named Pusterla, had no sooner won his spurs, than he must needs venture rashly beneath the very walls, and was taken. In Florence it was believed that Hawkwood was endeavouring to produce some rising or insurrection among the citizens of Florence, a thing possible enough, if Bernabo had been a tolerant person instead of a hateful tyrant.

Many of the English were taken prisoners at Prato, (January 16), whither they had ventured hoping to find favour.

Meanwhile in San Miniato, (January 10), which was again in the hands of the Guelphs, the Pope, the Florentines, Pisans, Venetians, Genoese, Bolognese, and Perugians, were stipulating one of their usual platonic leagues, to prohibit mercenary companies in Tuscany.

In any way Bernabo's army put itself in readiness to recross the Apennines, and Visconti notified (February 6) to Lodovico Gonzaga Lord of Mantua, that his captains Federigo Gonzaga, Achud (Hawkwood), Rieten and Rod, being unwilling to remain longer in Tuscany for lack of provisions, had demanded and obtained permission to transfer themselves with their brigades into Lombardy, where Signer

Guidosavina of Fogliano, once their comrade, had promised them supplies;—from this we gather that they were to have paid a "visit" to Signer Guidosavina and his territory.

Bernabo liked a jest and delighted in ironical language even in diplomacy, but it is certain that the Lord of Fogliano would willingly have done without that visit so politely announced. However, this might be the visit was put off. Hawkwood lingered by the way, to make a useless attempt at a *coup de main* on Lucca, (February 15), and on Pisa (this was certainly on account of the exiled *doge* Agnello) requiting himself by capturing prisoners both male and female, and damaging the country to the worth of 10,000 florins.

Giovanni Agnello was obstinate in determining to regain his lost dominion in Pisa, and to re-attempt this, he made an agreement with his friend Bernabo, taking into his pay a thousand horse, and twelve thousand foot-soldiers conducted by Johann Rieten and Andrea di Rod, under the supreme command of Hawkwood, who with these forces recrossed the Apennines in the spring, (May 19), and encamped under Pisa, where he tried to scale the walls but in vain. The Pisans even took, quartered and hung on the battlements of the walls a "slave of an Englishman."

As a slight recompense, Hawkwood took Leghorn instead of Pisa, and went on as far as Piombino, but having heard that six thousand horse under Rodolfo Varano were concentrated at Empoli (on the part of the Guelphic league) he recrossed the mountains (June 13), with the greatest solicitude.

Visconti was preparing new work for him in Lombardy, and with his usual hypocrisy wrote to Lodovico Gonzaga (July 18), that:

> Hawkwood, Rieten and Rod, with their comrades, without either his wish or command had entered the states of Parma; hence and in as much as Cardinal Albanese, and his colleagues of the Church, were opposing him in his pretences to the territory of Reggio, he had decided to make terms with the said companies, giving them money enough to induce them instead of damaging his lands, to aid his captain Wulf von Grovenich.

★★★★★★

Note:—Called Cardinal Albanese because he was bishop of Albano—he is known also as Cardinal Anglico or Angelica, and as Egidio Grimaldi or Grimoardi; he was a certain Grimoaldo of Grisant, of English origin, and he resided in Bologna as vice-regent of the Romagna for Urban V. He had risen because he was related to Pope Innocent VI, who created him bishop of Avignon, but was not liked in his office as we perceive from two epigrams which we have read on the frontispiece of the *Regestum Litterarum Camerariis apostolicis*, 1364-69, in the Vatican archives.

★★★★★★

He concluded with:

> We then will go to Parma, so that if our enemies want to fight, we may induce them to make a "good fat war."

He had blockaded Reggio, where his three thousand pioneers had rapidly constructed two strong bastions or ramparts, (August 1), a mile away (according to the measurement of the time). These were Hawkwood's chief support, and he displayed his resolution to take the city; but he let himself be drawn off by riding with two thousand cavalry to the gates of Bologna. The garrison of Reggio and the members of the league—who, conducted by Manno Donati (the hero of the first Battle of Cascina) and by Feltrino Gonzaga, had taken the field to help her—profited by this error; they attacked and took possession of the bastions, conducting into the city two hundred pair of oxen with their respective herdsmen, taken from among the baggage.

Hawkwood returned too late for the success of the action, he fought with valour but only just succeeded in retreating and enclosing himself in the fortresses of the Parmigiano. All this occasioned Bernabo immense regret. Hawkwood was unable to regain a victory till the winter, when Rosso dei Ricci and the Conte Lupo, captains for the league, retreated after a vain attack of Mirandola. He surprised and routed them when fatigued by marching through the snow, and took Ricci prisoner; and this time Bernabo could keep the feast with fires of joy.

The Florentines (February, 1371) next sent the Conte Lucius Landau against Hawkwood with five thousand *"barbute"* (lances of two men each) and he held his own with success, so that Bernabo was quite content to reconfirm those stout Englishmen in his pay, and was yet more content the following year when Hawkwood, together with Ambrogio Visconti, (June 2, 1372), who had finally been released from his Neapolitan dungeon, at length routed the army of the league at Rubiera.

After this victory the two *condottieri* had gone with four hundred lances to reinforce Galeazzo Visconti at the siege of Asti, and they fought in various bloody frays against Count Verde's followers, who took the field in aid of the town, in this way they had taken one bastion erected to damage the camp, and had completed two. which placed Asti in great peril.

Hawkwood had always distinguished himself amongst adventurers for his fidelity; the astonishment was consequently universal when it was understood (September), that he had struck his tents and deserted with all his band. The cause of this defection is not very clear. According to the *Annali Milanese*, Hawkwood withdrew because he was not allowed to make a serious attack on the Conte Verde, even though he felt certain of victory. This was probably because the youthful Conte di Virtù was among the troops with many other young Lombard nobles, and his mother Donna Bianca Visconti had commanded Stefano Porro and Cavallino de' Cavalli his chancellor or notary, not to allow these young sprigs of nobility to run the risk of an engagement.

It must have been in this way that the advice of "those scribbling notaries" prevailed, and possibly for this reason Hawkwood protested that "he did not choose to regulate himself in military matters according to the counsel of scriveners" (*de escrivans*). We may observe that Bianca Visconti was the sister of Conte Verde, and hence it was most natural that she sought to prevent decisive battles, in which either her son or her brother might be much injured. That the siege failed on account of the departure of the Conte di Virtù is confirmed by many other sources. They add also that Hawkwood just then received orders from Bernabo to ride towards Reggio with his three hundred lances and his two hundred archers, and that Galeazzo Visconti complained to his brother that the Englishman had not done his duty before the walls of Asti, not having obeyed orders, and having spoiled the country.

It seemed to Bernabo a good reason to diminish the pay of his captain. Hawkwood wanted nothing better: he came to an understanding with the Legate of Bologna and passed straightway into the pay of the "shepherds of the Church" and under the orders of Aymero di Pommerio and Dondacio Malvicino, captains of the league. By his aid the Visconti were prevented from erecting two new fortresses as they had intended to do near Modena. Borgonovo was taken, and after a fierce battle Broni also capitulated, and all the territory was laid waste between the Rivers Panaro and Trebbia.

Beginning of January, 1373, winter quarters were not necessary to *ultramontane* adventurers: they made campaigns in all seasons, and Bologna being menaced by Giannotto Visconti's eight hundred lances,

Hawkwood hastened thither, where the mere announcement of his vicinity was sufficient to induce the Visconti to retreat. Seconded by the Bolognese, Hawkwood confronted them on the Panaro and after a fierce engagement of one hour, Visconti was completely discomfited, losing two thousand out of his three thousand men, some being killed and others drowned; he himself found difficulty in fleeing with only three hundred lances. The victors triumphed at Bologna, on account of the many knights they had taken prisoners, and the abundant spoil, but they did not long remain idle.

At that time John Brise, one of Hawkwood's comrades, being dispatched as ambassador of the company to Pope Gregory XI, returned from Avignon (January 15), with two letters from the pontiff to his captain.

★★★★★★

In the documents at Avignon the name is written Britz, the Perugian chronicler has it Breccia, elsewhere it is Birche, but in the Lucchese Bris and Briz; therefore we write Brise, a name still known in the county of Essex where Hawkwood lived.— (It might be also one of the more common names of Brice or Birch.)

★★★★★★

In one (the ostensible one) the Pope asserted that he had listened benignly to all that Brise had explained in the interest of the company, and that his reply would be given by Brise *viva voce*, adding a warm exhortation to fight the villainous Bernabo (*lo scellerato Bernabo*); he prayed the English to have patience in the matter of stipends, promising that they should be carefully provided by the Cardinal of St. Angelo.

The other letter (private) gave notice that the Abbot Berengarius, legate at Piacenza, was planning some schemes there, for the execution of which he would require Hawkwood's men; he therefore prayed him that, on the request of the abbot, he would mount quickly and secretly, with all or a part of his brigade: "in fact it is needful as you know, that this should be kept secret and performed with rapidity."

The abbot had bribed several of the nobles of the district of Piacenza against Bernabo they talked of occupying the forts and ruling them for the Church. The Pontifical instructions were precisely followed out (February) in spite of very bad weather, and although the Pope did not pay the stipends either punctually or in full.

Some little money was sent from Avignon—we have a curious

document respecting it—the order of the Papal treasurer (May) to pay to Issarmida the Jew the small sum due.

Hawkwood therefore remained creditor for a large sum, but he resigned himself, well knowing that means would not be wanting wherewith to reimburse himself on the States of the Church, as we shall see.

CHAPTER 11
A Battle Regained

To ensure the success of the Guelphic League, a French corps led by the Lord of Coucy was added to their forces, Bernabo Visconti however did not lose courage, on the 1373. contrary he borrowed some troops from his brother Galeazzo, and disposed himself to "requite in good earnest the Lord of Cossi" (Coucy) and Sir John Hawkwood, as well as the Count of Savoy. (April 20 1373.)

The Conte Verde was just at that time rashly employed in throwing a bridge across the Adda at Brivio; it was of great importance to the league to disengage their ally; consequently, at the solicitation of the Papal Legate and the Pope's letters, Hawkwood, Coucy, and Aymer de Pommerio, captains for the Church, left Ferrara and crossed the Po by the bridge of Stellata. Visconti's army marched against them led by the Conte di Virtù and Annechin Bongarden, and the opposing ranks confronted each other on the River Chiese. (May 7.)

The ranks of the Visconti numbered a thousand five hundred lances chiefly Germans and Hungarians, and four thousand foot. Hawkwood and de Coucy only had six hundred lances and seven hundred archers besides the *provvisionati* (peasant infantry recruited in haste, and poorly paid), infantry, and some civic volunteers under a certain Malatesta; nevertheless Coucy with his French impetuosity did not hesitate to make the attack, and Hawkwood was constrained to support him; indeed if we may believe Froissart, he willingly did so "because Coucy had married a daughter of the King of England." After a short conflict of an hour, the army of the league being discomfited began to flee, and that of the Visconti, stipendiaries and plunderers, dedicated their attention to spoil.

Hawkwood, taking refuge on the heights of Montechiaro, saw that they might make an attempt to retrieve their defeat and though he only had the *provvisionati*, the volunteers, and very few mercenaries under his standard, he reorganised them, and with Malatesta fell unexpectedly on the enemy while they were intent on spoil. His quick glance and resolution changed defeat into victory. Bongarden's Germans gave themselves to flight on the instant; the Lombards made a long and useless resistance.

Not only the camp remained in the English possession, but two hundred prisoners besides, amongst whom were Francesco d'Este, Gabriotto di Canossa, Francesco di Sassuolo, and about thirty of the best nobility of Lombardy who had to disburse great ransoms. The Conte di Virtù left his helmet and lance, he was thrown to the ground and he too would have been in the enemy's hands, if a good many of his faithful followers had not defended him and found him another horse. The maternal presentiments of Donna Bianca were thus fulfilled.

Hawkwood however was not intoxicated with success; he, coolly considering the superior forces of which the Visconti could yet dispose, the many dead and wounded which the battle had cost the conquerors, the difficulty of finding provisions, and the hostility of the peasants, feared he might be cut off from his base of operations if he advanced. He thought it would be rash to attempt to join Conte Verde, though that would have been the total ruin of the Visconti; so, riding day and night he retreated to Bologna to recover his strength and dragged to prison there all the captives who had been unable to pay their ransoms. He justly considered that the effect of the defeat would be enough to prevent the Visconti from attacking the Count of Savoy who was able to rejoin Hawkwood at Bologna, and concert a plan to lay siege to Piacenza, which was not carried out, solely because the Conte Verde fell ill.

The knowledge of these successes did not reach Avignon very rapidly: a certain Francesco, messenger of the Lord of Mantua, was the first who carried the news of victory, (June 2), and he got a present of twenty-five florins. Then there came the official report, brought by the noble *douzello* Pietro di Murles, who had been sent to the camp with a letter from the Pope to exhort Hawkwood to join Conte Verde. Being an *employé* of the court and of noble birth, Murles had a present of thirty florins; and Hawkwood received an eloquent Papal letter which exalted the triumph "of the few over the many, of the invaded over the invaders" (?).

The Pope also added that he had heard of the retreat to Bologna, but he limited himself to expressing his opinion that it would have been better to continue the onward march, and besought Hawkwood that he would effect as soon as possible the junction with Amedeo Count of Savoy, captain general of the war, on the upper Milanese territory; so as "not to give the defeated enemy time to take breath."

He sent no money for the arrears of pay; he promised however to provide against these, as well as other arrears, assuring Hawkwood that he and the cardinal legate were engaged on the subject and he recommended the English meanwhile to have filial patience (*figliale pazienza*). He could hope for little while paying nothing— besides the victory of the Chiese had cost Hawkwood's company very dear, and therefore in a successive letter, while expressing his astonishment that "Bernabo, that son of Belial, should have lost neither city, fortress or town of any sort," the Pope enlarged into most tender expressions towards the English *condottiere*:

We have in our own heart to regard with serene countenance and to anticipate at all times with our best favours your most amiable person, who rests nearest to our heart.

This last letter served as a letter of recommendation to the noble Ugo di Rupe, cavalier and master of the *sacro ospizio* (Knights Hospitaller) who was sent to Hawkwood with verbal instructions, and then the campaign was recommenced.

July 17, Bernabo wrote to Gonzaga:

We have heard that Hawkwood and his brigade are reformed and all united together.

In fact, the English provided for the defence of the territory of Piacenza, and entered into the lower Milanese province thus rendering possible a rebellion of peasants in the Bergamasco, which cost Ambrogiuolo Visconti his life.

It cannot be said that Hawkwood failed in his duty; for, as in the preceding winter, (January 1374), he repeated an incursion in which Castel San Giovanni was taken for the cardinal legate, and finding that the Visconti, profiting by his withdrawal, had marched to menace Bologna, he rapidly retraced his steps falling on the flank of the invaders. They attempted to fly, but having found a broken bridge, they were constrained to fight with the English, and with the populace who had emerged from Bologna, and thus being taken in the midst they sustained a complete defeat.

The Pope on the other hand continued to pay the English with fine words. Hawkwood therefore first sent the noble knight Sir John Brise, then he wrote, and not receiving anything but vague promises by message or letter he sent his secretary, with instructions to propose some formal agreement. Amongst other things he demanded that the number of lances should be augmented, which would only have served to increase the amount of arrears. Perhaps this was exactly what he would have liked, hoping to get himself paid in landed possessions, but it was denied. On the other point we only know that the secretary had to give him verbal answers conveying the good intentions of the Pontiff. We may believe that these were sufficiently satisfactory, as Hawkwood continued in his service.

A little while after the Pope sent his *donzello* (usher) Giovanni de Canis with ample letters of recommendation and orders to follow out the commissions which this gentleman should communicate either verbally or in writing.

Meanwhile the Visconti had laid siege to Vercelli: every day the besieging forces increased, and the city suffered greatly from famine. On this account the Pope, who had at first commissioned Hawkwood to keep in the vicinity of Parma and Piacenza, finding that the enemies in those parts had withdrawn, begged him to fly to the succour of the besieged town, leaving a sufficient garrison at Bologna, in agreement with Cardinal Sant'Angelo, vicar general; and he assured him that "the prince of the apostles in person would accompany him in his march."

The Pope wrote a separate letter in the same tenor to John Thornbury marshal, praying him to exhort Hawkwood to the enterprise, he recommended his *donzello* De Canis to Thornbury as well as to Hawkwood. He had given Pietro de Murles recommendations to several of the other marshals—Brise for example; and he had written letters like the one to Hawkwood, to both the above, as well as to Cook, constable, and Thomelino de Bellomonte marshal and Guglielmo Martedonis (?) captain, to beg them to be patient in regard to pay, which serves to show that in the English Company, the authority of the captain general was tempered by the counsel and consent of the officers.

The march to Vercelli was not effected after all. Hawkwood continued to encamp near Piacenza and the lower Parmese territory, spoiling the land "so that the corn could not be sown in the fields, which proved a great injury for the following year." Then, having nothing to do when a truce was concluded between the Church and the Visconti, he passed into Tuscany.

CHAPTER 12

The Exhortation of Saint Catherine

And here at length the long account of the incessant wars with which the foreign mercenaries outraged Italy is interrupted by a few words of peace. She who pronounces them is a humble nun, but a worthy woman both in mind and heart—Catherine of Siena.

Gregory XI had inherited from his predecessor the idea of liberating the peninsula and the ultramontane countries from the adventurers, by inducing them to go across the sea to fight for the Holy Sepulchre. He thus deemed that in any case, whether they were victorious there, or better still were destroyed by the Turks, Christianity would thereby derive either great benefit, or a great relief. For this object he sent a brief to the Dominican and Franciscan provincials, and especially to Fra Raimondo of Capua, in order that they should prepare the ground for the Crusade. The influence of the monks was at that time immense, both with the nobles and the populace.

Raimondo of Capua enjoyed an universal reputation, and was not less appreciated for his preaching than Catherine of Siena was for her writings. The nun and the monk often worked together for the Church and for the peace of the world; and by the sole means of moral persuasion, sometimes succeeded in moderating events, in an age when brute force seemed to have absolute reign. It appears then that in 1374 Catherine of Siena sent to Hawkwood, by means of Fra Raimondo, the famous letter which is one of the most remarkable in her magnificent epistolary. It is addressed *a Messer Giovanni condottiero e capo della compagnia che venne nel tempo delta fame.* (To Messer John *condottiere*, and head of the company which came in the time of famine.) The ancient manuscript collection of her letters does not contain a precise indication of the date; but the passage of Hawkwood into Tuscany in the summer of 1374 is certain.

In company with Count Conrad of Hechilberg, he then appeared on Sienese ground with the pretext of wishing to fight other bands who were hostile to him, and menacing a sack, if they did not use towards him the courtesy which was his due. The *Sienese Annals* of Piccolomini (Pope Pius III) say the same thing. Meaning that if they often suffered hunger, in that year the suffering was greater, it was indeed "a year of famine." For the rest the date is of little importance, we have rather to note from the context of the letter, that it appears that Hawkwood had already engaged himself to go to the Holy Land, and Catherine reminds him of it, wondering that he should now wish to make war here. If anything, this engagement dated from the year 1365 when Urban V had commissioned Cardinal Albornoz to induce the mercenaries to take the Cross.

★★★★★★

The most authentic biography of the celebrated cardinal would be that of Genesio da Sepulveda printed at Bologna in 1521, and compiled from the documents preserved in the Archives of the "College of Spain" in Bologna, founded by this cardinal himself. But Sepulveda, a member of that institution, occupied himself (as he declares) more in writing good Latin than anything else after having loosely arranged the materials extracted in confusion from the Archives, by a Bolognese named Garzoni. There results, however, a confirmation of the facts that in 1365 the cardinal, availing himself of the services of Gomez Albornoz his nephew, a soldier by profession and a friend of some of the English, conducted long and repeated treaties with these bands, but only the ephemeral agreement already cited was concluded, so much so that not long after he had to go and defend the Perugians against them.

Sepulveda does not talk of a crusade, whilst Raynaldi's *Annales ecclesiastic!* certainly do mention one. For the rest the biography is very concise, and not always trustworthy; he perhaps exaggerated the part of the Albornoz in resisting the English near Perugia, and he certainly errs when he says that Gomez put to death the leaders of the English who were defeated and taken prisoners in that engagement, leaving the others free on giving their word to abandon Italy. We have already seen the very different facts given, even to the most minute particulars, by the Perugian chroniclers.

★★★★★★

Contrary to the epistolary custom of St. Catherine the letter is very short. Tommaseo, who is not always very happy in his comments, supposes this to be "because it was written to an Englishman and a hasty soldier perhaps ignorant of the language." Now Hawkwood, who for thirteen years had fought in Italy, treated with Italians, and had Italians in his company, besides employing Italian secretaries, attorneys, chancellors and scriveners, should certainly by this time be familiar with the vulgar tongue. Tommaso d' Alviano and Alberic of Barbiano were not known as more patient soldiers than Hawkwood, and yet to them Catherine wrote in her usual diffuse and exuberant style. The reason of her brevity appears rather to be that St. Catherine sent the letter by Fra Raimondo and begged Hawkwood to listen to him. She merely gave the theme in her epistle, leaving to the powerful eloquence of the Franciscan the care of developing it.

The theme lies entirely in this affectionate exhortation:

Therefore, I pray you sweetly for the sake of Jesus Christ, that since God and also our Holy Father have ordained, for us to go against the *infidels*—you who so delight in wars and fightings, should no longer war against Christians; because that is an offence to God, but go and oppose them (the Turks), for it is a great cruelty that we who are Christians should persecute one another.

The holy woman prayed that he "from being the servant and soldier of the devil, might become a manly and true knight."

Hawkwood might have answered that that same Holy Father had paid him to fight Christians, and that hence it was the Pope who acted the part of the devil in the Christian republic. However in the Aldine edition of the *Letters of St. Catherine of Siena* it is said (we do not know on what foundation) that Hawkwood and his *caporali* promised Fra Raimondo to go to the Holy Land, and that the promise was inscribed in a document furnished with their seals.

★★★★★★

Canonico Luigi Balduzzi acutely observes that "perhaps the arms of Hawkwood—which are a chevron sable charged with three scallop shells surmounted by a cross, as we see in his effigy in the Duomo—may have some relation to this affair" (*Atti e Memorie della R. Deputazione di Storia Patria per la provincia di Romagna*, 3rd series, vol. II, fasc. I). Hawkwood however did not use this seal only, which is really the arms of his family, and though we cannot always distinguish the seals still adhering to his documents, on account of the old custom of covering the wax with a piece of paper, across which the name was written, yet one can sometimes distinguish on a seal the figure of a hawk, which would have been a rebus to his name, and which we also see repeated in the parish church of Sible Hedingham his native home and burial place.

★★★★★★

It was in any case a mere repetition of preceding promises, which bound them to nothing and were only made out of courtesy.

As the Saint shewed between the parentheses of her letter, thorns were not lacking in the career of an adventurer. Hawkwood had experienced both defeats and captivity, though on the whole, he beheld his fortunes increase, and could still hope much in carrying arms at the expense of the Italians.

There was another Englishman in Tuscany at that time, William Flete (Fleet?) B. A. who dedicated himself to study in the penitential solitude of the hermitage of Lecceto, and was a great admirer and devoted disciple of Catherine of Siena; but Hawkwood no more felt the vocation to make a holy war for ascetic enthusiasm, than he did to drink vinegar and water to follow the example of his hermit compatriot.

★★★★★★

We do not wish to say by this that the *condottieri* and soldiers of that time were incredulous, or that they laughed at indulgences as the Lutheran bands of "*lanzenknechts*" did in later days. When the remains of Cardinal Albornoz were transferred from Assisi to Toledo, and Pope Urban V granted jubilee indulgences to all who had gratuitously carried him on their shoulders from one place to another, many adventurers (says Cardella in his biography of the cardinal) willingly profited by the occasion to cancel a great part of their sins: but to demand that they should entirely renounce their calling would have been too much.

★★★★★★

Even supposing that St. Catherine and Fra Raimondo had touched his heart, it was not long before a tempest burst over Italy, provoked by the infamous misgovernment and tyranny which oppressed the people subjected to the temporal power of the Pope; a misrule and tyranny in proof of which we have eloquent documents in these same letters of St. Catherine of Siena.

The prelates who governed the provinces and cities of the Church, chosen by the nepotism of the Avignonese Popes to be proconsuls in Italy, being covetous of riches, given up to every excess, and daring to practise the most systematic injustice, were a scourge worse than the mercenaries. With the latter, one might find ground for a compact, but against the former nothing remained but rebellion.

Hawkwood having increased his company to one thousand five hundred lances, five hundred archers, and a great number of infantry, and taken as his lieutenant his countryman John Thornbury (which Italian documents vulgarise as *Tornabarile*), had gone to winter on the Perugian territory, where they robbed towns and villages, hardly permitting provisions to be supplied even to the city. But the citizens suffered a worse torment within.

The Benedictine almoner Gherardo de Puy, abbot of Montemaggiore, was a relative of the Pope and governor of Perugia; the learned and pious brother in Christ, Gazzata, thus speaks, in his description of him:

> He did many detestable things, this among others. One of his kindred, enamoured of the wife of a noble, entered her house during her husband's absence and made infamous overtures to her; she replied: 'Noble *signore*, as you desire it and lest my husband should discover anything, enter this room, I will send away the servants and come to you.'

It was a stratagem to preserve her honour; "she closed the outer door and tried to pass by the window into the house of a neighbour, but fell and was killed." The case becoming known, the citizens complained to the abbot who contented himself with saying: "Do you Italians suppose perhaps that all the French are eunuchs?" and he sent them away.

The same kinsman, thus encouraged, three days after carried off the wife of another citizen, which being denounced to the abbot, he interrogated his nephew who confessed. Then the abbot in the presence of all, condemned him "to restore to the citizen his wife under pain of death. . . . within fifty days."

Other possessions of the Church were not more fortunate than Perugia;—now, "*he who sows the wind must reap the storm,*" the exasperated people only waited a propitious occasion. And the occasion came when Cardinal Guillaume de Noellet, pontifical legate, attacked Florence without any plausible motive, and provoked the famous "war of the eight saints" (*guerra degli otto santi*). (The history of this war has been recently well told by Gherardi; it is enough for us to extract and fill up that which refers to Hawkwood's part in it.)

The cardinal had the English Company which had returned to Lombardy in his stipend, but he had neither the means wherewith to pay them, nor a fair excuse to dismiss them.

He asked a loan from the Florentines, (1375), but could not obtain it, and by reason of the truce with the Visconti. he was unable to throw off the troops across the Po, so he thought to get rid of them in Tuscany.

Florence had for some time suspected this peril; when she foresaw the truce which was afterwards concluded, she thought of sending ambassadors to find out the designs of Hawkwood. (Spring 1375.) He having received the pontifical instructions from the legate, and from

Biagio of Arezzo, the Church official at Piacenza, in a few days reunited to his own soldiers a great many of the troops of the Church and the Visconti, and forming them into a great Holy Company (*Compagnia Santa*) manned the fortresses around Piacenza; and as the Gonzaga had not been willing to put his hand into his pocket, he ravaged the Mantuan territory along the Po.

Bernabo Visconti wrote to Gonzaga (June 18), promising to interfere and added:

> We hear that the English are waiting to receive a certain sum of money from the "pastors,"—that is the officials of the Church—and they assert that they cannot depart until they have received it.

Hawkwood, instead, had transferred his general quarters to Bologna, and in Tuscany people were trembling at his approach which had now become evident. The Florentines sent men-at-arms to the passes of the Pistoiese Apennines, but they had much more confidence in their florins, and also sent two orators to Hawkwood. These were Simone Peruzzi and Spinello di Luca Alberti, named della Camera (of the chamber) on account of his office of Treasurer, and hence he was the most appropriate person for the occasion.

★★★★★★

> Simone Peruzzi, as following events will shew, was one of the most prudent among the political men of Florence. Spinello belonged to the noble family of the Alberti, a very rich commercial company who then possessed, and long preserved, important factories also in England.

★★★★★★

At the same time the commune of Pisa sent Ranieri Sardo (the chronicler we have often cited), Oddo Maccaione, and Lippo Agliata on the same errand of offering money, if he would spare the land. All the gold of Tuscany was thrown at the feet of the Englishmen.

To the Pisans, Hawkwood and his leaders responded that they must first arrange with Florence; to the Florentines they replied amicably, but made them understand that the florins must be many; and then they continued their march without breaking off the negotiations.

Was the cardinal legate cognisant of this or not? A popular Florentine poet answers:

Dissesi, poi che furono aocordati
Che 'l cardinale ne fu poeo lieto:

Ma biasmar non poteva il capitano,
Perche gliel' avea scritto di sua mano.
(They said when all the terms were fully signed
Small pleasure was there in the cardinal's mind:
He could not blame the captain in command,
For he wrote the order with his own right hand.)

A significant comment on this is found in a letter of the *Signoria* to Messer Carlo di Durazzo, saying that "by advice of the Ecclesiastics, Hawkwood had demanded a sum which it was believed the Florentines would be unable to pay. Then seeing they consented, they tried to break off the agreement." There was a credible rumour that the Legate and Hawkwood had an understanding that half the money extorted from the Tuscan communes should go towards the pay which the Church owed to Hawkwood, and the other half to the advantage of the *condottiere* and his soldiers.

CHAPTER 13

Two Millions and Half in Three Months.

The Florentine ambassadors wrote from Bologna, *before sunrise in the morning* (June 21, 1375), the urgency of the affair did not let them sleep) a letter to the *Signoria*, of which a copy, like many other intercepted epistles, went to repose in the archives of Siena. (For precaution two copies of important letters were sent, one by the direct route and the other by way of Vernia and the Casentino.)

Very interesting circumstances result from this.

The company was encamped near Imola; it was very numerous, and well provided with *bombarde* and with iron implements for use in war against walled towns; the soldiers threatened to take the Italian cities of whose internal discords they were aware, and foretold new invasions of companies as soon as peace should be concluded between France and England, then belligerent: they would not specify precisely the object of their imminent march, but the envoys suspected that once the company had penetrated into Tuscany, they would take the Pisan road or that of Montepulciano where it was thought they had an understanding with the inhabitants.

The Florentine ambassadors acted in accordance with those of Pisa, and kept them informed how the negotiations were going, and the Pisans on their part, knowing that Hawkwood was not willing to come to terms with all Tuscany at once (for he shewed himself especially ill disposed towards Pisa on account of arrears of pay and because they had not kept their promise of giving him a fortress), advised the Florentines to make their own agreement, reserving the right to aid Pisa—which aid it appeared they could not deny, because if Pisa were conquered, Florence and other Tuscan cities would be lost.

In respect to Florence, the company had already formulated its pretensions, *viz*: 130 thousand florins in four rates between June and September: and yet they seemed to repent having asked too little, in comparison with what they might have gained by taking prisoners for ransom.

The personal opinion of the ambassadors was not very favourable to the agreement. According to them, the citizens ought to have shut themselves up in Florence and let the company burn up the country as they chose, because "that which did not take place today, would very soon happen" (*quello che non è oggi sarà tosto*). In fact, some good men had forewarned them that the company kept its promises but badly, and would not abstain from plundering on the way. At least the ambassadors wished to make the first rate of payment to the English, as small as possible.

But they had instructions to conclude the compact at any cost, and that same morning went to the camp accompanied by Pietro di Murles agent of the cardinal legate, by Ruggiero Cane and by the Viscount of Savoy "captain of Piedmont," which three persons were to take the part of mediators.

★★★★★★

As we shall see, this Cane took part in many successive negotiations during the war of the "eight saints," because he was a man much trusted by Bernabo Visconti. and familiar with Hawkwood. He was the son *nobilis viri Adoazzi Canis de Casali de Luagij Pedemtium* and perhaps of the same house as De Canis, the Pope's usher.

★★★★★★

The agreement was concluded, drawn up, and signed at the camp near an old bridge on the *Via* Emilia, built by the Countess Matilda. The signatures on the part of the company were those of Hawkwood captain general, the two marshals, the constable, and twelve more between councillors and *caporali* (knights).

This deed is important as a type of those *condotte* which we might call "guaranteed" or "reserved;" it will be sufficient to cite the principal clauses:

That neither the company nor any of its men shall for five years injure the commune, the city, the country, or district of Florence, nor her dependent towns unless the company should be regularly engaged by some lord or commune, and even if legally hired, it shall abstain from hostilities for three months, excepting only in case that the Republic of Florence should make war on the Pope, Bernabo Visconti, or the Count of Savoy (because the Pope had an alliance with the one, and a truce with the other).

All those who enter into the company shall be bound to take the above oath.

The Commune gives in recompense 130,000 florins in gold, of just weight and of the Florentine mint, of which 40,000 shall be paid in June, 30,000 in July, 30,000 in August, and 30,000 in September, (1375.)

Moreover in case the Communes of Pisa, Siena, Lucca, or Arezzo should come to terms with the company, the latter may pass over the Florentine territory, on the condition of giving four days' notice to the Priors and Gonfaloniere, and of marching by reasonable and fit roads, according to their destination, and under the guidance of those deputed by the Commune for that office: and that they shall pass by amicably, paying the price of provisions and doing no damage, nevertheless they may take without payment wine, poultry, and litter for the horses.

That during their march, the knights and men may enter Florence so long as not more than one hundred are within the walls at the same time.

That the Commune of Florence shall have the facility of denying passage and provisions to the company, if it be not in the pay of either Pisa, Siena, Lucca or Arezzo, and of subsidising the said Communes her allies, with money or troops, against the company as against any other enemy.

Finally, that for the said term of five years, the Commune shall not treat of taking any one or more persons out of the company, to engage them in her own, or other service.

This agreement was immediately approved (June 26), by the Florentine *Signoria*—which in consequence deliberated, that the chamberlains of the Commune might pay the sums decided on, either to Hawkwood or to his procurator.

Meanwhile the company crossed the Apennines at Firenzuola. Two new Florentine envoys, Doffo de' Bardi and Giovanni Ducci, accompanied it in the quality of commissaries. Bardi on account of preceding embassies was already intimate with the English, and Hawkwood seemed, at least in words, to carefully regulate the march in good faith. But in fact, the soldiers only abstained from capturing prisoners and from incendiarism, while they robbed with a free hand;

> They go wherever they please by ones, twos, or threes, finding out every crag of Apennines and cutting down the corn.

The mountaineers demanded from the commissaries permission to fight these plunderers, but when Spinello Alberti interfered citing the terms of the compact, the commissaries were obliged to command the mountaineers to abstain from every hostile act, and to sell to the English the commodities they required. It ended of course in the English "taking the commodities and paying no money."

The Florentine "orators" ventured to speak to Hawkwood in favour of the Sienese, but the captain loftily replied that:

> The Sienese needed advice, and that he would go and reason with them so closely that they must needs hear it.

Thus, menacing Tuscany, and amicable only with Florence, Hawkwood neared Prato. It appears that the cardinal had given him the commission, not only to starve out Florence by cutting off her roads, but to occupy Prato where an act of treachery was already arranged.

At least the *Signoria*, in a diplomatic manner, afterwards accused the cardinal of it, while in Prato they arrested as traitors the notary Ser Piero da Canneto, and a grey-friar priest, who, when tried in Florence, were convicted, tortured, and buried alive with their heads downwards. We may hold that Hawkwood revealed the plot, which would explain how (July 12) the *Signoria* "considering the terms" ultimately concluded with Hawkwood, "and inasmuch as his nobility and the exercise of his valour might be able in many ways to work for the honour of the Commune of Florence," should have assigned him an annual pension for life of 1200 florins. At the same time, besides liquidating the expense of 77 florins, contracted by the Florentine mission of Spinello Alberti and his companions, they deliberated to give 400 florins to the nobleman Gozzo Battaglia da Rimini "for his services and expenses in treating with Hawkwood on behalf of the Commune."

The first rate of 40,000 florins was not paid at the time specified, that is in June, perhaps on account of a short absence of Hawkwood, and therefore by a deed stipulated at the monastery of Nicosia in Valle di Calci, (July 3), it was agreed that the payment should be received by hand of the noblemen John Foy, knight, Bernard Rammise (Ramsay?), Robert Sever, and William Tilley as procurators of the company and of its captain general; and it was paid to them in Montopoli, (July 7.)

Thus, we see that the English had passed into Pisan territory; and as soon as they appeared on the Serchio, (June 28), amidst a rush of fugitive peasants, the great bell of the Campanile of Pisa was rung for the defence, and the citizens placed strong guards at the gates, and on the walls, day and night. The inhabitants of the valley of Calci felt themselves secure amidst the folds of Monte Pisano, but a squadron of eight hundred English, passing the mountain from the North, fell upon them, and thus assailed above and below, before and behind, they were easily routed and plundered.

Stationing their general quarters at Nicosia, the English at length deigned to listen to Maccaione and Agliata, again sent by the Commune of Pisa, and they agreed (July 3), for 30,500 florins, thus divided:—3000 to Hawkwood as his pension for five years at the rate of 600 florins a year: 2500 to John Thornbury and Cook. Englishmen (the chief lieutenants), these to be paid within a day—and to the company 15,500 florins due within ten days, and 12,500 in September. Besides this, the entry into the city was conceded to two thousand five hundred soldiers, provided they were only armed with sword and knife, and that they would leave it again in the evening.

The Pisans were punctual in payment; the English abstained from incendiarism and from "making prisoners and slaves,"—but not from other injuries—until they passed into the territory of Volterra.

Such vast sacrifices of money weighed very heavily on the treasuries of the Tuscan cities. Florence was obliged to have recourse to several extraordinary taxes and forced loans; for example, Piero de' Corsini was, on that occasion, obliged to expropriate certain rustic possessions, situated outside the walls in a place called *in Polverosa*, where we shall in future behold Hawkwood as peaceful proprietor.

Taxes not sufficing, Florence was constrained to make wretched exactions of small sums from debtors, and humiliating entreaties for subsidies to the Communes allied to her.

As it was well understood, in spite of the hypocritical protests of the cardinal legate, that the English had come down to Tuscany in agreement with him—the Tuscan republics were induced to turn against the Church, thus breaking the Guelphic Confederation.

Florence was the first to decide, and to set the example, (June 25), she notified to Pisa, Siena, Lucca and Arezzo that she had leagued herself with Bernabo Visconti:

> Considering the great peril in which we are now placed owing to the sudden and unforeseen coming of the English Company, and knowing how formidable and dangerous we may yet expect its stay in Tuscany to be.

She did not hesitate to impose rates on the clergy, defying ecclesiastical censure; and in this too she was imitated by the Sienese, who hearing from their ambassador, the notary Ser Iacopo di Ser Gano, how much money the English demanded, resigned themselves, only attempting to include Cortona and Montepulciano in the ransom and deliberating to raise a tax of 20,000 florins on the clergy, a forced loan of 3 florins on a thousand from the citizens, a loan of 12,000 florins from the Municipalities of the country, and the loan of a sum not determined, from the feudal lords of the Communes and their dependents. They were even reduced to the extreme measure of putting their hands on some hereditary moneys deposited with the bankers, for example on 300 florins which had belonged to the defunct bishop of Siena.

We perceive that Hawkwood carried out his threat of being exigent with Siena, for, besides the money, he wanted provisions and even wine and sweetmeats to feast merrily withal.

Having received the money from Pisa, the company passed to Laterina, (July 31), where they drew the second rate of the Florentine contract and menaced Arezzo; the third Florentine rate was paid at Bibbiena after Arezzo had been obliged to compound for 8500 florins, (August 28.)

The English were inexorable in exaction—would they have been so faithful to their contracts? They much doubted this at Florence, saying that:

> In mercenary soldiers there is neither faith nor pity. Their hands are venal, and they turn themselves where they can find the greater gain. (*Nulla fides pietasque viris qui castra sequuntur*—the quotation is from Filippo Villani.)

It was reported that Hawkwood would have taken the first opportunity to prove, the truth of the intelligence, and even to treat personally with the Pope's Legate.

To keep him in good faith, the Florentine Signoria, not content with sending Giorgio Scali to him as envoy, thought of calling from Milan that Ruggiero Cane who had assisted them in the treaty of peace, and had a great influence over the English captain, who seemed to have a very reserved and inaccessible manner. "He is the only one," they wrote to Bernabo, "to whom Hawkwood is accustomed to confide his most secret designs, and who knows his weaknesses and his good moments."

And as Cane was late in starting and then was detained some days by illness at Lucca, the *Signoria* wrote and rewrote to Hawkwood that he should "patiently put up with the delays of his desired friend, and most faithful counsellor." At length Cane arrived at the English camp, and soon understood clearly that Hawkwood expected the annual pension of 1200 florins would be assured to him even if he should leave Italy. (Second half of September.) The *Signoria* immediately consented, only making the proviso "except that he enter the service of the Church, when we do not choose to give him anything," and recommending Scali and Cane to persuade him to enter the service of Florence and Bernabo Visconti, or "at least keep him free from the Church." Like their captain, the English soldiers were evidently held in great estimation at Florence, for Scali, the ambassador, received the following instructions:

In regard to the other brigade, do the best you possibly can—especially with the English—to bring them into the pay of ourselves and Messer Bernabo, on such terms that those who come to us, shall be obliged to serve freely against every other man in the world, otherwise we will not give them a *grosso* (a small coin).

In fact, Cane procured for the league four hundred lances, and four hundred archers, who by their own stipulation must have voluntarily deserted the company, since their compacts forbade the Florentines to treat with, or induce any soldier to leave it.

While his friend Ruggiero Cane was busying himself with Hawkwood on account of the Florentines, the Lieutenant John Thornbury was exerting his persuasions on behalf of the cardinal legate, Hawkwood resisted for a long time, but in the end he gave in, and (October 3), Cane was able to write to the cardinal:

It has been a serious task to bring back your captain into your service. . . . he would no longer remember anything he had promised. I remedied this however, and he was satisfied with promises and my word of honour.

Hawkwood had found by experience that the money of the Florentines was much more certain than that of the Church; and precisely at this time the treasurer Alberti arrived at the English camp at Staggia, (September 30), to so effectuate the payment of the last rate.

In those same days Hawkwood exacted other large tributes from Lucca and Siena; the agreement with Lucca 1375. amounted to six thousand florins, against the usual promises to treat the Lucchese territory in a friendly manner. We cannot give the exact cipher of the contract with Siena, but it cannot have been less than fifty thousand florins.

Anyhow, between Florence, Pisa, Lucca, and Arezzo, the English Company had obtained in little more than three months 174,800 florins in gold, which with those of Siena would amount to nearly two millions and a half of *francs*—an enormous sum for those times—without counting the annuity of 1200 florins, assured to Hawkwood.

Perhaps the latter was persuaded that he had drained Tuscany quite dry, and therefore he decided to treat with the Church.

CHAPTER 14
A Cardinal as Hostage

The Florentine *Signoria*, (September 25), finding that the greater part of the English remained with Hawkwood in the service of the Church, hastened, by calling on the troops of Bernabo Visconti, to put the Genoese, Pisans, and Lucchese on the defence against the probable movements of the company.

But the latter marched on Siena instead, and Florence was warned directly, for Ruggiero Cane and Spinello Alberti accompanied the English camp and kept them diligently informed of its movements.

Thus, the Sienese received certain intelligence that Hawkwood had concentrated his forces at Moutepulciano, intending to possess himself of that town, and they placed a garrison there, paying 200 florins to him who had revealed the design.

The Florentines still preserved some hope of seducing Hawkwood, for they had secret assurances that the *condottiere* resigned himself unwillingly "to the deceit and treachery which he found in the priests;" and their agents at the camp received these instructions:

> If we cannot by any means obtain the service of Hawkwood with one of his brigades, and if he wishes to stay with the Church, do not bring us any of the English—but let the Church

bear the whole burden.

They calculated that the Church was not in a condition to pay the stipendiaries, in which case this would have created great embarrassment. They did not know, as we shall soon see, that Hawkwood had already provided himself a recompense for the lacking stipends.

October 18, Alberti returned to Florence with the news that the Church had engaged the English for 30,000 florins a month, the pay to begin from the middle of October, besides two loans and pay in anticipation, and that they were to be enrolled in November.

Great was the consternation—so great that Florence hastened the march of Bernabo's men-at-arms, (November 6), who had already arrived at Sarzana; although the faithful Ruggiero

Cane had forewarned them (October 31), that in eight days Hawkwood intended to pass into the Papal states, whereas if Bernabo's troops should come into Tuscany he would stop to fight them.

But in the meanwhile, nearly all the towns dependent on the Church rebelled, invoking by their deeds that *Libertas* which they inscribed on their standards. It was necessary for the Legate to employ all his forces to repress the rebellion, and leave Tuscany in peace. Consequently, no worse tribulations awaited her than the violence perpetrated by some sanguinary spirits, who on the occasion of the English invasion had seized the opportunity to join with a number of bandits from the various cities.

The cardinal legate had caused the English to encamp in haste under Perugia, sending a detachment to garrison Città di Castello—but even this town rose in insurrection, (November 7), about fifty of the English were killed, while the rest were blockaded on the *piazza* and scarcely succeeded in getting off with their arms and baggage.

The cardinal immediately sent Hawkwood with all his company against Città di Castello, but in those days a resolute defence sufficed for a walled town even with inferior force; Hawkwood could do nothing; on the contrary, two of his outworks were assaulted and taken before his eyes. Meanwhile, profiting by his withdrawal, the Perugians also rebelled, and constrained their diabolical governor the abbot to shut himself up in the castle where they held him in a state of siege.

The English being again recalled, encamped under Perugia, but as to any decisive action, they did not even attempt it; and as the rebellion spread over all the Papal states, they were next sent to the succour of the citadel of Viterbo. (December 5). Here the people and militia fairly opposed them in open fight, the attempts of the English were vain, and, leaving many dead and wounded in the ditches and trenches, they were obliged to return to Perugia.

The affairs of the Church were going so badly, and the temporal power was so shaken, that the *Otto di balia* (the Council of eight) of the Florentines were enabled, (December 10), to write to Bernabo Visconti:

> If they have the strength to hold out the campaign for a month, the domination of the French and other foreigners in Italy will be made an end of forever.

Moreover, they were still afraid that the English not being able to do anything on the Papal territory should again turn against Tuscany.

But if the English could not attack Perugia, neither could the Perugians succeed in their assaults on the castle, and so they had to treat openly with the besieged Abbot, taking Hawkwood as mediator. They tacitly established a species of armistice till the end of December, during which time the English frequented the city, and the Perugians risked themselves in the camp.

In vain the *Otto* warned the Perugians that "the foreigners could not possibly be on the side of liberty," and advised them rather to bargain that Hawkwood should go away, or at least cease from hostilities.

As a consolation for the siege, the Abbot of Montemaggiore received on his birthday a fine present from his kinsman the Pope—no less than a cardinal's hat, and the grade of pontifical Legate! his exemplary virtues could merit no less! but this did not suffice to raise the siege, nor was it enough to provision the three thousand men shut up in the castle with him.

On New Year's Day 1376, he was constrained to surrender himself to the Perugians, with the understanding that he was to be permitted to retire to Hawkwood's camp. But as soon as he entered, Hawkwood courteously placed a guard over him as a prisoner, saying, "We want our pay."

Avendo Gianni Aguto dal suo lato
L'Abate e altri died eron nella rete,
Disse: Signer, s' i' non son pagato,
Giammai da me voi non vi partirete;
Ch' io debbo aver del tempo valicato
Cento migliaia o più, e voi il sapete.
(John Hawkwood had within his net one day

81

The Abbot, with some others he had caught.
And said: "Sir, if you do not quickly pay
My dues, then you and I shall never part.
For all my time and labour lost you owe
A hundred thousand florins, as you know.")

Moreover, his unlucky reverence lost a great many of his belongings—according to the treaty, his own baggage with that of his soldiers had been retained by the Perugians, who after ten days consigned them to the Englishmen. The deed of consignment was made in the cloister of San Martino where Hawkwood had his camp, and there the delegates of Perugia met Marshal John Thornbury, the agent of Hawkwood. An incomplete inventory was hastily made, while Thornbury restored the goods to their owners, taking a note of them.

And also, a great number of things were without written formalities *restored* to divers persons and men to whom they *were said* to belong, which things they were not able to describe by reason of the great haste and eagerness, (which is to say that anyone who chose, took the goods.)

Although incomplete, the inventory is very interesting: we see for example how the mercenaries were clad, for there was returned to an Englishman "a Milanese *barbuta* (helmet) with its nosepiece, and another with three silver *cannonibus* and a steel neck-piece; also an old red doublet, with white and green fringes." The list of objects given back to the cardinal is most edifying, there were many sumptuous things, several women's gowns (!) and the episcopal mitre and rosary, thrust into the same valise as his shoes and hose; the only books were a breviary and a little volume of songs.

The hurry of this operation is accounted for, by the fact that Hawkwood was hastening to raise the camp, taking the cardinal with him as hostage for the arrears of pay, (January 21). Having reached Rimini, Hawkwood on proceeding to Cesena, left the cardinal under the efficient guardianship of Galeotto, (January 22), Malatesta, who conceded to the prisoner the use of the palace garden (*Orto dei Signori*), but he kept him in good custody, having promised Hawkwood to restore him on demand, under pain of a fine of 130,000 *ducats* (probably the amount of pay for which his reverence was hostage). And Hawkwood was a man to whom one could not lightly make promises without keeping them.

He had indeed received enough promises in lieu of money from the cardinal legate of Bologna, to whom (October 3), Thornbury wrote that his captain hesitated to resume the service of the Church "on account of that castle which had been promised him." But now that Hawkwood had another cardinal in his hands, and he a kinsman of the Pope, the Church was obliged to maintain its promises, and so gave the *condottiere* the lordship of Bagnacavallo, of Cotignola, and of the village of Conselice, contiguous estates in the neighbourhood of Lugo in Romagna; important enough to constitute almost a little principality, a gift which though it did not entirely balance the credit, yet constituted a large sum on account.

★★★★★★

The precise date of this event is not given; it was certainly before the 13th of July 1376, on which day the cardinal left Rimini, liberated after his confinement. It probably took place in the early months of the year.

★★★★★★

Many incorrect assertions have been made respecting this domain of Hawkwood's. Domenico Maria Manni would not admit its existence, saying that "adventurers were paid in money and not in lands." Ricotti in one place speaks of Bagnacavallo and Cotignola, and in another of Bagnacavallo and Castrocarb. Some constantly substitute Castrocaro for Cotignola, others discuss the nature of the dominion, holding that Hawkwood was only the governor of these places, which he held for the Church, all of which are uncertainties dependent on the various versions of the chroniclers.

Without staying to argue the point, it will suffice to make everything clear if we give the historical succession of facts and documents; and meanwhile we will note that there is nothing to confirm the supposition of Fra Bonoli author of a History of Cotignola, according to which the Pope had conceded those places to Hawkwood as Gonfaloniere of the Holy Church (!!) with the condition of not alienating them to anyone except to Niccolo II, Marquis of Ferrara.

It would seem that (February), Bagnacavallo was consigned, as soon as the English shewed that if they were not paid, they were determined to pay themselves, by infesting several places in the Romagna, taking Castrocaro, and putting it to the sack, by way of restoring it to its rightful lord Astorre Manfredi.

These events put Bologna, where Hawkwood and his men were quartered, in a ferment. The cardinal made the mistake of not giving heed to them, and sent Hawkwood to take the fortress of Granarolo,

83

occupied by Manfredi. The Bolognese wished nothing better, and openly rebelled against the Church for the cause of *Liberty*, aided by a thousand infantry under Count Antonio da Bruscoli, sent to them by Florence.

Nor did the English succeed in their enterprise at Granarolo, (March 20); the same luck fell to their share as at Perugia, and Città di Castello—they were obliged to encamp between Granarolo and Bagnacavallo, both their captain and themselves being, as may be imagined, greatly irritated, the more so because some of them remained shut up in Bologna in the hands of the citizens; altogether they were but too ready for the worst excesses, and even decided on a reign of terror.

Chapter 15

The Slaughter at Faenza

Here the figure of Hawkwood appears in a sinister light, and the only excuse we can make for him is that the authority of the captains over the mercenary companies was not so complete, as in a well ordered army, and so they could not always bridle the excesses of the soldiery, nor be held wholly responsible for them, as for things premeditated and commanded by themselves.

★★★★★★

In fact, it is only as an exception in some Florentine contracts with the *condottiere* that we find this clause: "That at the request of the commander the notary of the troop shall dismiss those stipendiaries who are not obedient, or do not give true service."

★★★★★★

The city of Faenza was governed by the Bishop of Tarragona, with the title of Count of Romagna. He fearing that the people of Faenza might follow the example of their neighbours at Bologna and participate in the general rebellion, called Hawkwood and the English to garrison the town—they came, but it was to plunder, not to man the forts.

March 24, the bishop-count had scarcely posted them within the walls, when he went off, leaving everything to their tender mercies; and they began to run about the streets crying: "Long live the Church." Hawkwood quickly made a proclamation that every citizen or countryman must consign me his arms whether of offence or defence, in the rooms of the fortress, under pain of fine and bodily punishment.

And soon after, without loss of time, the Englishmen, crying this time, "Long live Sir John Hawkwood, death to the Church", hurled themselves on the goods and persons; indeed to be more at their ease, they drove out the men, the old people and children, keeping in the city only young women and girls.

The Sienese chronicle says that two constables fought a duel for the possession of a nun, and that Hawkwood, like a new Solomon, plunged his dagger into the unfortunate creature exclaiming: "Half for each." This is probably a fantastic embellishment, the above-mentioned chronicle being very hostile to Hawkwood, from whom Siena had more than once to suffer oppression, and extortions. If we may believe Marchionne Stefani, the bishop-count was particularly greedy in the matter of this kind of spoil, for standing at the gate where the women went away (for many were spared by the knights, who were pitiful of them), he turned them back saying: *Torna addietro: questa sia buona per la masnada*, and besides he would not allow the convents to be spared, but had them put to the sack and treated just like the more worldly abodes.

Other historians and chroniclers, although deploring the excesses of the English in Faenza, do not speak of bloodshed, nor were useless cruelties habitual to those soldiers, who were more than anything avaricious of gain.

"Everything that was in Faenza was appropriated by the company," this we can easily believe, the more so that the company laid claim to large credits for arrears of pay—while the captain, for his part and account, had obtained the castle and land.

When this news reached Bologna, the indignation was general, and the temptation to make reprisals was very great, since the citizens had in their hands Filippo Puer one of the principal constables, Cook the cavalier, and several other soldiers, together with the illegitimate children of Puer and two young sons of Sir John Hawkwood, who had remained there when the company marched forth on the Granarolo expedition. But they were afraid to take strong measures, and contented themselves by treating them as hostages, confining Puer in the house of Salvuccio Bentivoglio, and putting the other soldiers in prison.

Even this was enough to excite the anger of Hawkwood, and to provoke fierce menaces. The Bolognese sent Eoberto da Saliceto to try and make terms, but he wrote that:

He could do nothing, because there are no worse people in the world (*perche al mondo non v' e pegyior gente*), they demanded such tremendous terms that if they had been citizens of Faenza they could not have wanted more.

Saliceto returned to Bologna, terrified out of his wits, and thanking God that Hawkwood had not taken him prisoner.

The question became grave, so much so as to preoccupy also the Signoria of Florence. The Florentines were anxious that the Bolognese should enter into a decisive campaign, as their allies against the Church, and would have wished to procure an agreement between them and Hawkwood, as a preparation towards detaching that valuable captain from the ecclesiastical service; but they feared to make matters worse by interfering, and they moreover doubted whether peace between Bologna and Hawkwood might not mean war to Florence. It was therefore resolved to let Bologna alone, as best understanding her own business, and to remind her that the Florentine men-at-arms were already in the field. (April 21 and May 18.)

This much we find from the *Consulte e pratiche*, or report of the business transacted in the councils of Florence, in which there met together with the *Signoria* (or in war time with the *Otto di balia*) the *Gonfalonieri*, the twelve *Buonuomini* and the captains of the Guelph party.

★★★★★★

The *Otto di balta*, which was called in war times the *Otto di guerra* (Eight of war), was a council first created during this very war, and it took the place of the *Signoria*, or was added to it, in the general war council. Its office was to decide on matters of expense, and means of raising funds etc. in time of war. In peace, it was a council of eight which ruled the political economy of the city.

The *Gonfalonieri* were the heads of the different quarters of the city. Each quarter had four *gonfalons* or standards, the bearers of which were called into council on special occasions. The twelve *Buonuomini*, or good men, was a council formed of three elders (*Anziani*) from each quarter. Its sittings lasted three months, and it was called into council with the *Signoria* on especial occasions.

★★★★★★

They are therefore documents of great interest, because they reflect, day by day, the public opinion then prevalent in Florence, and reveal the mechanism of government from behind the scenes, and the private reasons of the events in which the Florentine Republic took part.

Hawkwood, without so many councils, passed directly on to practice. Exhorted thereto by the cardinal legate who had taken refuge at Ferrara, he invaded the Bolognese territory, (May 16), treating it "with fire and the sword," which decided Bologna to formally enter the League of Florence against the Pope.

The English were encamped at Medicina, (May 25), and Hawkwood flashed out from the camp in person, with four hundred lances, and for three days rode towards Ponte Maggiore, sacking, burning, and taking prisoners about four hundred peasants. Thus, hard pressed the Bolognese took courage, and this time threw into prison all the English who were in the city, not excluding Hawkwood's two little sons. This was all that was necessary; paternal affection outweighed the fury of the captain. To regain the hostages, a truce of sixteen months was accorded—while the prisoners, and even the cattle taken as spoil, were restored.

Having got his children back, Hawkwood employed the armistice in arranging his affairs and insuring his territorial lordship.

Having by this time squeezed out of Faenza all that was worth having, he decided to cede the empty husk to Alberto d' Este Marquis of Ferrara, some say for 60,000 *ducats*, some 40,000, others 24,000 florins.

In agreement with the Pope who, above everything, feared the city getting into Bernabo Visconti's hands, the Marchese settled the account with the English, taking from them the pledge which they had in hand: and the cession was made the following year, (1377).

Meanwhile the affair being concluded, Hawkwood took up his abode at Bagnacavallo, a well-fortified town in which nothing was lacking, and without more ado, he began to enlarge and strengthen his contiguous possession, Cotignola. In those days, fortifications were of the greatest efficacy, as artillery was either not yet employed, or used in exceptional cases and rudimentary form. We might even say that Cotignola was reconstructed by him from its very foundations; hitherto we have only seen him as the rapacious vandal, now we behold him as an architect.

A century before this, the people of Faenza and Forli had made a strong fortress at Cotignola, but in Hawkwood's time it was in a very bad state, perhaps because it no longer corresponded to good military rules, the town being very small and not capable of holding a sufficient garrison. Hawkwood enlarged it to five times the size, surrounding it with new walls, a deep moat, and bulwarks. A plan is still existing in the Archives of Cotignola which minutely describes this rebuilding, and shews us that besides several small forts, and the various suburbs, he also erected a "large and royal palace with dungeons like a very stronghold."

According to Bonincontri, an historian little trustworthy in regard to facts, he had even thought how this enlarged town was to be populated, and proposed prizes to immigrants—but in practice he seems to have done the opposite thing, seeing that to build the above-mentioned strong palace, he had to take away from Giovanni Attendolo, son of Muzio and father of the Sforza, a possession which was contiguous to his own and imposed a tribute in favour of Giovanni and his descendants on all those who wished to build houses within the new circuit.

This shews that the English captain was not a tyrant without a sense of justice, capable of expropriating possessions without recompense, and it proves besides that the tradition of the rise of the great family of the Sforza from a poor peasant was unfounded.

Hawkwood kept for some years the lordship of Bagnacavallo and Cotignola; that he had leisure to complete the works we have mentioned, which he began towards the middle of the year 1376, is placed beyond doubt by the map we have cited, in the Archives of Cotignola.

★★★★★★

Another mention of Hawkwood's dominion might be perhaps gleaned from Pietro M. Carantho, a learned man of Cotignola, who wrote of the events happening in his native place as he had heard of them from his ancestors, or seen them with his own eyes. Thus, says Leandro Alberti (*Descrizione d' Italia*), but this Carantho does not appear in the *Bibliografia storica degli Stati pontifici*, by Ranghiasci, nor do we know whether his history has ever been published.

★★★★★★

Near Cotignola, arose in those days, the Castle of Cunio, afterwards completely destroyed in the 16th century; the ruling count was Alberico da Barbiano, whom we shall soon find in the field as *condottiere* of some troops (Italian ones at last), and fighting even against the English, and against Hawkwood. In Cotignola there was also that Muzio Attendolo son of the Giovanni mentioned above, who was then a boy of seven years old;—he began the career of arms, (1381), at the earliest age (Giovio asserts without foundation that he was a pupil of Hawkwood's), and by this career the Sforza had the good fortune to found their dynasty.

Indeed, some years after, when Hawkwood, as we shall see, was despoiled of his lordship, this same Muzio Attendolo was created Count of Cotignola, by Pope John XXII, (1414), and the lordship passed to his descendants the Sforza, who gave to Cotignola the title and privileges of a city, amongst which privileges may be classed the ancient jocose spectacle of the *Sega vecchia* (old saw) at mid-lent, which has lingered to our own days.

It is probable that Hawkwood fortified and built also at Bagnacavallo, but no memorial of this exists except some possessions left to his heirs and a street which still has the name of *Strada Aguta* (Hawkwood street). This opens towards the east of the city and terminates in an open space marked on the old maps as *Commenda* (Commandery) *di San Giorgio*; near there was a fortress called the "Bastion of Villanova," so it must have been a military road opened by Hawkwood, to ensure communication between the capital of his feudal territory, and that rampart, which was perhaps built by himself and certainly was held by him to be important.

On the other hand, we have at Cotignola a well-preserved monument of Hawkwood, especially interesting from its military character. We may therefore be permitted to linger awhile in this little city, an inheritance of two of the most celebrated *condottieri* who held the sword of command in Italy.

CHAPTER 16

The Tower of Cotignola

Till towards the middle of the last century, Cotignola retained the circuit of walls, the moats and bulwarks, with which Hawkwood had enclosed it four hundred years before. The bulwarks however were in a ruined state, and the moat half filled up by the drainings left by frequent inundations of the Senio, a torrent stream at that time badly dyked.

A weapon of war which had suffered neither siege nor assault—its fortifications fell slowly into ruin, from mere decrepitude, and no longer served any other purpose than to mark out the square boundaries of the little city. The three gates in the wall stood always open, the most ancient of them being the one towards the bridge over the Senio.

In our day neither walls nor bulwarks remain, the moats are entirely filled up, and the Senio is tamed with magnificent dykes, behind which the little city, now open, is nearly hidden. To the eyes of one coming from Faenza nothing is visible but the square tower of the Church, and a round tower, emerging at the southern extremity of

The Tower of Cotignola

the inhabited part.

This last is all that remains of John Hawkwood's architecture. The cracks in its masonry testify to its antiquity, but by the aid of iron clamps it is integrally preserved, and offers an elegant and curious example of military architecture at the end of the 14th century. It is built of brick, broken at regular intervals by square holes, and rises cylindrically on an escarped basement; it is crowned by a high drum-like gallery without apertures, slightly projecting on light corbels of brick, in the form of reversed pyramids. This is bordered above and beneath by two string-courses of brickwork of pleasing design.

Below this, at about two thirds of the height of the tower, were once eight small round-arched windows, now almost entirely walled up, though traces in the masonry still remain to indicate them.

On the drum are now four pilasters which support the roof, and the woodwork for a bell, but this is of posterior construction.

Hawkwood had erected a watch-tower, in connection with his *magnum et regale palatium in modum fortissimi loci*, (royal palace in a strong and great manner), which accounts for the elegance of its construction—something between the lordly and military, and for the name of *Castellina* which to this day is given to the locality where the tower rises.

The turret is now isolated; it may be entered by means of five iron bars in the wall leading to a little door placed at about a third of its height, which gives ingress to an *entresol*; from here four ladders bring you to a platform where the inscription of the fine bell (fused at Bologna in 1616) offers almost a resume of the history of Cotignola in the 17th century: *arma—ignem—excubias—Senium—sontes—senatum—jubila. . . . cano.*

It was no longer in the warlike times of Hawkwood, nor of Attendolo Sforza; on the contrary by way of making the bell useful from time to time, the people of Cotignola arranged that it should ring out its strokes, on the passing by of any wayfarer.

But although Cotignola does not count more than 7000 inhabitants, the tower which they call *del Campanone* (the tower of the big bell) and which we call "Hawkwood's," is not the only interesting thing in the place. Setting aside objects which do not concern our history, there is a grand old building, which from its architecture might be attributed to the end of the 14th, or beginning of the 15th century, and which has the merit of preserving almost intact the internal distribution of rooms of that epoch. One might at first sight almost seem to recognise that "great and regal palace" of Sir John Hawkwood; but on the capitals of two marble columns which sustain the arches of the "Loggia" are sculptured the arms of a lion rampant bearing the quince of Cotignola. The lion rampant was given by the Emperor Sigismund to Attendolo Sforza in 1401, and in a large *terra cotta* medallion on the facade at the back of the building the same arms are repeated, with the well-known crest of the Sforza—a winged dragon with a human head.

So, we treat of a palace either radically modified, or entirely rebuilt by the Sforza.

Hawkwood then was domiciled in his new possessions, (June), and restraining his English Company from spoiling the lands about Faenza—and here ere long a letter reached him from the *Otto*, who, in Florence were directing the war against the Church. The letter, (June 9), which referred to June 9 the intentions communicated by Hawkwood through his chancellor Ruggiero Cane, and Spinello Alberti, simply expressed a hope of coming to terms; and added that Ruggiero Cane, the faithful friend, and usual mediator, would explain to him the wishes of the *Otto*.

The captain seeing that the Church and her enemies were disputing for his sword, naturally raised his demands, he could exact the more from Florence and her allies, because a company of fierce Bretons commanded by most ferocious captains, and led by the Cardinal of Geneva who was more ferocious than captains and soldiers put together, had crossed the Alps on the Pope's behalf; and one of the captains, Malestroit, had boasted he would enter Florence as easily as the sunlight could get in, while the cardinal threatened the Bolognese that he would wash his hands and feet in their blood. In fact, he disposed of both Bretons and English.

★★★★★★

Baluzio cites a codex (56 of the Colbert library in Paris) which contains a prospectus of the men-at-arms under command of the cardinal, and the payments made to them by Domenico Francesco d'Incisa bishop of Acqui, who was lieutenant of the bishop of Bologna, and the Pope's treasurer general for Italy. In the first place is nominated G. Acuto captain of the English, then comes Malestroit captain of the Bretons.

★★★★★★

Then the *Otto* wrote to their ally Bernabo Visconti, (June 16), that he should order his dependent Ruggiero Cane to obtain for the League "as many Englishmen as he could" even up to 1500 lances and 800 archers. They doubted the result "because Hawkwood had demanded impossible things, and an intolerable price," however they had sent Spinello Alberti their treasurer to begin the negotiations, and were "ready to participate in the expense, because it was important to prevent the union of the Bretons with the English."

The fear of contracting "intolerable" expenses was very soon overcome, (June 20), for the peril seemed so urgent that it was agreed in consultation that:

> The *Otto* should manage to obtain the English brigade at all costs; to which end they should employ every means both secret and open; that they should make the deeds and remissions, requested by Hawkwood; and it was only in case they could not possibly get him, that they were to obtain a captain of war and every other possible means of defence.

On that very day the *Signoria* wrote to Hawkwood that while acceding to his requests they accorded him full pardon for all past injuries and evils, praying him to reciprocate it.

We may believe that Hawkwood and his Englishmen did not care to measure themselves with the Bretons, whose "ferocity" they had probably experienced in the French wars. At Florence it was known that negotiations were commenced for an agreement between Hawkwood and the Church, and hence they deliberated (June 21):

> That the *Otto*, as they have hitherto done, shall use every means to procure that the Bretons and English shall not injure us, providing nevertheless that there shall be no agreement between them. That in this peril the citizens shall be called on to assist the Commune with money. And that they shall use every effort to do this, and the *Otto* shall provide how and when the companies shall eventually leave the country.
> That the *Otto* shall provide for the well-being, liberty and defence of the country, and for the fortifications of the towns.

We can feel what trepidation the Florentines were in, we might say hour by hour; they feared beyond everything that Hawkwood would agree with the Bretons, and make one company out of the two.

Notice arrived that his contract with the Church was concluded, (June 22), but at the same time secret assurances to the contrary must have been received. The captain had decided to keep both feet in the stirrups to take money from each side and do nothing serious for either, avoiding the dreaded conflict with the Bretons, and having respect to the Florentines. The latter in fact wrote to Bernabo begging him to corrupt the Bretons at their united expense, whilst they themselves undertook to keep the English at bay.

And in the *Consulte*, (June 23), although foreseeing that they could hope nothing from Hawkwood's words, and agreeing with the opinion of those who wished to fortify the passes of the Apennines, and make every provision for war, against him, as well as the Bretons; yet Filippo Corsini advised them "nevertheless to make haste in consulting about an agreement with Hawkwood."

It being known (June 25), that the Bretons were at present aiming at Bologna, the prevailing idea was, that by closing the passes, clearing out the country, and displaying the crossbowmen, they could give efficacious aid to Bologna and "yet keep an eye" on Sir John;—but "meanwhile" (the orders ran) "try to procure a contract with Hawkwood." To render this less difficult, the *Signoria*, by means of the Scaligers, persuaded the Marquis of Este not to lend the Church the 30.000 florins necessary for the stipends of the English.

Whether this were the cause, or the brave resistance of Bologna had made it clear that the Bretons were not so formidable in war as they were ferocious to the defenceless, certain it is that Hawkwood began to yield again to the golden seductions of Florence.

In conformity to his request the *Signoria* assured him, (July 10), that they had made arrangements, for his annuity of 1200 florins to be paid him in Venice, and continued even if he should leave Italy. But even this was not enough to decide him: he still maintained such an ambiguous part, that in Florence they gave credence to rumours of the most insidious perfidy on his part.

News arrived (July 22), that three Genoese archers (of that troop sent to the Romagna by the Florentines, to help Bologna) had schemed to give Hawkwood the castle of Granarolo, which lay near his possessions of Bagnacavallo and Cotignola, and that Giorgio Grimaldi, the captain of the Genoese, having discovered the plan, had hanged the three archers by the neck.

Then came notice of the discovery (July 29), of a treaty made by certain men of Arezzo, to betray Arezzo to the Church, for which purpose the traitors had changed the lock of one of the gates so as to have the key; it was said that "somebody's head was cut off," and as to the treaty, "John Hawkwood and the Bretons had a hand in it."

But it was all empty talk, for rumours will circulate in time of war for terror. It is more probable that the Florentine Doffo de' Bardi, who had been successful on some previous missions, and was at this time sent to Faenza to confer with Hawkwood, found that the captain had gone to Medicina to hold an interview with the Cardinal of Geneva. The Englishman prudently attended this conference with an accompanying guard of five hundred lances. The interview took place in the tower of Giovanni Isolani, and all the day was consumed in parleying, without coming to any agreement, so that when the cardinal presented himself at Faenza with the Bretons, he was denied admittance.

Hawkwood persevered in his double game: he managed to send word to the Florentine captain of war Rodolfo da Varano, requesting him to send a person of trust: the treasurer was sent, as being the most fit envoy, but he was taken by the cardinal's men-at-arms.

★★★★★★

There is a tradition that the Varani, Lords of Camerino, were of Anglo-Norman origin, in common with the English Warrens. Litta however in his *Celebrated Families* holds this theory to be unfounded—it may perhaps have arisen from the fact that towards the year 1260, Gentile da Varano obtained assistance from Pope Alexander IV, and was put in command of an English brigade, which had either stopped in Italy after the Crusades, or came when the Pope offered the crown of Naples to the Duke of Lancaster, son of Henry III.

★★★★★★

Vice versa when the Florentines inflicted a defeat on August 22. the Bretons near Faenza, Hawkwood went out to help them, if not "they could not have held their own." And then the English and Bretons together attempted Forli and were repulsed.

Hawkwood, though enriched by the sale of Faenza, and well furnished with provisions, yet received very tempting proposals from the Bretons: he might even have schemed to have the overtures made to him. as he was not at that time content with his men, nor were they with him. Then the Florentines, Bernabo, and Bologna agreed to make the attempt to break up the English Company and take into their pay as many as seven hundred lances, and three hundred archers. They made a secret understanding with Philip Puer (Power), John Berwick and with another "Messer Giovanni" to bring their men, promising the high pay of from 22 to 24 florins a lance, but these knights only succeeded in bringing two hundred and fifteen lances and ninety-two archers. "And this I know, for I enrolled them, being employed in Bologna on behalf of the Commune," says Marchionne Stefani.

To sum up, the Florentines had reason in encouraging the Bolognese to resist, for they sent them as captain the expert Rodolfo da Varano; but they could also persevere with good hope of success in the attempts to deprive the Church of Hawkwood and the English, its best leader, and finest soldiers.

CHAPTER 17

Hawkwood against the Church

If the English *condottiere* had more promptly decided to abandon the Pope's service, he would have saved himself the shame of figuring as an actor, although repugnantly, in one of the most atrociously bloody deeds recorded in history. It is too true that on this occasion he was still under the orders of Roberto Count of Geneva, a cardinalpriest of the order of the "Holy Apostles," ugly and deformed of body, whilst in character he could rank first among those Avignonese bishops, who scandalised the world with injustice, simony, avarice, gluttony, lust, luxury, pride, and all the cardinal vices; adding to these, as an especial characteristic, bestial ferocity, so much so, that catholic ecclesiastical history is pleased to be able to classify him amongst the antipopes, though it cannot cancel the fact that he was first the legate of the legitimate High Pontiff Gregory XI, and commissioned to restore the temporal power.

The cardinal had failed to enter Bologna, and he revenged himself by putting all the country under the horror of fire or bloodshed; rewarding, and absolving with great rejoicings such of his Bretons as recounted to him the murders they had perpetrated, he even blessed and consecrated their bloodstained swords.

Then he took up his winter quarters with these unbridled soldiers at Cesena, the only city in the Romagna which would receive him with "a joyful and reverent spirit," the only one which "benevolently favoured" the head of the ecclesiastics; but the Bretons illtreated the unfortunate Cesena in such a manner as to reduce the citizens to despair. The cardinal gave no heed to their remonstrances, while the captain-general, Galeotto Malatesta, told them to take justice into their own hands.

The leaders of the Bretons in their turn complained that provisions were dear, (February 1), so the cardinal gave them leave to procure them without payment; the soldiers then fell to and plundered the butchers' shops;—the measure was full, the Cesenese armed themselves and killed a good many of the brigands. The cardinal then matured and carried out an unparalleled scheme of revenge. He made a solemn promise of pardon to those citizens who turned to him with repentance for their rebellion, and for that almost excusable manslaughter on the sole condition that they should consign their arms; this he swore by his cardinal's hat, and to inspire them with more faith, he asked, and obtained fifty hostages, whom he immediately released again with benign words.

Having thus rendered them defenceless (whilst he had called Hawkwood and his Englishmen from Faenza, secretly causing them to enter the fortress known as *la Murata*), as soon as night came, he gave orders, for the captain to fall on the city and "administer justice." Hawkwood attempted to lead him to milder measures, declaring himself ready to constrain the citizens to disarm, and to promise obedience, but the cardinal had already attained this, and wanted quite a different thing:— he explained that by *justice* he meant *blood and more blood*. Hawkwood insisted, showing the cardinal that he ought to look to the result, but he finished by resigning himself to the reiterated commands.

His repugnance may possibly help to diminish our horror of the part he took in the affair. It arose perhaps from his intention not to compromise the already advanced understanding with the Florentine League, any way it showed that he did not approve of useless ferocities.

On the other hand, was he certain of securing the obedience of his Englishmen, if he denied them the chance of a sack? And did not Alberico da Barbiano himself, whose praises are sung by generous spirits and Italian sentiment, take part in the fierce repression of Cesena together with his two hundred lances? In fact, both Bretons and English threw themselves on the defenceless and trusting city.

For three days and nights, they made such horrible slaughter of the citizens that the pen refuses to describe the particulars. It may be admitted perhaps that authors have related it with some exaggeration—for example how are we to believe the Sienese chronicle which calculates that the little town contained 40,000 inhabitants? But on the whole, there is a formidable array of chroniclers, historians, diplomatic documents, and popular poets, all agreeing in describing the slaughter of Cesena as an outburst of insuperable barbarity.

The letter of the Florentines to the King of France written by Coluccio Salutati, chancellor of the Commune, is a circular *manifesto* sent to the different powers, denouncing the horrors committed in the name and defence of the Papal dominion, by two bands of robbers.

Even if we doubt the interested eloquence of this witness, we may believe Poggio Bracciolini, the secretary of eight Popes, and we may trust the archbishop St. Antonino. The latter without reserve compares the cardinal to Herod and Nero, and the Bolognese chronicle says:

> People no longer believe either in the Pope or cardinals, for these are things to crush one's faith.

There is a short Latin comedy in four scenes which has been erroneously attributed first to Petrarch, and then to Salutati, the subject of which is a description of "the slaughter of the unhappy city of Cesena." It agrees with many of the chronicles, and asserts that five thousand inhabitants were killed in one day;—the most moderate reports say "about two thousand five hundred Christians." Naturally the men did not let themselves be butchered like lambs: three hundred of the murderers were killed, a few in the town and more disbanded about the country, but the mass of the citizens, being unarmed, were only able to seek safety by flight. Those who did not flee in haste, or were overtaken, found no quarter.

The chronicler of Rimini, who is especially trustworthy from his vicinity, says more than all:

> As many men, women, and nurselings as they found, they slaughtered, all the squares were full of dead. A thousand drowned themselves in trying to cross the moats—some fled by the gates with the Bretons pursuing, who murdered and robbed and committed outrages, and would not let the handsomest women escape, but kept them as spoil; they put a ransom on a thousand little boys and girls, neither man nor woman remained in Cesena.
>
> Then they methodically began to plunder—sending the best things in cars to Faenza, and selling the rest of the furniture to the people of the neighbouring towns.
>
> By the 15th of April neither corn, nor wine, nor oil, remained, except what the mountaineers supplied them with, and even they took away a load of blankets or clothes, whenever they brought a load of straw, and so the city was undone.
>
> About eight thousand between great and small came to Rimini, all begging for alms, save a few artisans who found work, and thus the said *Bretons* consumed Cesena inside and out till the 13th of August.

It seems then that the worst was done by the Bretons, who, being naturally fierce, were rendered more so by revenge for their lost comrades. St. Antonino specifies that the English preferred plunder above everything, and on this account, they urged to flight the people of Cesena. Ammirato confirms this, and the *Cronaca estense* says:

> Sir John Hawkwood, not to be held entirely infamous, sent about a thousand of the Cesenese women to Rimini.

But even his men did not entirely relinquish atrocities in search of prey.

> All the survivors left in the city were constrained by the English to ransom themselves; they barbarously illtreated men and women, to make them reveal where real or supposed treasures were to be found.

To conclude, the slaughter was such that the following year when means were taken for the restoration of the city, many deep trenches for the conservation of corn, and two large cisterns were found full of corpses. Hawkwood had hastened to inter the dead in that manner, because his company was quartered at Cesena.

Remembering his reluctance to execute the cardinal's orders, it may not be out of place to suppose that disgust at these doings contributed to his resolution to leave the service of such rulers.

It is certain that very soon after this, the negotiations which were already begun, to employ him on the part of the League, were brought to a conclusion. This news (April 10), seemed to the Florentines "good news, for you have disarmed the power of the Pope and strengthened yourselves."

The Pope was so bitter, that he revenged himself by excommunicating and interdicting Florence, and the Florentines replied by obliging their priests to officiate notwithstanding.

We have a rhyming echo of the Florentine joy on the *conversione* of Hawkwood, in a verse of a song composed after the war, by Franco Sacchetti, in which he magnifies twelve great enterprises, achieved by Florence in his days, by comparing them to the labours of the mythic hero, Hercules. (Communicated by Sig. Salomone Morpurgo from his monograph on the poet story-teller—Hercules was the patron of the Florentine Republic, whose seal bears his figure.)

Brave Hercules doth burn the fearful snake
Which nature has endowed with num'rous heads,

So that for one cut off, three more awake
And he who dares to combat it is dead.
But on a fire of gathered sticks he flings
That Hydra dread, which dies and no more stings.
Fair Florence, ah! how oft thou hast to one
The English serpent turned thine arms to fight
Whose heads increase the oftener they're cut down:
But ah! in warm sweet words, how great thy might!
Although no fatal fire for him doth burn
Beneath thy standard doth the dread one turn.

Bernabo Visconti, whose influence had been the principal means of gaining Hawkwood, so disposed, that his brigade should be placed at the service of the League between Cesena and Forli; its stipend was fixed for a year beginning on the 1st of May, 1377, and it was to be composed of eight hundred lances and five hundred archers (of these two hundred with two horses each, and three hundred with one), at the monthly rate of 21 florins each lance, 14 florins for the archers with two horses, and 8 florins for the others, which with 3200 florins for the *provvisioni* and *preminenze* of Hawkwood, of the leaders etc. etc. made a sum of 25,200 florins a month.

Of this sum a third was at the cost of Bernabo Visconti, the other two thirds were divided between the Florentines and the other allies; and these were apportioned in the following manner by Florence, who kept the accounts for all, advanced the money, and had, it is said, some trouble in getting it reimbursed: Bologna had to pay 9000 florins, Perugia 4000, Siena 3000, Arezzo 2250, the Prefect of Viterbo 2250, Ascoli 600, Forli 1500, Urbino 1340, Fermo 1800, Città di Castello 600, Guido da Polenta Lord of Ravenna 1200, Bartolomeo di Sanseverino 300, Bertrando Alidosi Lord of Imola 450, Rodolfo Varano Lord of Camerino 600 florins.

This last, who had been until now captain of the League, took offence at being required to cede the supreme command to Hawkwood, and went over to the Church not returning to his alliance with Florence till after the death of his rival. In any case half Italy was tributary to Hawkwood, and it being an affair of gold, Florence paid for everybody; it was a lucky day for him when he arrived at Bologna to assume the baton of command. (May 1st.)

★★★★★★

On account of the defection of Rodolfo, the Florentines deprived him of the citizenship, and in several places painted infamous effigies of him with a mitre of devils and with figures of the vices on his face. They sent Count Landau to fight him, but Hawkwood did not go with him, as Litta asserts in his *Famiglie celebri*.

★★★★★★

Together with his magnificent pay Bernabo Visconti had adopted another means of seduction; and to make sure of his brave captain, he gave him one of his daughters in marriage—it is true she was illegitimate, but in those times, even the bastard child of the lord of Milan was considered an honourable match for the son of the modest landowner and tanner of Sible Hedingham.

A famous *condottiere*, rich in pay, lord of feudal estates, and now become also the son-in-law of the most potent of Italian princes, Sir John Hawkwood here reached the climax of his fortunate career.

CHAPTER 18

Marriage to Donnina Visconti

Bernabo Visconti's prolificacy was proportionate to his extremely energetic temperament. His wife Beatrice Scaliger, called Regina., bore him fourteen sons, and he had many others by less legitimate mothers, amongst which his favourite was "Donnina," daughter of Leone Porro, a lawyer and Milanese noble.

This favourite "Donnina" had by him two sons, Lancellotto and Palamede (who is indicated as a counsellor); her daughters were Ginevra and Soprana, who were unmarried at their father's death, and Donnina who espoused Hawkwood, and who by the error of some genealogist has been named as daughter of Montanaria Lazzari, another of Bernabo's "favourites."

That Hawkwood's mother-in-law was the favourite of Bernabo, is proved by his donation of towns and castles to her, and we shall find other proofs to follow; but however, this be, the wife of the *condottiere* was only a natural child. It would appear that Hawkwood was at the time, (1376), a widower; as from the manner in which the chroniclers speak of his two sons at Bologna, it would seem they were legitimate; there is besides a document (1379), in which he himself speaks of a "son-in-law" (see chapter 21), hardly two years after his marriage with Visconti's daughter; and some memorial, relating to his monument in England—now destroyed, (see last chapter), shews that he was there represented in effigy with his two wives. Still we cannot absolutely

101

affirm that those sons may not have been less lawfully born in the course of camp life, and the more so that there is no mention of such offspring after his marriage with the Visconti. The only mention of children is in the deeds of the Brandolini family at Bagnacavallo, where *the heirs of the late John Hawkwood* are cited: he had perhaps, on his legal marriage, made provisions for his sons whether natural, or born of more humble wedlock.

Following this wedding, we hear of several matrimonial alliances with the Visconti which served to insure to the interest of that family the most famous *condottieri*. Filippo Alaria Visconti married Beatrice di Tenda, widow of Facino Cane, so as to get her men-at-arms under his banner, and he gave his relative Antonietta Visconti to the Conte di Carmagnola; Bianca Visconti espoused Francesco Sforza: but Bernabo, reserving his legal daughters for princes, made bargains for the others with the *condottieri*: thus he gave Riccarda to Bertrand de la Sale, one of the leaders of the "ferocious Bretons;" Enrica to Franchino Rusca da Como, Isotta to Carlo son of Guidosavina of Fogliano, and Eliza-beth to Count Lucius Landau.

According to the *Annali Milanesi*, the last-mentioned marriage was contemporaneous with that of Donnina to Hawkwood.

Fortunately, Hawkwood obtained a most beautiful woman for his wife. (May 1377.) Some English authors call her *Domitia*, and want to specify even her *dote*, which they give as an annual income of 10,000 florins. The extreme improbability of this cipher, enormous for those times, releases us from the necessity of seeking the origin of informa-tion so evidently unfounded.

In his will, Bernabo left 6000 florins to his unmarried daughters by Beltramola de' Grassi, and 20,000 to those by Donnina Porro. To Eliz-abeth, who married Count Lucius Landau, he gave a *dote* of 12,000 florins and many *jocalia* (bride's dress). We may then argue that the wedding portion and trousseau of Donnina would have been equal, or not much superior to those of the last mentioned.

As to the marriage, the following letter from the ambassador of Lodovico Gonzaga at Milan, gives us plenty of information:

> Last Sunday, Sir John Hawkwood conducted a bride with all honours to the house where he was living, that is to say to the house once belonging to Gasparo del Conte, in which the late bishop of Parma lived, and the wedding was honoured by the presence of the lady Duchess, and all the daughters of Signer

Bernabo. After the dinner the said lord Signer Bernabo with his Porina (mother of the bride, Donnina Porro), went to the house of Sir John, where there was jousting going on all day. They tell me that after dinner the Lady Regina made a present to the bride of a thousand gold *ducats* in a vase.

The Signer Marco gave her a *zardino* of pearls, worth three hundred *ducats*, and the Signer Luigi, a gift of pearls of the same value, and in like manner did many of the nobles. So much silver was offered in *largesse* to the Englishmen, that it is estimated at the value of a thousand *ducats*. They had no dancing, in respect for the late Lady Taddea. I have heard that Sir John was near Parma on Thursday, and according to what Signer Bernabo told me amongst other things, he will soon be starting towards Modena with his English soldiers; and when I was in Cremona, there came some *provvisionati* (country militia) from Signer Bernabo's towns, who they say are to be quartered there in place of those who were ordered off. I also understood that they were preparing a great many projectiles and gunpowder.

******

Lady Regina the legitimate wife of Bernabo had enough superiority of mind to treat the children of her rivals well; this might contribute to explain the great ascendancy she always maintained over that terrible man.

Marco and Luigi (or Lodovico) were two of the legitimate sons of Bernabo; at that epoch they held Parma as an appanage, in common with their brothers, Rodolfo and Carlo.

The late Lady Taddea, we do not know what Taddea this can refer in unless it be that daughter of Bernabo's, who married Stephen duke of Bavaria: if this is the case, Litta erroneously assigns her death to the year 1381.

******

Other sources also confirm the fact that Hawkwood passed his honeymoon at Cremona, where, besides being occupied by his bride, he was making preparations for war.

He had for instance to provide for the defence of his possessions, in Romagna, now that he had broken with the Church. For this purpose, he asked Lodovico Gonzaga, (May 7), to grant a pass free of tolls through the Mantuan territory, as he had to send by way of the Po a quantity of battle axes, crossbows, and many other things necessary to garrison his castle at Bagnacavallo.

He also prepared to resume his place at the head of the troops, and therefore requested the same privilege of a free pass for his secretary of war, Giovanni da Cingoli, (May 26), who brought his servant Giovanni da Napoli, with his attendants and furniture from Ferrara.

Everything spoke of an imminent renewal of hostilities. The Florentines reinforced themselves by hiring the English constable Philip Puer (Power) with a hundred and two lances and thirty nine archers, the German Heinrich Paer with seventy five lances, and several other German and English captains of ten and thirty lances, and some Italian *caporali* with two or four lances; in fact they took anybody, in spite of the trouble they had in getting their allies to refund the part which they had advanced, (amongst the others, the Sienese and the Perugians were in arrears), towards the Englishmen's stipends.

Although the Bolognese had profited the most by the agreement with Hawkwood—seeing that after the slaughters of Faenza and Cesena, both the English and Bretons were menacing them more than Tuscany—they yet refused assistance on the ground that Hawkwood had only been engaged in the name of Bernabo Visconti. At this "the Florentines marvelled and Visconti was indignant." (Letters of 2 and 4 of July 1377. *Sign. Curt. Miss. XVII*, State Archives of Florence.)

June 19. But he soon found a remedy for it by signifying to the Bolognese that they must contribute 30,000 florins or give Hawkwood's company passage and provisions. In fact, the English did pass through that friendly country, committing serious injuries which the two Florentine ambassadors at the English camp were quite unable to prevent. Such was the oppression of the country that the Signoria of Florence wrote to Hawkwood, (July 12), begging him:

> For pity's sake to have some compassion on the poor Bolognese, who had been so illtreated the previous year, and that he would at least leave the Bolognese territory as soon as possible, and pass into the Romagna against the enemy.

The letter arrived too late; on that very day Hawkwood left the neighbourhood of Bologna, and encamped that night at Faenza. Here he helped Astorre Manfredi to recover the dominion of his hereditary city (the English thus wresting from the Marquis of Este the pledge consigned to him). The following day he constrained the Bretons, who wanted to enter Faenza, to retire towards Cesena; he was then reinforced by the company of Astorre Manfredi, and by some infantry from Forli, and finally to deprive the Bretons of their provisions, (August 25), he rode towards the rich salt-springs of Cervia.

There the territory of Ravenna had to suffer. Guido da Polenta complained to Florence very resentfully, and the Florentines answered him that:

> They had recommended all respect to his land, writing with as much earnestness as though Guido himself held the pen, and not content with writing they added the authority of Bernabo, (September 1st), by sending his kinsman Ruggiero Cane.

Remonstrances were of little importance to Hawkwood who fulfilled his intentions in spite of them; the Bretons were compelled to evacuate the Romagna and pass into Umbria; Hawkwood surrounded them, and wrote to Florence (September 9), demanding archers, because being only four miles behind the enemy he had stopped them from crossing the Tiber, and intended to fight them if they came near him: but instead of archers Florence sent advice.

It is the celebrated Coluccio Salutati, chancellor of the Commune, who in his almost Ciceronian letters shows himself the guiding genius of the war against the Church.

★★★★★★

The Italian Historical Institute promises at length a complete edition of Salutati's *Epistolary*, and the programme which Signer Novati has announced in the *Bulletin* of the Institute (no 6) assures us that the undertaking will prove worthy of that learned man, and confer great benefit on literature and history.

★★★★★★

He, writing to Hawkwood in the name of the *Signoria*, (September 11), prays him to avoid fighting, so as not to give the enemy a chance of victory:

> Curb the generous impatience of your men, so near the discouraged enemy, who being already reduced and enraged might fight desperately—wait till they are more demoralised, or till they rashly risk themselves in an insecure position.—For the rest we trust in your prudence and well-known capacity.

In the postscript he adds:

> If you see that the enemy turns towards our territory, then at once with all your energy take the surest and shortest paths as may seem most convenient, and make every effort to precede them.

These suggestions were reasonable enough, for Hawkwood did not disdain them as he did those of the *escrivans* of Bianca Visconti at Alexandria, nor did he reply as he once did to Andrea Vettori:

Go you and weave your cloth and leave me to guide soldiers.

In fact, for that time he evaded a battle.

CHAPTER 19

Hawkwood as a Mediator for Peace

Still following up the Bretons in the valley of the Tiber, the English *condottiere* descended into the Perugian territory, where he spoiled the towns which sided with the Church. As to Perugia, although one of the League, it did not lend itself to the requirements of the captain with the expected zeal. This he complained of, writing to Florence that:

The Perugians would not furnish him with mounted guides who knew the country, as it was necessary to take fresh ones from one place to another, because they are thus familiar with the district, and are able to spy out the intentions and movements of the enemy.

And he said that the Perugians had also refused to proclaim a recruitment of archers, and that they would not even send some musicians to the camp for a few days, (September 13.) And therefore, the Florentine chancellor besought the Perugians to reinforce Hawkwood with foot soldiers, horses, and archers: or at least, as it would cost them nothing, that they would oblige him to terrify their enemies withal.

These enemies took the road, (the end of September), through the Sienese Maremma, and with a thousand eight hundred lances blockaded Grosseto. Hawkwood, who had but few forces to dispose of, was encamped in observation, on the narrow table-land which forms almost a bastion from Montepulciano to San Quirico.

Here he remained almost two months:

As a friend, and the Sienese ambassadors with many of the citizens were constantly in his camp. The Sienese sent him a horse with caparisons worth a hundred and fifty florins, much confectionery and corn, amounting in all to the value of three hundred florins.

Whilst here the Florentines sent him, (September 25 and 26), commissions to reassure Siena—which he did—and to assist Grosseto, which was not at that moment convenient to him; for one reason he did not feel strong enough to attack the Bretons, and for another, because by his means the Church was attempting to commence negotiations with the League.

This is the only occasion in the career of Hawkwood in which we see him as a mediator for peace but even this mediation was unheeded. The *Signoria* answered (September 27), with badly concealed ill humour, recalling him to his duty of vigorously conducting the war:

> We have understood the request made by you on behalf of the High Pontiff, about a contract of peace and concord with our 'magnificent' brother Signer Bernabo, or with him and ourselves on one part, and the Roman Church on the other. . . . . We recognise that you have undertaken to establish peace on worthy conditions and that you are moved by sincere and pure intentions; we thank you for your counsels, but we pray you to pursue the war in the manly way you have commenced it, because this is, or at least we believe it to be, the only path which will lead us with honour to the wished for peace.

The same kind of "bitter-sweet" was repeated more concisely three days later, (September 30), with the addition that they had written to Bernabo for advice. They informed him (October 1st), besides that his brother-in-law Count Lucius Landau, who was also in the pay of the League, had returned from the March of Ancona and was at Perugia; and that he should hold a conference with him, and arrange to give a decisive blow to the enemy, who infested all the Sienese Maremma, and was threatening Florence.

In spite of this it appears that Hawkwood still pursued his negotiations. Beginning of November, he went to San Quirico to meet as a friend "certain commissaries of the Church, who were coming to make peace," but who at the moment had a good reason for not coming. Anyhow the negotiations were broken off, the Bretons besieging Grosseto were obliged to retreat; indeed, in the following year a certain number of them passed into the service of the League.

On this account the campaign closed in a manner favourable enough, and Florence could joyfully send the treasurer Spinello to the English camp with the usual pay; but he returned bringing very unwelcome news, which was that Hawkwood's brigade intended to winter on Florentine territory under certain given conditions, and that they were making their preparations. In plain terms this was equivalent to having the enemy at their gates.

Without even waiting for Spinello to explain the propositions, the *Signoria* sent a dispatch to Hawkwood, (November 16), regretting he had such intentions, as:

> A thing very displeasing to Bernabo as it would be a cause of exultation to the enemy, and dishonourable to him. What would he say to the invincible English flying the foe, and seeking repose afar from the war? And what will happen when the enemy occupy the confines of the League, as they will lose no time in doing? And would not the Bretons boast of having forced him to retreat?—Dispose then your company to honourable deeds with your usual prudence, either return to the Papal States to help the allies, or go to the Marches where you could stay very comfortably in the territory of Camerino or other places. Whenever you make your decision, the Florentines will immediately remove from thence the Germans (of Count Landau) and other troops, so that in those opulent and rich places the English Company may fight alone with great slaughtering of enemies, to their glory and advantage.

The following day Spinello had the opportunity of explaining himself better to the *Signoria*, and he made it clear that Hawkwood had done all he could to persuade his troops to remain where they were, but that the Englishmen would not listen to reason, and had obliged him to seek winter quarters where they were sure of finding every convenience—that is, on Florentine ground:—that the captain had still tried to move them, and in any case he gave the best advice to the *Signoria* how to manage things with the least possible injury to themselves.

A general counsel was held on this elucidation. The *Signoria* sustained that the coming of the English would be perilous to the towns, on account of strife and depredations, *and for words which are often spoken, and many others which might be said, against Bernabo* (it would appear that the alliance with the Visconti was not very popular) it would be even profitable to spend something to send them elsewhere.

The *Gonfalonieri* resigned themselves with heavy hearts to the wish of the English, trusting in the opportune precautions of the *Otto di balia* (Eight of war) recommending them to keep their eye on San Miniato and other towns in the Val d'Arno, besides placing soldiers in towns of proved fidelity and, *if possible, to arrange that Sir John and others should stay in Florence*, almost like hostages.

On this last point the twelve *Buonomini* also insisted, (November 11), saying: *make sure that Haiokwood remains in the city with as many of his company as possible*; they also advised that the fortresses should be well garrisoned.

It was deliberated to write again to Hawkwood immediately, reiterating the desire that he should march into the Papal States or the March of Ancona; if that were not possible, they would be content to follow out his counsels and the plan he had made: they advised however that:

> He should arrange to preserve from injury the territories of Florence and her allies, providing that each brigade should quarter in the place destined to receive it, and where such order was established that all should be content.

He was also recommended to provide against any scandals, either on the entry of the English, or after it, and to place the smallest possible number in each town, and that one of the *Otto* should go to Hawkwood in person to make the required arrangements. (November 24.)

The fact was, the Florentines were in great distress at the near vicinity of those dangerous mercenaries, and they made a last attempt to pass them on to Siena. They wrote to Siena, (November 26), that they had heard from Filippo Bastari, envoy at the camp, that Hawkwood would willingly quarter his troops in the territory of Montepulciano, observing that during the winter, the country could not be injured by this, and it would be a very useful position enabling him to oppose the enemy, and to protect the Sienese and Perugian territories.

For the rest Hawkwood himself must have conferred with the Sienese ambassadors: they ought therefore to take immediate steps, and if need be, Florence would decide the campaign according to "that wise counsel" (*a tal salutare consiglio*).

However, they hoped so little from this, that the same day they discussed the benefit of making the English return towards the enemy, even if it entailed expense (*magari spendendo*), and whether they should not send one or two of the *Otto* to Val d'Arno to collocate the English there, and arrange for the fortifications and garrisoning of the strongholds, placing the fewest number possible in fortified places, and in any case to keep about three hundred lances of *our troops* in the city.

The next day brought the definite resolutions of the *condottiere*. Wherefore it was written to Gioannello di Vico Mercato, commissary at the quarters:

Bastari on his exit from the interview with Hawkwood informs us that the captain is content that the English shall be stationed in our territories of Val di Nievole, Val d'Arno, Pistoia and Prato, and that they will personally swear to the preservation of the towns which are in the hands of our officials. Over and above which Hawkwood himself would write to him and the other officials placing everything in his and their hands.

The Florentines were now obliged to take ill luck with a good grace. Some still wanted to try and get the English away as soon as possible, giving Hawkwood every satisfaction, for he did not seem quite content with the Commune, but Giovanni Dini, one of the *Otto*, was of the opinion that:

With the English it is needful to proceed prudently so that no scandal shall ensue. And as they must remain a long time in our service, we must treat them, and act with them in such a way as not to enrage them, because if they are made to march against their will, they will do things to the Commune which we shall not like—indeed quite the contrary. Here they have to be stationed for the present; and we must try and manage that they shall leave spontaneously. (December 1st.)

His troops being thus on their way to winter quarters, regaled by the Pisans with barrels of white wine, confectionery and other gifts, Hawkwood celebrated his triumph.

Today (December 7), Sir John Hawkwood entered Florence with his company at the twenty third hour (hour before sunset) and dismounted at the Palace of the Archbishop of Florence, and great honour was paid him by our *Signoria* and other councils, and a great deal of wax, and sweetmeats, and draperies of silk and wool were presented to him. They made a great feast for him and his company in the palace of the *Signoria*, and he was much honoured. God give him grace never to injure us, either in goods or *person*, Amen.

He departed again the morning of the third day (December 10), "to go to his castles in Romagna," says the diarist, adding this ambiguous augury: "May he never return here" (*Non ci possa più tornare*). We may suppose he went to see his newly made bride, who had been so neglected in favour of the camp.

But the exigencies of command were such that in twelve days

(December 22), he returned to Florence, and the next morning at ten o'clock he went to his brigade at Fucecchio.

CHAPTER 20

Serving Two Masters

If Hawkwood was a Florentine warrior, he was also the soldier of Bernabo Visconti; indeed he felt himself especially bound to that prince by his new relationship, therefore in serving the League he paid respect above everything else to the especial views of his father-in-law, and (beginning of January), went to Milan to consult with him.

Whilst he was there the Florentine *Signoria* wrote to ask him to speak in favour of the request they had made to Bernabo; which was, that he would disburse his share in the pay of the troops they had hired in common. They begged him also to confirm, even on his own responsibility, the explanations which were given to Bernabo, (January 5, 1378). Perhaps this referred to Ruggiero Cane and to some suspected relations with the enemy. Lastly, they entreated him to return quickly to Tuscany, "otherwise the management of the English will be rendered very difficult, and without a leader many things are in disorder." As he delayed, they thus insisted, (January 21):

> Come and command your troops as soon as you can, especially as the Ecclesiastics have become very strong in the Sienese district, and are doing some injury every day. And as to the English, they were, as you are aware, placed in such narrow quarters that it is now necessary to change them on account of scarcity of fodder and other things; without you we can neither control them, nor send them to the help of the allies, which may be the cause of consequences displeasing both to you and to us.

He was to come then, to arrange, consult, and effect all that was necessary to the honour of Florence and all the League.

This letter crossed Hawkwood on the way, and as soon as he returned to Florence, he again started to his soldiers' quarters. (January 25 and 27.) The soldiers were behaving very badly: fifty plunderers of the brigade commanded by that Cook who had won his spurs under the walls of Florence, rode to Corliano, (February 7), insulting and even wounding the peasants; sacking all the houses, carrying away the cattle large and small, clothes, and everything, just as though they were the enemies' belongings. The *Signoria* claimed compensation from Cook for damages, and warned him that such an occurrence must not be repeated: they also wrote to Hawkwood adding, that:

> Similar things were happening every day, which they were sure
> would displease him, and Bernabo would be more sorry than
> if the men were his own subjects. It was the captain's office to
> immediately repress this scandal, going at once to the place
> where his presence and prudence would be sufficient to re-
> establish order.

Hawkwood had other affairs to see to; he was at San Quirico in
close contact with the ecclesiastical camp, and requested of the Florentines (February 3), a pass for himself, and of the Sienese a safe conduct for two months, for the Papal ambassadors and for their escort
of two hundred horse. The Florentines delaying to send the required
permission, he insisted and obtained it. (February 8.)

Then the schemes for which he had journeyed between Milan
and Florence became clear; Bernabo having other projects of war in
view wanted to propose negotiations with the Church by means of
Hawkwood, and demanded that the League should give leave to all,
or to part of the English to serve him. As to the safe conduct, the Florentines dared not refuse it, indeed they consented that Hawkwood
"should go with other commissaries of Bernabo to the camp of the
Church party." (February 12.)

There were serious apprehensions about dismissing the English;
according to what Piero Canigiani, one of the *Buonomini*, explained:

> This dismissal is very perilous; firstly, because if Bernabo wishes
> to invade the Genoese territory with the English troops, that
> would set the Genoese at enmity with us, and in the same way
> if he wants to invade the Marquis of Mantua or act against
> the Veronese—his aggrandisement is perilous to us. Besides it
> might be that he has a secret understanding with the Pope and
> may set the army of the Church on us, or the Sienese. If we
> really are forced to dismiss the English, we must recall our own
> troops from all parts, (February 15.)

It was besides considered that the Ecclesiastics menaced the territories of Perugia and Siena, the latter of which was ill adapted for
defence. To ensure himself on that side, Hawkwood proposed to take
up his position at San Quirico with a hundred lances (the position
was in fact very well chosen, and he thought he could thus leave the
rest of the company at Bernabo's disposal). But the English refused to

move till they had received their pay for February; and yet by reason of their continual depredations, their presence on Florentine ground was very annoying.

To resolve all these difficulties, the *Otto*, the *Buonomini*, and the *Gonfalonieri* were unanimous in deciding that the English must be paid without ado, anticipating also Bernabo's share, and thus making sure of their marching against the enemy without delay.

Hawkwood having returned to Florence, (February 24), was given to understand this decision, and (February 26), according about the 18th hour (which, to Florentine astrology, was the propitious hour to begin a military enterprise) he rode off without delay to take command of his troops.

According to the plan adopted by the Florentines, Hawkwood was to go to the defence of Perugia, with all, or at least the greater part of the English. The Perugians were therefore written to, that they should prepare quarters and provisions, and send a commissary to conduct the English as soon as possible to the quarters designed for them.

But to go to Perugia it was necessary to cross the Sienese territory, and the people of Siena, although allies, would not hear of giving them a pass. On this the Florentines wrote to Siena, greatly marvelling, and reminding them how they had, *even with importunity*, entreated for the *invincible hand* of the English, and exhorting them, shewing them the need they had of it; this dispatch was communicated to Hawkwood, (February 25), who, if he made difficulties in starting, was perfectly justified. In any case he would not have moved, and had in fact scarcely reached the quarters of his troops, when he began to open treaties for a truce with the Ecclesiastics, going himself to meet the Pope's ambassadors. (March 2.) This being known at Florence, there was a clash of opposite opinions such as frequently happens at critical moments. Andrea Salviati's advice was that:

> As soon as possible an upright and honourable man shall undertake an embassy to Hawkwood, advising him to leave the negotiation in the hands of Bernabo.

Simone Ranieri proposed that:

> We send to say that in peace or war the Commune intends to do that which pleases Bernabo—let the captain abstain then from concluding an armistice, but if after all he should have orders from Bernabo, let it be made for a month.

The *Gonfalonieri* wanted to "boldly continue the war" allowing no truce, which is dangerous, because capable of being prorogued. Let a bold envoy be sent to Hawkwood and to the other commissaries of Bernabo, who would explain the great astonishment of the *Signoria*; and at the same time dispatch an embassy to Parma (where Bernabo was) so that the intentions of the Commune should not be thwarted.

The *Dodici* and the *Otto* put forth a more complex counsel:

Let us signify to the commissaries of Bernabo by means of an envoy, that we do not consent to a truce, or at least that the negotiations for it must rest entirely with Bernabo. If they already have his command for it, the truce should be for fifteen days rather than a month. At the same time let Hawkwood have orders to go to the frontier on the Perugian side with his men, which will prove whether or not he is free to act. (This was to measure better the projects of Bernabo.)

Almost as if foreseeing this request, there arrived a letter in which Hawkwood explained his inaction; he wrote that the Perugians had no need of troops, because they had received security from the Pope's ambassadors and that his Englishmen would not mount till, they had received their pay.

To which the *Signoria* replied with resentful wonderment:

How can you possibly make treaties without our knowledge or that of Bernabo? We admit that you have acted with a good object; but we warn you it was never our intention to suspend hostilities till peace was concluded, nor to lose time which we can never regain. Let us have no truce; now that the Pope is unfurnished with means, on account of his discords with the Romans, is just the time to leave the confines of the League and carry the war into the enemy's country, if your men will only mount according to the orders given. Go then at once with your men to Perugia, where all is ready to receive them. Spinello is in Val d' Arno ready to pay the troops as soon as they are in marching order. Every day we are having complaints of homicide, violence, and rapine, at which the people already begin to murmur. This is another reason for hastening your departure, (March 4.)

In confirmation of this letter Filippo Alamanni, a keen man, was sent as envoy; but Hawkwood had already gone to meet the Pontifical ambassadors (the Cardinal of Amiens, the archbishop of Pampeluna, and the archbishop of Narbonne), who were on their way to Pisa. (March 6.) He escorted them with Ruggiero Cane and some other cavalry soldiers, dismounting at the house of Ser Jacopo d' Appiano, the next morning he continued his journey with Cane to Lucca, thence to Sarzana where the ambassadors found Bernabo and began the negotiations.

> The English had promised the treasurer Spinello to commence action as soon as the stipends for February were paid; but when they had received the money, they again refused; meanwhile the towns they occupy, are entirely destitute of forage, and the enemy is still domineering in the Perugian territory, (March 16), greatly to its injury.

These were the Florentine last and still ineffectual remonstrances to Hawkwood, who certainly would make no move now that Bernabo in person was negotiating a peace with the Church, and to render it more easy the death of the Pope took place just at that time.

Nothing was now left to Florence but to liberate herself from the disobedient Englishmen: the peril of keeping them in San Miniato and other towns in the lower Val d' Arno had increased, because it was necessary to quarter there some other stipendiaries of Florence— the German Company of the "Stella" commanded by Count Lucius Landau. If they united, they might put the state in danger, therefore it would be worthwhile even to give the English their pay for March, on condition that they would go elsewhere, and immediately arrange to remove them from the towns on which they were quartered.

In one of these towns the English captain, Tomellino was dying, and without doubt all the cavaliers would come to his funeral; this seemed a very good opportunity, so it was proposed to commission Sig. Lotterio to shut the gates upon them everywhere when they had gone away, and to advise the country people not to let themselves be caught in the open country, where the Englishmen might take revenge on them, for the trick.

But it does not appear that this practical joke, which was suggested by Ghino Bernardi, was put into practice. A better idea was to keep Count Landau's Germans in the service as a guard against the English, but first to endeavour, by peaceable means, to send them to serve Bernabo, in which case they would be contented with an assurance from them, "not to oppose the Commune in the form of a company, and for this the proper price would be paid." This was done; Hawkwood came to Florence, (April 3), for the necessary understanding, and then returned to Lombardy, (April 5), where he was preceded, or soon followed by his troops.

CHAPTER 21

A Father-in-Law Badly Treated by His Sons-in-Law

Florence could congratulate herself but little on Hawkwood and his services. But this frequently occurs when one is the servant of two masters. In comparison with any other *condottiere* he might yet pass as a pearl of fidelity, and if there were still much to fear from him, something could also be hoped; hence we do not wonder that the Florentines deliberated to "keep the promises made to Hawkwood," (May 18), that is to continue his life-annuity.

Besides, while campaigning in Lombardy he might favor Florentine interests with Bernabo: in fact they wrote to remind him that the latter with Ruggiero Cane had made an agreement with Florence, about the payment of the Germans, of Hawkwood's own brigade, and of the Bretons, that is, of all the mercenaries who fought for the League during the preceding campaign. Now Bernabo—the truce being concluded, and he treating for peace with the Church—made a show of knowing nothing about it, and therefore Florence applied to Hawkwood that:

> He should, as it were, cultivate the alliance between Florence and Bernabo, availing himself of the influence of the illustrious lady Regina or any other personage.

Bernabo was at that very moment making war, with Hawkwood's help, against the Scaligers of Verona, his wife's family; and his consort the *illustre Signora Regina* herself was, in fact, the one who most violently urged her husband against them; but although the Visconti had hired the new and exclusively Italian Company of *San Giorgio*, formed by Alberico da Barbiano, it was a long drawn war.

In the archives of Mantua there exist several letters from Hawkwood, written to the Marquis Lodovico Gonzaga during this campaign, (between April 16 and August 8): they are severally dated from the "Entrenchments of the camp under Verona," from "Piadena," from the "camp of Villafranca," from the "camp of Monzambano" and other places between the Mincio, the Adige, and the Po, but none of them refer to military events of any importance.

We find that Hawkwood had orders from Bernabo to respect the Mantuan territory, but notwithstanding this, frequent violations occurred, which were inevitable, as the Mantuan land lay between that of Milan and Verona. We learn that the Mantuan soldiers sometimes ventured to steal some horses or baggage belonging to the English, or to intercept letters and dispatches, that every now and then skirmishes took place with Veronese freebooters—the letters therefore treat of excuses, protests, restitutions, indemnifications, and punishments. Generally, it is Hawkwood himself who writes to explain these "little incidents;" sometimes it is William Gold, constable-general of the company.

There being very goodwill on both sides, the relations between Visconti's army and the Lord of Mantua continued to be amicable in spite of the "little incidents," so much so that Gold did not hesitate to ask for special favours. For instance, he requested that the custom-house officials at Mantua would arrest three servants, who had fled from the camp after stealing two horses, with their respective breast-plates, and a silver flagon; and also a certain Janet his domestic, who had taken the road to Venice with 500 of his master's florins. Then finding himself ill provided with forage, he also begged that some might be provided by the captains of the marquis.

Amidst his numerous occupations as captain, Sir John Hawkwood did not lose sight either of his possessions in Romagna, or of interesting events in general politics.

One of his letters (April 7), demands a free pass on the Po for six boats going to Ferrara laden with arms, woodwork, tools, corn, and other supplies, all destined for Bagnacavallo; and in the postscript he informs the Marquis of Mantua that he had received notice of the election of the Cardinal di San Pietro (*in Vinculis*) as Pope (Urban VI).

At Bagnacavallo some English brigades doubtless held the garrison. In fact, Nicholas Clifton, Englishman from Bagnacavallo, treated of entering with his brigade into the service of the *Signoria* of Florence, (July 17), which promised him the same terms as those made with another of his compatriots named Berwick.

And thus, it is confirmed that many of the English fought on their own account in Italy, after having formed part of Hawkwood's company, and even when secure of returning to it.

Each leader, even of two or four lances, constituted a small independent atom, which disintegrated itself from, or united with the brigade under a *conestabile*; and each brigade either separated from, or joined with the permanent nucleus, according to reciprocal convenience, or to the course of events.

For example, that John Thornbury who had often acted as lieutenant to Hawkwood, had passed into the service of the Scaligers, (May); was taken prisoner by his old comrades and fellow-country-men, and obliged to pay a ransom: this we find from a letter in which he begs Gonzaga to allow him to live quietly in Mantua, and pay expenses at the inn. Such extreme mobility in the elements constituting the companies explains how little dependence could be placed on their discipline, and might excuse the frequent breaches of trust, for which history usually holds the captains responsible. And this renders the habitual fidelity of Hawkwood yet more meritorious.

It is said that he gave a brilliant proof of rectitude during this very campaign. The "Ten" of Venice, offered him a large sum if he would devastate the Paduan territory, and he refused because he was a friend of Carrara, Lord of Padua. Such delicate regard for friendship seems doubtful, because it is not known that before this there were any relations between the Carraras and Hawkwood.

The Paduan chroniclers substantially confirm the fact which they also attribute to 1378, but they recount it thus:

Lucius Landau and Hawkwood being dismissed Toy Bernabo Visconti, the *Signoria* of Venice wrote officially to them proposing to give them 30,000 *ducats* to harry the Paduan territory for fifteen days, and 1000 *ducats*, for every day over that time. They communicated this to the Carrarese, who with "good means" (which is to say money) so arranged that Hawkwood should go across the Po without touching the Paduan soil. Now since Landau and Hawkwood did not leave Bernabo's service till 1379, the date would contradict this; in any way the two *condottieri*, honestly and without risk, gained as much, as it had been offered them to gain dishonestly and sword in hand.

Without doubt the Florentines were in great distress, fearing a new visit from the English Company, and the *Signoria* wrote in confidence to its annuitant, the captain, (August 7):

We understand that Bernabo wishes speedily to send the English brigade to another destination, asking for transit either by our territory or wherever it is most convenient to him. We earnestly pray that you will take the road through Romagna, where there are frequent cities and towns, and where abundant provisions and forage will not be wanting; while on our lands it would cause great injury to the country and also serious scandals.

The Florentines were not ill-informed: Hawkwood himself writing to Gonzaga from the camp of Monzambano, (August 8), on account of the usual damages, confirms the fact of his having to march elsewhere "for certain services required by his masters."

It seems he replied to Florence with a variation of the usual song, alleging that the English were their creditors to the sum of 10,000 florins. And whether this credit existed or not, the motion was carried in the Florentine and councils, to "take this measure to content them": while the proposal to hire them for the city was negatived.

The usual contract for six months between Bernabo and the company having run out, (end of September), it was renewed, and the forces increased by the German Company of Count Lucius Landau who also passed into Lombardy, uniting with his brother-in-law Hawkwood in the service of their father-in-law Bernabo.

A considerable force was indeed necessary, for the King of Hungary had sent, first against the Venetians, and then in aid of the Scaligers, five thousand Hungarians conducted by the "*Vaivode*" of Transylvania and the "*Ban*" of Bosnia, and these had already entered Verona. (August 15.)

Neither Hawkwood nor Landau prevented the Hungarians from domineering as they chose in the Brescian territory, whence they pushed their way on to Cremona, they were even defeated and put to flight (September 1st), under Brescia, so that Bartolommeo Scaliger was able to attack Brescia and take several outworks.

Bernabo immediately agreed to a truce for forty-five days, (middle of October), and Hawkwood tranquilly placed himself in his autumn quarters at Cremona, from thence he sent his domestic *Pierino della Latta*, to provide ten cart-loads of Gazzoldo wine for his own use and that of his household.

The truce expired, (middle of November), the Lady Regina in person left Milan with her eldest son Marco, to take part in the war, with a thousand four hundred lances, and numerous infantry. She took with her the companies of both Hawkwood and Landau, then rode on to Brescia and urged all the troops to devastate the Veronese country between the lake of Garda and the River Adige.

The Hungarians disputed the passage of the river with Hawkwood and Landau; there were some killed and drowned on both sides, but the two brothers-in-law crossed safely, and giving themselves to plunder, penetrated as far as Valdagno.

Meanwhile the Hungarians and the Scaligers in revenge, pushed on across the River Oglio, returning with six hundred prisoners, and twenty thousand head of large cattle.

Hawkwood and Landau were at Caldiero, (January 29, 1379), when the news of the enemy's return with such immense spoil reached them. The temptation was too great, they crossed the Adige by night, lay in wait for the enemy near the river, fell upon them while they in their turn attempted to pass over, and, cutting up their forces greatly, they recovered a good many prisoners.

In spite of this, rumours were circulated that they allowed themselves to be corrupted by the Scaligers; at least, it appeared to Bernabo that they did not conduct the war with a zeal proportioned to their immense salaries (the two companies cost at the rate of 250,000 florins a year), nor yet as behoved two sons to their father-in-law, and hence arose ill humour and discord, which the vehement lady Regina certainly contrived to fan.

This explains why Count Landau and Hawkwood wrote to Gonzaga, (February 18), that Bernabo denied a pass through his territory to the recently made prisoners. The time to present them at Verona and receive their ransom thus expired; the captains however, with the agreement of their soldiers, determined to prorogue it, sending the noble and prudent Ulrich Ofsteten, and praying that he might be received at Mantua, and that it might be conceded to him to go and return from Verona with the prisoners, under the necessary escort.

The next day they wrote again to Gonzaga informing him that:

A little misunderstanding had arisen between themselves and Bernabo, but that, with the help of God, they hoped to regain the favor of the Visconti, and that whatever should be the result they would keep him informed.

They sent an analogous communication to Florence on which the Florentines "deliberated" to send an envoy to their camp with the mission of procuring concord, for "it grieved them not to be in harmony with Bernabo:" but also to fathom their intentions. (March 2.)

If free of engagements those two *condottieri* might take a course of action which would be perilous to Tuscany;—indeed the Visconti had hastened to secure the concourse of the Florentines against his sons-in-law, but they replied by showing him the danger that would accrue if Hawkwood and Landau should unite themselves with the Italian

Company of San Giorgio, brought to the Po by Alberico da Barbiano.

Marchionne Stefani, the chronicler, was sent to them, but he could conclude nothing, and the rupture became complete; a son-in-law of Hawkwood left Milan (beginning of March), where he had lived a long time, and took refuge in the camp of his father-in-law, who seat him to Bagnacavallo with an escort of sixty horse, for whom he demanded a safe conduct from Gonzaga.

★★★★★★

The son-in-law was perhaps that Lancellotto del Maino who according to Corio had married Fiorentina, a daughter of Hawkwood, by his first unnamed wife. See the last chapter.

★★★★★★

And the Visconti's two sons-in-law, Hawkwood and Landau, considering themselves dismissed, provided for themselves by forming an Anglo-German Company of a thousand two hundred lances.

Which party was in the right? Some chroniclers say that Bernabo did not pay the two *condottieri*, perhaps calculating that the bond of relationship was strong enough to make them patient creditors. Others would make us believe that the whole was an understood game with Bernabo, and that he hoped by the aid of his sons-in-law to subjugate Tuscany, but successive facts do not justify the supposition: and later, (October 25), Bernabo though silent about Hawkwood, who was not a subject of the Empire, made a formal accusation to the King of the Romans, that Count Lucius, his brother Eberhard Landau, and other German captains had betrayed him in the enterprise of Verona; indeed at the time of the rupture the fury of Visconti was so great that he published a reward of 30 florins for every adventurer whether taken or killed.

CHAPTER 22

Hawkwood Fighting for His Possessions

The brothers-in-law Hawkwood and Landau, with their respective Englishmen and Germans, only stayed a few days to spoil the territory of their father-in-law (1379); then having crossed the Po they encamped in the Bolognese district certain of finding good employment ere long. Meanwhile, (March 19), Bologna, to obtain quiet, disbursed them 2500 *ducats*; and Peracchino (of Padua), just then made Cardinal of Santa Cecilia by Urban VI, proposed to the Florentines that they should engage them.

Florence would willingly have done without this new burden, especially as the two *condottieri* were bound for two years more to re-spect Florentine property; however while protesting their own loyalty to this contract, the two captains gave them to understand that there was a danger of Count Eberhard, brother of Count Lucius, moving his brigade against Florence on his own account. Wherefore the good Marchionne Stefani observes:

> Thus, they broke faith with the city; which thing though not done openly, was yet more than evident. I don't oblige you to buy us again, but, even if you don't want us, you have got to give us money, whether you will or not.

At the same time, they sought a pretext for litigation, addressing veiled and polite menaces to the Sienese, and to all the cities in Tus-cany. On account of this Florence sent a notary to Bologna, together with the cardinal's envoy, with the mission of verifying the adventur-ers' intentions, "secretly, and through the medium of trustworthy per-sons who have access to the company." To the cardinal, they declared themselves disposed to make a treaty if the money were not required immediately, and if he himself would undertake the negotiations, stip-ulating that the company should not touch on the Florentine terri-tory. At the same time debates took place in the *Consulte* (Councils), how they could be hindered from passing the Apennines. (March 17, 18 and 20, 1379.)

Having received the required information, the Florentines resigned themselves to sending commissioners to attempt an agreement, but as a precaution they disposed that the peasants should evacuate the open country and the district, taking refuge within the walled towns, and that the fortresses should be garrisoned and manned by archers. By this time, (March 31), the Tuscans were quite accustomed to measures of this kind.

The Cardinal of Padua opened negotiations on the base of 250,000 florins a year; but one fine day he unexpectedly departed, leaving everything uncompleted, and the *Signoria*, who had already disbursed some money, had the trouble of finishing the treaties, (April 22.) This office was given, as usual, to the treasurer Spinello Alberti, but this time he did not so easily bring affairs to a conclusion, perhaps because Landau was harder or more particular than Hawkwood.

End of May the Germans and English had passed into the Perugian territory, nominally as friends, but in reality, they comported them-selves more like enemies, not keeping their contracts, even after having extorted 8000 florins from Perugia, and molesting Montepulciano, and Val di Chiana. Much ill humour fermented amongst the people in Florence, which often degenerated into tumults; outside the city several companies of disbanded adventurers and rebels were raging, so it was urgent that the *Signoria* should make sure of the two captains.

They therefore sent couriers to Spinello Alberti, (May 22), to make the contract at all cost, then they sent a man on horseback (May 27), with "full powers" (*ampia balia*) in a dispatch in cypher, and orders not to move from the camp till the matter was concluded, (May 28); together with other instructions, to the effect that after having signed the agreement with the *condottieri*, they should form a defensive league between the Tuscan Communes, and those of Bologna; that the companies should be hired in the name of this league, dividing the expense of the pay between the allies.

At the same time, they wrote longwinded thanks to Hawkwood for all the good "which they hoped from him."

The diplomatic energy of Spinello resulted in the contract concluded at Torrita, between Hawkwood and the two brothers Landau (Lucius and Eberhard), on the one part; June 10. Florence, Perugia, Siena, Arezzo, and Città di Castello, on the other.

The agreement was to the effect that each of the cities should take a certain number of lances into their service and at an exorbitant price not including extras. Florence had 450 of them.

We are minutely informed of the sums paid by the Sienese:—to the two Landaus and to Hawkwood a royalty of 6000 florins promised by Spinello, besides a remuneration of 1600 florins; to Count Lucius 2000 florins for "damages before time *suffered* (!) by him on Sienese ground;" to Count Eberhard 100 florins for a palfrey, and 500 for his registrars and procurators; to the Sienese commissioners 200 florins; besides 32,000 florins, for the pay of 200 English and German lances which fell to the share of Siena at the rate of 20 florins a month each lance, from June 4 to February 4, that is to say 100 German lances, 77 English ones under Giovanni Gulione (?) and di Monte, and 23 of Hawkwood's.

The latter as usual showed himself relatively discreet. During the hostilities preceding the agreement, a Sienese gentleman, Stefano Maconi, had been taken by Gulione and had bound himself to pay a ransom of 100 *scudi* in gold, but this was remitted by the solicitation of the Senate to Hawkwood. (From a letter dated November 6 1379, written by Francesco Casini of Siena, doctor to Pope Urban VI, and cited by Tommaseo in his comments on the letters of St. Catherine of

Siena. He might in error have mistaken the Britons for Bretons.) The company dissolved at Grecciano near Montepulciano, and everyone went to his destination. (June 26.)

Hawkwood had left (or reconducted thither) the greater part of his brigade in his possessions of Romagna, where his neighbours Manfredi Lord of Faenza, and Polenta Lord of Ravenna, were both hostile to him. He himself writing from Bagnacavallo to Gonzaga, (July 3), said he had gone there to reside, and added that he had 300 lances without pay on the Faentine territory, and that Count Lucius had gone to the March of Ancona with 500 lances: the rest of his troops, that is to say 600 German lances and 500 English, were engaged at service in Tuscany.

In the same letter Hawkwood recommended one of his men Nicholas Tanfield, who had gone to Mantua to obtain the consignment, or the ransom of a prisoner who had escaped from Astolfo, one of Hawkwood's officers—the said prisoner had been taken in "our territory at Gazzolo" (terra nostra Gazoli).

We have thus an indication that, besides his possessions in Romagna, Hawkwood had land also on the Po; but we do not know at what time, or on what title he had acquired this land at Gazzolo, nor indeed how long he kept it. We cannot even decide which it was of two places, both called Gazzolo, nor can we say it may not have been that Gazzuolo which at the end of the 15th century belonged to the Gonzaghi, by whom it was adorned with a noble fortress (destroyed by the Austrians in 1772) and with beautiful porticoes which still exist, (1889).

The possession of Gazzolo explains the care with which Hawkwood cultivated friendly relations with the Marquis of Mantua, and of which we also have an interesting document in a courteous letter of thanks and compliments written to Gonzaga (September 7), by Donnina Visconti of Milan, consort of Sir John Hawkwood.

Hawkwood was in open hostility with his neighbours in Romagna, especially with Astorre Manfredi; so that Florence, who judged that this did not conduce to her interests, sent an envoy to attempt making peace between them. By this time (July 2), Florence had the opinion that Hawkwood was the best, and the least false of the *condottieri*, and as she continued to pay his annuity she wished to have him always at her disposal; therefore the *Signoria* wrote also to Bernabo Visconti, (July 30), to try to reconcile him to his son-in-law.

For his own safety Hawkwood took care to reinforce himself

against his hostile neighbours, and to excite other enemies against them. He himself (July 7) informed his friend Gonzaga (in this letter Hawkwood signs himself "English knight"—*miles anglicus*), that he had called up a considerable force from the Marches, of which 100 lances entered the service of Bologna, and the remainder consisting of 250 or more, comprising archers, under the command of constable Gold, had gone towards Forli "to certain barons of the Romagna who were waiting to make an attack on Guido di Ravenna, and Astorre Manfredi." (From other sources we find that Galeotto Malatesta, Lord of Rimini, was at the head of these barons.) He stayed at Bagnacavallo with about 60 lances, and there he provided himself with provisions and arms, (August 28), ordering from Gazzolo 500 battle axes and 100 head of cattle, large and small.

While attending to his own business he did not lose sight of the affairs of Florence, for his bonds of interest with this city were strengthening daily. The government was at present in the hands of the conservative party, but it was menaced by the chief burghers (*popolani grassi*) and by the low populace (*ciompi*). It chanced to come to light, that the Florentine opposition was plotting nothing less than a revolution, and that the leaders of the conspiracy were some exiles at Bologna; the agitation of. the *Signoria* was great when a letter arrived from Hawkwood (December 10), saying it had been revealed to him in confidence by a citizen, that there were *great plots going on in Florence.*

He added that he was in relation with a person who knew the whole scheme, and would explain it .to him in full, in the presence of an emissary of the Commune; that he was ready to serve Florence in such a serious emergency, but if they wanted the complete revelation of the plans, and of the conspirators he would demand 50,000 florins and the facility of saving six men—"their lives and property, excepting only exile." If they were satisfied in knowing the plot without the names of the conspirators, he would be content with 20,000 florins—the money to be taken to Bagnacavallo where the revelation was to take place.

The prevailing idea was to spend as little as possible, and the delicate mission was confided to Guccio Gucci. He was a wise man, wealthy and loyal, who would not allow himself either to be deceived or corrupted.

They thought that Hawkwood wanted too much profit, first on the Commune, and then on those citizens to whom he reserved the right to sell their impunity. Consequently, Gucci haggled about the price, although the *Signoria* in its anxiety sent a man every day to Bagnacavallo for news. It ending by obtaining a reduction of terms: 20,000 florins and impunity for six persons, if everything were revealed with the names of the conspirators; and 12,000 florins if the names were kept back. The last proposal being accepted, and the necessary understanding arrived at with Hawkwood, the Florentine emissary was introduced by night into Sir John's room, where there was no light except a little charcoal in a brazier, and where the unknown informer, who did not even remain unknown, was admitted: Hawkwood had already him tracked several times in vain, but that night, after the colloquy, with success.

The *Signoria* now knew, all that was necessary to counteract the plot, and did not regret the 12,000 florins, especially as it was afterwards confirmed from Count Antonio da Bruscoli and many other sources, that a very serious rebellion was treated of. The Commune was thus able to take precautions, secure proofs, and discover and condemn those who were culpable.

After this secret and profitable service against the internal enemies of Florence, Hawkwood had soon occasion to lend other service more open and not less lucrative, against the external enemies of the same Republic. To complicate the troubles of Italy (1380), a new element was added. Carlo di Durazzo of Anjou came from Hungary to sustain his pretensions to the crown of the Kingdom of Naples, and, in agreement with the Pope Urban VI, threatened the Tuscan cities who were hostile to the Pope. (Buonincontri—*Annali*—says, we do not know with what foundation, that the Pope called the Hungarian prince of Anjou into Italy, after having held counsel with John Hawkwood.) The prince of Anjou had large forces at his disposal, and the chief of them was that Italian Company of San Giorgio, with which Alberico da Barbiano had become quite an important military power after his famous victory over the Bretons near Rome.

To provide for their own defence, the Florentines immediately turned to Hawkwood, whose sword was at present disposable, his hostilities with the Lords of Faenza and Ravenna being for a time suspended. Venice too, who found herself involved in the critical war of Chioggia. wanted him for her captain, but he refused, for he had a better understanding with the Florentines; so, the Venetians gave the command to Carlo Zeno instead, and then took into their pay Gold, Cook, and some others of Hawkwood's tried comrades and compatriots.

He lent a much more willing ear to the proposals of the Florentines, because his brother-in-law Lucius Landau had also accepted them.

CHAPTER 23
The Contest with Astorre Manfredi

At the beginning of March, the Company of St. George, being masters of Arezzo, were menacing the neighbourhood of Florence: it was therefore provided to bring the corn into the city, and arm the people, but there were dissentions in the Florentine councils as to the choice of a captain.

The *Otto di balia* proposed Hawkwood, and would even have received him into the League as a potentate, engaging to induce the Bolognese and Perugians to accept him; but many others wanted a man of noble birth, faithful, honest, and "not of too much weight"; some resigned themselves to take Hawkwood, but were diffident about it, they did not want him "in the city, nor to distribute the garrisons in the fortresses, elsewhere they might make use of him as long as it was necessary." Marchionne Stefani thus explains the case:

> Those who were suspected, or had been *ammoniti*, and their friends wanted him, and they made the people believe he was necessary to them. Others did not want him, some because he should not favour the above-mentioned, and others because they did not want to spend more than they were obliged.
>
> ★★★★★★
>
> Note:—To be admonished or *ammonito* under the Republic of Florence was to be excluded from the power of holding public office; it was a punishment a degree less severe than exile for the disaffected.
>
> ★★★★★★

They were doubtful, in fact, of his interfering with the sword, in the civic questions which were continually arising in Florence. Meanwhile they sent him a messenger with proposals, reserving his nomination to the captaincy, until they had received replies from their allies.

The approach of the enemy cut short all delays and hesitation. The *Signoria* passed a motion (20, 21 and 22 March), that they should themselves conduct the election of a captain, together with the councils, and other officials and the *capitudini* (that is a consul elected from each of the twenty-three *Arti*). The *capitudini* being elected, Hawkwood was unanimously proclaimed captain without loss of time (March 26); the only dispute was that some were disposed to take him with the 300 lances offered by him, and others only wished for 200, but they begged him to make the best terms he could for them. There was no time to lose, they had already come to blows. (April 1st.) Eberhard Landau repulsed an attack of the Company of St. George taking 70 horses, together with Count Giovanni brother of Alberico da Barbiano (in which action John of Berwick, *a brave Englishman*, was wounded); but this little success was not enough to reassure them.

The following day Hawkwood's election as captain-general for six months was announced to him, and (April 6):

> He entered into Florence at the 22nd hour of the day (about 4 p.m.) with the *Signoria* and a large company of citizens. The great bell was rung, and he entered with great honour, and sounding of trumpets, and ringing of bells, as our captain of war in the name of God and of good fortune. In the morning of April 14th, he received the *bâton* in the name of God, at the palace of our *Signoria*, as our captain-general of the war, to the undoing and death of our citizens (exiles) who had come back, and were with that cursed company (of St. George). At *tierce* he rode forth from Florence with all the men-at-arms and they were considered fine and grand troops.

The fame of his name was enough for the exiles and the Company of St. George who had approached Lucca, with a demand for 20,000 florins, for they hastily compounded for half the sum, and took the road into the Maremma.

Having made the first defensive preparations in the upper Val d'Arno, Hawkwood with many of his men returned to Florence (April 20), to regulate the conditions of the *condotta*. Now the Florentines were in an economical mood, especially as they had made some proposals towards a compromise with Barbiano, and wanted to await his reply. They desired Hawkwood to be content with 130 lances, but rather than let him go away they preferred to grant him the 300 he wanted, (April 27, 28), dismissing the other stipendiaries.

They had the prudence not to let him guess how much they depended on his services; it was not without good reason that they had become the most astute merchants in the world. Thus, Hawkwood was induced (April 29) to accept only 200 lances, and 1000 florins a month for his salary; and on these conditions he was nominated captain-general till All Saints' Day, (April 30) accepting the office by a public attestation.

The Florentines did not wish to attack the army of Carlo di Durazzo now made master of Arezzo. Hawkwood always said to the Florentines: "If you wish, I will conquer those troops for you"; and they would not let him on account of the bad condition of Florence, and out of regard to the King of Hungary (a kinsman of Carlo).

The "Eight of war" provided for the defence, the "Eight of peace" for making negotiations with the enemy.

It has however been noticed in preceding campaigns that Hawkwood always showed a great wish to fight when he knew his masters would not give him the means of doing so, and liked to drag out a slow war when they wanted decisive action; such little hypocrisies were useful to the reputation of adventurers and served their interests.

It is probable that in his own mind Hawkwood was very well content that the wishes of the Florentines did not go beyond the defensive, and in providing for this he displayed his undeniable abilities.

He placed a camp of observation at Montevarchi, where on all sides, wherever the enemy appeared, he opposed an efficacious resistance, so that Carlo of Anjou was induced to make those terms in earnest, which he had at first only proposed to blind the Florentines.

With this kind of plan of campaign, the immediate presence of the captain is not always necessary. Hawkwood was sometimes able to demand and obtain leave of absence, perhaps to run up and glance at his estates in Romagna. (May 19.) He had finished by gaining the entire trust of the Florentines, who chose him as arbiter in a question (probably that of an armistice for the treaties already begun) with the hostile Company of *St. George* (June 1st), they tried to wean him from the project of entering the service of the Duke of Bavaria, (July 16); they recalled his troops into the city and followed minutely his advice to be as cautious and carry arms, exactly the same as if they were not treating for peace, or as though the Hungarians with whom they treated were their enemies.

They accorded him extensions of time in the execution of their orders, nominated him and another Englishman William Chorsal (Kursel?) constable of a small brigade, on the same conditions as though they were actually fighting, granting them the usual benefits of toleration about the supply of better horses and ponies, and absolving them from the obligation of registering the names of pages (with all which little extras every captain made considerable profit on the pay).

Hawkwood returned to Florence (September 24), when the troops of Durazzo moved away towards Siena and Montepulciano, and notwithstanding this retreat of the enemy he was on All Saints' Day re-elected captain-general for another six months. He sent verbal instructions to the Defenders of Siena through his comrade the noble Antonio di Porcaria, but during the winter, having nothing to do for the Florentines he returned against Astorre Manfredi, his own particular enemy, and occupied some towns over which the Commune of Florence asserted a right (they were probably in the upper valley of Lamone). The Commune discreetly deliberated to provide that *those towns should not pass into other hands*, unless restored to Manfredi, but above everything else to extinguish that fire, by hastening to procure peace between the two combatants. (January 8, February 6 1381.)

The Florentines were anxious to suppress this contest, for, although they disputed how many lances should be paid for, all with one accord wanted Hawkwood as captain, renouncing, if necessary, the services of Eberhard Landau, who had also served them faithfully. They so firmly believed that, he "would have observed and maintained his written word," that in their Councils they absolved the *Otto* in anticipation from all responsibility, (January) in case things fell out differently.

By force of diplomacy, they succeeded in concluding a truce (March 20), as the *Anonymous* diarist informs us:

> John Hawkwood and Astorre Manfredi are coming to Florence; it is said that the *Signoria* have procured peace between them, for the honour of the Commune. And if I had anything to do with it, I should pay them off and have done with it, and we needs must have a truce for two years. And so, goes the affair. God send peace to all the world.

This done, the captainship of Hawkwood was immediately renewed by the *Otto*, and because stipulated without the full powers necessary, it was revised and confirmed with an official commission, (April 10), in which the form is as remarkable as the substance. It solemnly begins thus:

> The Priors and *Gonfaloniere*, principally because the men-at-arms of the Commune should be led when occasion requires by a good captain, with sound judgment, also one approved in valour, and circumspect in military arts, especially in feats of arms, of wide experience, and self-confidence, cast their eyes on the magnificent cavalier John Haukcuod (Hawkwood) Englishman.

He was nominated captain for seven months with thirty lances at the expense of the Commune. He was not required to serve immediately, it was enough if he placed himself at their disposal, but he could not without leave absent himself more than eighty miles from Florence. He might however enrol the thirty lances even at Bagnacavallo, where he resided.

Consequently, the pay was less than usual, being fixed at 333 florins, 6 *soldi*, and 8 *danari* for Hawkwood himself—10 florins and 10 *soldi* for the lances of three horsemen each—6 florins, 10 *soldi* for the lances and archers of two horses each—and 4 florins for the archers with one horse.

If it should afterwards be deliberated that Hawkwood and his brigade were to be wholly at the orders of the *Signoria*, his stipend was to be tripled and that of the brigade doubled.

And here we have an additional proof of the especial consideration shown to Hawkwood, for at the same time, (April 18), William Gold (called Coccho), whom we already know as a brave veteran, was hired with fifteen lances on the same terms, except that to him personally the pay was only to be doubled in case of active service. The terms made, (September 23), with another Englishman Richard Romise (? Romsey) were even less liberal.

Every proposition made by Hawkwood (May 4), was listened to with the greatest deference—hence they promised him 600 florins "for those Englishmen of whom he had written."

Hostilities were very soon renewed with Astorre Manfredi; the truce was not observed; so Florentine envoys were sent into Romagna, to enjoin the two parties to "do nothing new" (*non far novita*), and in accord with the Bolognese commissaries, they were to give sentence as arbiters in the litigation. (May 13.)

Then they made efforts to arrive at a good treaty of peace, to be stipulated at Bologna or on her territory, inviting the Bolognese to summon the two litigants—proroguing, if necessary, the date of the umpirage. It was the opinion at Florence, that Manfredi was in the right, but they recommended that justice should be rendered if it were possible, and they were also inclined to maintain the truce, (May 24), leaving the disputed question in abeyance. Not coming to any conclusion in Romagna, Manfredi and Hawkwood had repeated invitations to come to Florence, and *with good reasons*, leave of absence was refused to Hawkwood, who, foreseeing that the arbitrator's sentence would be unfavourable, intended to protest by going farther away.

The arbitration was conciliative, although when it came to the execution, the Bolognese had orders to punish Astorre if he rebelled, and to reassure him if he obeyed. The Florentines then took on themselves to write to Hawkwood reproving him for his attempts against his neighbour. Anyway this long litigation, and the hostility which had embittered it, convinced Hawkwood that it did not suit him to keep his estates in Romagna among such perilous neighbours, and that he could not with advantage be at the same time a feudal lord and hired captain. He must choose between the two positions, and he with practical English sense preferred to continue his lucrative and now honourable career as a soldier, rather than waste himself with his few forces in the poor little principality of Bagnacavallo and Cotignola. He liked better to be the first of the *condottieri*, than the last of the lords of Italy.

Chapter 24

Hawkwood Sells His Possessions in Romagna and Has Florence at His Feet.

Just beyond the ford of the river near Bagnacavallo in the territory of Lugo (either in the open fields or at an hostelry near the ford) the two contracting parties met on the 10th of August 1381. They were Hawkwood on the one side; and on the other Tommaso de' Gilli di Terdona, proxy, and the noble Paolo di Lendinara, a confidential friend, both procurators of Niccolo and Alberto Marquises d' Este. There were present the chamberlain, the captain of Lugo, the Englishman John Rayner, and others as witnesses to the legal act which was there stipulated between them, and drawn up as a public document.

In it Hawkwood acknowledged the receipt of 60,000 gold *ducats* from the Marquises d' Este, and promised to restitute the said sum, at any time and before any court the said marquises shall be pleased to require it. As a guarantee he pledged all his possessions present and future, but especially the estates of Bagnacavallo and Cotignola, with the fortresses, palaces, towers, gates, bastions, and their respective buildings and lands, together with every jurisdiction, and every right which had belonged to him; besides all and every stronghold which at present was held by him, or by others in his name, in the province of Romagna, except the bastion of Sezada.

Further, Hawkwood rendered all the aforesaid possessions responsible for the expenses which the Marquises d' Este should sustain for restorations, repairs, and custody of the same, whenever the expenses should outweigh the receipts, in which case the Marquises d' Este might retain and demand legal compensation from any person holding the goods so pledged. We conclude then that Hawkwood declared that he possessed those estates on a precarious title, and promised to restore them to the Marquises d' Este or their agents, in their charge and absolute free power, just as above specified, excepting always the single bastion of Sezada.

> And this in consideration that the said Sir John is not himself powerful enough to defend the said territories with honour to the Church, from the enemies' incursions and from their persistent machinations; and observing that the said marquises have been, and will be, faithful sons and servants of the Pope our Lord, and most true defenders of the Roman Church, and its rights; and being thus powerful, they know how to defend the said lands to the honour of the Church, and the Pope our Lord.

Hawkwood besides solemnly renounced all his rights to these possessions in favour of Pope Urban VI, or his successors and their commissaries; to the effect that the Marquises d' Este might be invested with those rights in his place, and for this object, he nominated the procurators of the Marquises d' Este as his procurators in the contract, pledging himself never to revoke the nomination. And this under penalty of 1000 *ducats* without prejudice to the validity of the contract.

All which, according to this faithful summary, would at first sight appear to be a contract of mortgage, but containing certain clauses by which Hawkwood on one part takes 60,000 *ducats*, and on the other he cedes to the d'Estes all his possessions in Romagna, excepting the bastion of Sezada, which doubtless served as a military precaution against Astorre Manfredi.

If we do not style it a sale, it is a loan against a cession of property, and interesting to us not so much from its legal singularity, as because it renders the fact evident that Hawkwood was in Romagna a true territorial Lord of feudal character, under the high domination of the Pope; and it also shows that he resigned this principality because the trouble of defending it was not convenient to him, the expense exceeding the income. The Marquises d' Este, being rich and ambitious, endeavoured to extend their dominion between the Po and the Adriatic by every possible means, and for this they had bought from Hawkwood the possession of Faenza, and although they did not long retain that place, yet they now risked spending 60,000 *ducats* for Bagnacavallo and Cotignola, where their lordship was less precarious. It was they who brought the Jews into Cotignola, allowing them a *ghetto* with a synagogue, and a bank for usury, which lasted till 1598, in that part named *Castellina* where Hawkwood's ancient tower still rises, (1880).

The d' Estes sent as their commissary to take possession of Bagnacavallo, Cotignola and the annexed village of Couselice, Filippo Guazilotti of Prato, brother of one Alberto Guazilotti, commissary general in Lugo, now deputed to the government of Faenza.

★★★★★★

Bonoli, *Storia di Cotignola*. This author says that Hawkwood was induced to sell the estate for lack of money, after having spent too freely in the fortifications of Cotignola, and not being able to pay his soldiers, who had now for some months been his creditors. But although he cites an ancient MS. in the library of the Duke of Modena and another MS. of the Signori Trotti, one can put little trust in a writer who makes one affair of the two sales, that of Faenza in 1376-77 and this of 1381, giving the date as 1380.

★★★★★★

Having sold all his estates Hawkwood was still irritated at the little favourable interference of the Florentines in his dispute with Astorre; they besides delayed in granting him a sum of money to buy a house at Florence, as he intended to do, now that he no longer had a residence at Bagnacavallo, and they were rigorous in the liquidation of his pay. Hence, he formed a league between his company, that of Eberhard Landau and that of the Ban Johann of Hungary, lieutenant and captain-general of Carlo Durazzo, which he was free to do, as in October he ceased to be at the disposal of the Florentines, and was in every way free from active service.

He sent an embassy to the Florentines, (end of August), to obtain an absolute dismissal; but by this time, they could no longer do without him, and deliberated that it would be well to give him a verbal reply, sending Spinello Alberti, a pleasing person who was well acquainted with him. They did not wish to dismiss him without knowing his intentions, so they would proffer him "sweet and good words" accepting him as a friend and servant. As to the affair with Astorre, they would justify the rights of the Commune in such a manner as to satisfy him, and in agreement with the Bolognese, they would clear him of every reproach. They would arrange the account of his stipends so as to content him, respond graciously to his good wishes, offer him the house he required, rather than pay out the price of it, and endeavour to re-nominate him as captain, or at least to bind him not to injure the Commune, her allies, or the Lord of Milan.

In fact, Florence threw herself at his feet; and yet as a precaution she prepared men-at-arms and defences as though Hawkwood's company was to be her enemy.

But on hearing of the league with Landau and the Ban, and that they threatened to ask a loan (!), they sent Spinello at once with secret instructions to break the league, and bring away Hawkwood, taking him into their pay as captain, and to quiet Count Landau with smooth speeches. (September 2, 3, and following days.)

Spinello did better, he succeeded in making an agreement, (October 3), concluded at Isola Romanesca near Assisi, where Landau and Hawkwood were encamped. They stipulated, also in the name of the Ban, to keep the peace with Florence, taking the oath for three months as stipendiaries (*in modum stipendii*) and for eighteen months as good friends (*in modum societatis*). Five thousand florins were paid them (which proves they had not a large brigade) and they were granted a pass on the aforesaid conditions.

A little after this, (November 18), Siena and Florence were obliged to disburse 30,000 florins to the great bands of *St. George*, of the *Uncino* (Hook) etc., who were encamped near Arezzo. This was enough to convince Florence that she must by all means have Hawkwood as her captain, (December 19), and he was re-elected captain-general for six months, but this time it was for active service, and consequently with the more favourable conditions contemplated in the "*provvisione*" of April 10 (see last chapter) and besides with the faculty of taking as many as ninety lances as his brigade, and with the extraordinary power of dismissing them.

For the time during which he delayed presenting himself in Florence he was to receive the third of his pay and his men the half. Moreover, he was accorded ten *per cent* on all which was gained in war by the stipendiaries of the Commune under his command.

No *condottiere* had ever obtained like favours; he was at the same time drawing more money from the Sienese, on his own account, and that of Count Landau and the Ban. Nevertheless, there flashed across him the longing for his native country, since he had expressly reserved the faculty of returning to England, or to cross the seas, even during his engagement with Florence.

In truth the 60,000 *ducats* recently received from the Estes must have rounded into a very respectable fortune in his hands, and the prospect smiled upon him of peaceful enjoyment in his own country, if it should please God, after he had been purged from his sins by fighting his last fight against the *infidels* beyond the seas, thus accomplishing the vow and promises sealed by him in answer to the exhortations of St. Catherine of Siena.

But habit and circumstances are often stronger than our resolutions, and always more so than our intentions. One who has a business well started cannot easily decide to leave it. Moreover, Donnina Visconti had already made him the father of several children both sons and daughters, without counting his other offspring legitimate or otherwise preceding that marriage. Nobody ever seems to have enough means when there are children.

Hawkwood therefore stayed in Italy, and at Florence he had a part to sustain in the service of the public order; the part of a man-at-arms in the tumults which too frequently afflicted that democracy. It was his office to provide for the internal peace, as well as the external defence of the Commune, and this was the reason the *Signoria* had made such efforts to have him in Florence and quickly.

Chapter 25
Enters the Pay of the Pope

Serious disturbances broke out in Florence, (January 1382), provoked by the rebellion of Giorgio Scali, Scatizza, and their companions. To assist the captain of the people in arresting the rebels, Hawkwood appeared on the *piazza* of the *Signoria,* (January 16), with his ninety lances. The sight of those three hundred veterans on horseback was enough to intimidate the mob.

The tumults were renewed at night; and in the morning, behold Hawkwood fully armed again arrived on the *piazza* with a great many soldiers and the seven consuls of the greater "*Arti*." Unable to maintain order, the captain of the people threw away the *bâdton*, and said "he resigned his office;" on which Hawkwood with his men-at-arms "went all round the city shewing themselves" so as to re-establish peace, and if nothing else, he managed to make an end of the excesses of that brutalised mob. He met a brigade who had mortally wounded Simone di Biagio, and with a halter were dragging him to execution and he said: "Lead him away" (*menatelo via*).

The enemy profited by these disorders: the Company of the Uncino, commanded by Villanozzo at Roccafranca, which formed the *avant*-guard to St. George, had approached as far as Marcialla, (January 24), a few miles from the city. It was quickly decided that Hawkwood should defend it if possible; if not, that he should come to terms, taking care not to compromise the State; that he should fight only if he were certain of success, and in any case, they would hear his opinion before negotiating. (January 26.)

With these instructions, with 800 lances, 200 archers, and 600 infantry, Hawkwood immediately left the city, attempted in vain and with some loss to make himself master of the hill of Marcialla, and encamped at Santa Maria Nuova where he fortified his position and awaited reinforcements. The two camps entrenched and fenced, faced each other as though they would come to action. At the end of three days the Company of the Uncino was obliged to commence a retreat, which they continued, masking it by skirmishes of the rear-guard. Hawkwood followed them as far as Berardinga where he had orders to retire to Val d'Arno.

The report of Piero Buoninsegni "that Hawkwood had had speech with the corporals of the *Uncino*" does not seem to be justified, neither does that which Marchionne di Coppo Stefani wrote "it was thought he did not do as much as he could in the service of the Republic." On the contrary we have numerous documents, showing his activity in organising and conducting the defence, bringing forward also the Sienese forces, and procuring good soldiers for the united service, and watching that their pay was adequate, and if the Uncino Company was able to retreat with spoil and prisoners, while it seemed to the good Florentine citizens that they had them in a trap, Hawkwood, it must be remembered, had instructions not to run any risk. It was the *Signoria* who, seeing the internal condition of the city, (February 15), wanted to have him at hand.

In fact, when the *burghers* and populace again invaded the *piazza*, they were once more stopped by the "halt there" of Hawkwood with many soldiers both horse and foot. (March 10, 1382.) Then at the sound of the hammer-struck bell, every man took arms. "Moscone with the other misguided men, ready to do evil," led on by the aristocratic party, "made a rendezvous at St. George," intending to increase their numbers and fortify themselves on that hill, "but finally Sir John Hawkwood managed to get them into the *piazza*." The rebels being thus hunted down, they were soon brought back to their duty.

These experiences persuaded the *Signoria* that the stipendiaries might render invaluable service to them in maintaining public peace, and therefore in a contract (April 12), with two English constables of sixty lances, is this unusual clause inserted:

> Item, if the aforesaid constables or any of their company shall be informed of anything which treats of, or is designed to, the prejudice, injury, or offence of the Commune, or of its peaceful condition, he shall immediately by letter or messenger notify the same in good faith, as soon and as fully as possible, to the Priors and *Gonfaloniere* etc.

Relative peace being established in the city, the *Signoria* desired Hawkwood to march into the Arezzo territory with one or two hundred lances, (April 10); he had also some infantry, but with such poor forces he could accomplish nothing. The "Anonymous Florentine" explains the secret: Hawkwood was only to place himself on guard at the frontier, and the treasurer Spinello went with him to buy the Company of St. George if it were possible.

What a quantity of florins had by this time passed by means of Spinello, from the pockets of the Florentines, into the hands of the mercenaries! Stefani exclaimed with reason:

> This is the blessing of Florence, the money of the Florentines is so sweet that everybody wants it.

St. George wanted too much of it, so Hawkwood and Spinello returned to Florence, (April 15), without having concluded anything, and now the Florentines burned with unusual ardour and wanted to make every effort at the frontier. If Hawkwood felt secure in doing so, he might exterminate the company without coming to any terms; 1500 lances were to be put together against it, and if Hawkwood approved, he could also attack Wilhelm Filibach, a German, who among the many mercenaries, had made himself a nest at Arezzo. (May 2 and 4.)

And in fact, from his camp at Civitella, Hawkwood anxiously asked the Sienese to join him in the attack on their common enemy, and to send all their troops to Lucignano, where he would meet them and thus attempt some decisive action. But the warlike fit was of short duration, even a few hours sufficed to change the wind, and then the *Signoria* wrote to Hawkwood, (May 5), to do nothing fresh, nor to take the field, but limit himself to resisting if Filibach attacked him; finally they adopted a middle course, (May 8), and gave him faculty to make an attack, informing him of the enemy's numbers.

Amidst these uncertainties, an event happened which carried the war elsewhere. Louis due d'Anjou, a formidable rival to Carlo Durazzo, came down into Italy, with doubtful claims but strong forces, to wrest from him the crown of Naples. Hence all the troops which were warring in Tuscany for Durazzo, were recalled to the defence of the Kingdom of Naples—the Tuscan cities could breathe again, and Hawkwood might sheath his sword.

But new openings for war were offered to the *condottiere*, this time by the Pope, who, as High Sovereign, had espoused the cause of Durazzo regarding the crown of Naples.

The Florentines were informed that Urban VI intended to ask for their captain and his soldiers, and they had some trouble in deciding whether to let him go: they were so well satisfied with Hawkwood that they had accorded him the benefit of "ten dead lances," *dieci lance morte* (*i.e.* pay in the same proportion as though they were effective lances), for as long as the price of the house which he desired, and which had been promised him in Florence, remained unpaid; but on the other hand they did not want to offend the Duke of Anjou; they would, if possible, only have given leave to Hawkwood when the Duke had passed Romagna on his march towards the Kingdom of Naples, and then on condition of his promising to return in case of need.

Meanwhile they consulted on the eternal dispute with Manfredi, endeavouring to make an end of it once for all, and to induce Hawkwood to purchase a certain bastion which was the cause of the litigation (probably that Sezada which he had kept back in the cession to the d' Estes). They even offered him 4000 florins if he would leave it to Astorre, who would in return guarantee to furnish the Commune with 1000 *moggia* of corn.

The uncertainty lasted till the middle of August. In the Councils they wanted first to know whether the Pope were in Rome, and if the Romans would give a good reception to Hawkwood. There were some who maintained that to dismiss him would prove *the destruction of Florence*: in any case such a grave affair as this ought not to be discussed except in a full Council, at which all the Consuls of the Arts and many citizens and artisans would intervene, forming almost an universal suffrage. (August 13 and 14.)

At length the ambassadors arrived from Rome, (August 20), bringing the following brief from Pope Urban VI, (July 31):

For a long time, we have desired that our beloved son the noble John Hawkwood knight should with six hundred lances militate in the service of ourselves and of the Roman Church. And inasmuch as it conduces no less to our benefit, honour, state and well-being than to that of your city, whether the said knight fights in your service or in ours, we pray most urgently, that as soon as the time shall come to prove the sincerity of your devotion and to display it in your deeds, you will efficaciously and without delay arrange that he shall enter our service, and everything which you shall pay as stipend to him shall be deducted from the debt which you owe to us and the Church.

The war of the "Eight Saints" being ended, the Pope had remained creditor of the Florentines for an indemnity, and thus suggested to them the mode of paying the debt, for which they were still under an interdict.

There were great discussions in the Councils, (August 22 and 23), and seeing there was not money enough to pay the Pope, the general opinion was that his request should be granted.

There were besides a great many merchants decidedly partial to entering into a league with King Carlo Durazzo, but they wished to do so in a manner not to compromise themselves with the Duke of Anjou.

The following wary subtilty was suggested by Simone Peruzzi—that they should give the Pope's envoys a written reply, refusing the dismissal of Hawkwood requested of them, but if Hawkwood himself should demand it, in another written document, alleging the contracts of the *condotta* (which in fact did not exist), the resignation should be accepted. When once Hawkwood was placed in a condition to act as he chose, and to go where he pleased, who could blame the Florentines if he passed into the service of the Pope?

It was so decided, and Bernabo Visconti, as soon as he heard a rumour of the affair, wrote protesting against the *condottiere* hired by the Florentines, passing into the service of an enemy to himself—their ally; they answered him immediately that on their own account they had repeatedly refused Hawkwood to the Pope and the King of Naples, (August 30), but that according to the contract he had a right to go. And when Bernabo again attempted to raise the same objection, he received the same answer. (February 13, 1383),

The affair being arranged, Urban VI authorised Cosimo Gentili, clerk of the chambers, to give the Florentines a receipt for the sum

(September 6, 1382), which they would in succession pay to Hawkwood, up to the amount of the 40,000 florins, they owed.

But before leaving for the camp Hawkwood wished to arrange his affairs in Florence, (October 2), and settle his wife there.

Such was the devotion of himself and Donnina his consort to the Commune, that they intended to reside in the city and its neighbourhood, and to possess property there, which they could leave to their heirs, demanding as foreigners the necessary privileges, and subjecting themselves to the taxes on the contract they were about to make.

The Englishman Richard Romsey (hired together with Tyliman and 333 lances) made the same petition, alleging that he had contracted marriage in Florence, although with an Englishwoman, and that he wished to collocate there the greater part of his property.

The general Council of the Captain and People consented with 211 affirmative notes against a minority of only 12. Hawkwood requested a loan of money on interest, (October 3), from the Commune, but it was not granted, nevertheless it is probable that the purchase of the houses outside Port' al Prato may be dated at this time.

Everything being in order, he took the road to Rome, (October 22), with 2200 horsemen, stopping a moment at the Abbey of Isola to demand from the Sienese 14,000 florins, of which he declared himself their creditor from the preceding year, when in league with the Ban of Hungary. The Sienese complained to Florence, but they ought to have applied to the Pope by whom he was now engaged.

Chapter 26

Deeds and Affairs of Hawkwood in the Kingdom of Naples

With a rapid march Hawkwood, accompanied by Carluccio Brancaccio and Andrea Carafa, arrived at Naples, (October 1382), bringing a brief from Urban VI to the archbishops of Naples and Capua which presented *dilectum filium nobilem virum Joanni Agut militem Anglicanum,* (our beloved son John Agut a soldier of England), as *condottiere* in the pay of the Church.

★★★★★★

In fact the Florentine chronicler Marchionne Stefani says that Hawkwood stayed in Rome some days, that the Pope gave signs of going to the crusade of Naples with him, or of returning to Corneto, for greater security from the Duke of Anjou: that then the Roman populace went to the house of "Mesaer Giovanni Acuto" and because he was taking away the Pope, they threatened him that if he did not go away at once, they would do him some injury. So, on the 6th of November Sir John Hawkwood left Rome and went to Naples.

But the authority of the chronicler loses much of its value by treating of things which happened so far from his own sight, and it would seem wiser to believe rather the Neapolitan Diarist, the Duke of Monteleone, who determines the date and the company of Hawkwood on his arrival at Naples. This would exclude the possibility of his stay in Rome, and the hostility of the people there, which Stefani was willing to believe, as he was of the opposite opinion when the Council discussed the question of favouring the Pope and King Carlo, by giving the leave to Hawkwood.

★★★★★★

His intervention in the war seemed of such serious injury to the French Anjou party, that the Duke of Anjou, without much heeding the subtle distinctions of Simone Peruzzi, wrote orders to France that reprisals should be made on the goods and persons of the numerous rich Florentine merchants in that kingdom.

With his concourse the army of King Carlo reached the number of 14,000 horse. The Duke of Anjou only had 7000, concentrated at Maddaloni, whence the superiority of the enemy, together with cold and hunger, compelled him to move into Apulia, losing on the road a good half of his forces.

It is to be supposed that in this retreat Hawkwood followed obstinately at the heels of the Anjou Army, and made not a few prisoners of rank, for he afterwards (December), boasted of being the creditor of Iacopo di Capri, Ugo di Sanseverino, and Antonio Carracciolo, for 1000 florins each; of two others for 500; seven more for 400 each; of twenty-one for 300; and finally four more for 200 florins each. The greater number of the debtors bore the most distinguished names of the Anjou faction, and were qualified as *militi* (knights). These circumstances, together with the round numbers attributed to each debtor, and the gradation of the sums in proportion to the importance of each, whether military, political, or economical, leave no doubt that taxes under the form of ransoms are treated of.

Hawkwood had granted liberty to the prisoners on receipt of promissory notes. When these fell due there was a deficiency of an aggregate sum of 10,900 florins; and he appealed to the king against his thirty-seven debtors, and in fact obtained from King Carlo, (December 24), a mandate to Donato d'Arezzo, judge of the Supreme Court, that the debtors should be constrained to pay.

Here then we see our *condottiere* involved in the difficulties of the forum, and in the tedious delays of a lawsuit. But for him Themis and Astraea showed themselves resolute and solicitous, thanks to the personal intervention of the sovereign. The jurisdiction of the civil causes did not pertain to the judge of the *Magna Curia* (Supreme Court), but the king's mandate gave Donato d'Arezzo the necessary competence and special jurisdiction. It was necessary to cite the debtors, but it was not possible to administer the summonses to all of them. The Neapolitan ushers could not reach Ugo Sanseverino who was out of the kingdom, nor Iacopo da Capri, who was imprisoned at Nocera, nor Aserello da Capri among the rebels at Ischia, nor Andrea da Messina in the army of Louis of Anjou. Hawkwood again appealed to the king, who commanded the judges to cite them by public edict. (January 14, 1383.)

Hawkwood succeeded in getting a great part of the 10,900 florins if not all, for the same year he sent his savings to Tuscany where he invested them in landed property, buying from Raimondo Tolomei of Siena a possession, composed of house, tower, and a palace, with several *poderi* (farms) in a place called la Rocchetta in the parish of Santa Maddalena, in the Commune of Poggibonsi near the River Elsa.

Although it is said "*out of sight out of mind*," Florence showed the same regard to him as if he had been near; it was discussed whether he should be called on to pay the property tax, and by common consent it was decided that if he were not a citizen he was exempt by right, but if they considered him a citizen (on account of his purchases), they should exempt him by favour. (January 7.)

★★★★★★

Like the captain, the other Englishmen were always the mercenaries preferred by the Florentines. We find that on February 12 1383 they engaged the constables John Berwick with 30 lances; John Beltoft with 65 lances, 3 fifers and a trumpeter; and Johnny (Gianichino) Swin, Johnny Boutillier (Butler), and Ozochino (Hoskyn or Hodgekin?) Norton with 37 lances. On October 3rd 1384 John Gulion. John Cokum, Thomas Ball, and Richard Sticklet were engaged as constables with 100 lances and 4 trumpeters. Robin Corbeck, and Johnny Barry with 50 lances, John Liverpool with 10; and on the 6th of October, John

Trickell with 100 lances, and 2 trumpeters.

★★★★★★

The winter being over, the king wished to advance to meet the enemy, and left Naples (April 4), with all the troops now increased to 16,000 horse and a great number of foot. After the Count Alberico of Barbiano, the commander in chief, the chroniclers give the first place amongst the foreign captains to Hawkwood who had the official title of captain general of the Church; but none of them had to fight in earnest.

The king having arrived at Barletta (April 12), sent the gauntlet of battle to the Duke of Anjou, who accepted the challenge; the two armies were displayed in battle array, but by the advice of Otho of Brunswick the king let prudence prevail, and it all ended in an insignificant skirmish of a few cavaliers.

There was a battle at Pietracatella instead, but it is not stated whether Hawkwood took part in it.

Moreover, while in these troubled waters the Duke of Anjou was taken away by a natural death; and King Carlo, who had garrisoned Apulia, returned towards the capital. He employed his men-at-arms (October 4), to keep his ally Pope Urban VI almost as a prisoner at Aversa, for five days, while he imposed his will on that Pontiff, who had thus unluckily arrived on the scene of action; he then re-entered Naples, (November 10), and Hawkwood seeing that there was nothing conclusive to be done down there, again drew near to the beloved and fruitful Tuscany, accepting in his company two first-rate soldiers, the Italian Giovanni Azzo degli Ubaldini, and the Englishman Richard Romsey.

His first menaces were for the Sienese, who sent three ambassadors to him (December 7), hoping to escape for 3000 or 5000 or at most 8000 florins, but they had besides to resign themselves to giving him a year's pay, (December 12), at the rate of 100 florins a month, and thank him into the bargain for his services. The Florentines had paid him on account of the Pope, first 12,000 florins, then 8000, but the captain asked for another ten thousand.

At first they wished to refuse, but afterwards they thought better of it, and while they maintained that he could not demand any of the King's money, they judged it wise to pay him, still on the Pope's account, provided that he should obtain absolution from the interdict which the Pontiff still kept suspended over the Florentines since the war of the "Eight Saints," and that he should ensure Florence from injury by his company.

✶✶✶✶✶✶

What this King's money was is explained by Marchionne Stefani. It was a sum of 38,000 florins deposited with the Commune at Florence, by the Duchess of Durazzo, when she found herself in the enemy's power, with orders not to dispose of it in favour of any person, as long as she were not free and in safety, or dead. And therefore, although King Carlo's ambassadors alleged new and different orders from the duchess, the Commune would not infringe the primitive conditions of the deposit.

✶✶✶✶✶✶

From all this it results that Hawkwood, serving King Carlo directly, and the Pope indirectly, (January 5, 1384), was not content with holding out his right hand for the pay of the Church, but he extended also the left for the pay of the kingdom.

King Carlo had ordered the immediate exaction of the new tax (January 28), called the *tari* (*turi* or *tarena*, small Siellaian coin worth about 4p), in the Principato Citeriore and in Basilicata (2 Neapolitan provinces), declaring it to be necessary for the pay of John Hawkwood's company.

We must suppose that as Hawkwood tried to make the Florentines pay him with the King's money, the *tari* of those two provinces was insufficient, and in making up the accounts he remained creditor, so much so that in exchange for his credit the feudal village of Carinaro in Aversa and other properties in Capua and Naples were conceded to him.

In leaving the kingdom, he left the administration of these rural lordships to his procurator the Sienese Recupido Lazzari; *Recupido!*— an ill-omened name for an agent! Nevertheless, Lazzari showed himself zealous. Rumours having been circulated that Hawkwood had been murdered in Florence, these feudal estates were without delay assigned to three of the great functionaries of the kingdom, *viz*: the *Almirante* (admiral) Giovanni Stendardo, and Giacomo Gaetano. The new lords soon hastened to disturb Lazzaro in possession, and he appealed to the Queen Margherita di Durazzo (King Carlo being deceased, his widow became regent for her son King Ladislao a minor), showing that his master was alive, and declaring him to be always ready for loyal service. The queen accepted the petition, and ordered that Lazzari should be kept in possession. (January 4, 1385.)

CHAPTER 27

The Catastrophe of Bernabo Visconti

The inquietude of the Perugians, on the reappearance of Hawkwood in central Italy, was very great; they invoked the good offices of Florence, (May 18, 1384), and got the *Signoria* to deliberate on recommending them to his mercy by letter, or, if necessary, by means of an embassy. Nor was the intervention in vain. The Florentines had reason to send (June 1st), and thank him for *his doings towards the Perugians and to Assisi.* In growing older Hawkwood became somewhat more humane and tractable, as about the same time the Florentines dared to excuse themselves for being unable to disburse money, and to neglect to give an answer about some certain places which he had taken, and which he probably offered for sale.

It is nearly certain that this referred to the castle of Montecchio, the fortresses of Migliari in the valley of the Ambra, and of the abbey at Pino, which we shall see later were possessed and sold by Hawkwood, though there is no documentary evidence of the epoch, or probable occasion of the acquisition.

But if he were tractable towards Florence where he now considered himself almost as a citizen, he was not equally so with others. This time the blows fell on Siena, which refused to pay new extortions, and wanted to hinder him from spoiling the land; Hawkwood reinforced by the Prefetto of Viterbo, and a new band formed by his colleague Giovanni Ubaldini, routed and completely defeated the Sienese troops, (June 12), taking prisoner the captain, Niccolo dl Messer Galeotto (Malatesta?) whom, to the astonishment of everyone, he released a few days afterwards.

On their side the Florentines deliberated to continue the promised payments to Hawkwood, and also to interpose between Sir John, who declared himself creditor, and the Bolognese, who denied the debt, so that they should not come to a rupture.

He having arrived at Florence, (July 9), and being well received by the *Signoria*, they again took up the discussion on the still smouldering question with Astorre Manfredi, procuring a truce for two years, (July 29), and arranging things in his favour, also replying graciously to Bernabo Visconti, who protected Manfredi with the ardour of a father-in-law at discord with his son-in-law.

These councils kept him some time in Florence, whence being pacified towards the Sienese, he wrote (September 3), to recommend to them Pietro Boncompagni, doctor of laws and his *protégé*, as candidate for the office of Syndic.

Then he joined the camp above Cortona, forming there together with Richard Romsey, and Giovanni Ubaldini, the Company of the Rose with the money drawn from Siena, (September 23.)

★★★★★★

This title of "the Rose" appears several times in the mercenary companies: there was one in Provence in 1357; another of 300 lances, lasted from 1398 to 1410, it extorted money from Siena in 1404, and is cited as the last company which had a name of its own, not taken from its captain.

★★★★★★

With this then he must have gone into Romagna, where, as some historians say, he united with Lucius Landau, (October), and was able to take Ravenna and put it to the sack, selling it afterwards to the Malatesta.

But the Florentines did not lose sight of him; indeed they thought of hiring him together with Romsey, and before negotiating with others, they wanted his advice, and asked him to give information about the men-at-arms, trusting entirely in his judgment; they acquiesced in his counsels, and begged him to come soon. Moreover they dreamed of stipulating a league between Hawkwood, Florence and Perugia, thus considering him almost as a potentate. (A note from the *Signoria* to Donate Acciaioli, Bartolommeo Ridolfi, and Jacopo de' Medici, ambassadors, perhaps refers to this.)

Meanwhile a very serious event took place in Tuscany; the Sire de Coucy, that French adventurer and great baron whom we have already seen fighting with Hawkwood for the Church, had returned to Italy for the Anjouvine wars, and had taken Arezzo. (The castle of Coucy, in 1880, still exists in French Flanders, near St. Gobain, and among the noble armorial ensigns, similar to that noted in Rohan, is recorded *Roi ne suis, Prince ni comte aussi Je suis le Sire de Coucy.*)

It was a case for action on the part of Florence: a number of men-at-arms were immediately engaged, (September 28), as and Hawkwood, though still receiving his pay, being employed beyond the Apennines, Giovanni degli Obizi was taken as captain of war. But as Coucy let himself be persuaded to sell Arezzo to the Florentines for "ready money," the worst was over;—all that remained was to assure their possession of the new territories, to wrest from the Signori Tarlati the places they held on the confines between Arezzo and Florence, for which slight duty (between January and May 1385), it did not seem necessary to take a captain of such valour and expense as Hawkwood.

The Florentines contented themselves with his counsels, and confided the execution thereof to Giovanni degli Obizi and Vanni di Michele di Vanni.

On the other hand, the fall of Arezzo left Hawkwood undisputed Lord of Montecchio and other towns recently occupied by him in the Aretian territory, of which the Florentines did not even dream of contesting his possession. He had a little leisure to see to his own affairs, to liquidate his debts and credits and he was reposing in the bosom of his family, in Florence, when (May 9), there reached him the most astounding news, which was of the greatest importance to him, his family and also to Florence.

This was, that Gian Galeazzo Visconti, the Conte di Virtù, nephew of Bernabo, had disloyally overcome his uncle and ruling lord, and shut him up in the castle of Trezzo, and was now over-running Milan on his own account, usurping the lordship without opposition, and that one of Bernabo's sons, the young Carlo Visconti, had fled to Crema and thence to Cremona. (The official announcement of this dynastic *coup d'état* was received by the *Signoria* in a letter from Gian Galeazzo on May 13.) The other young men and Donnina Porro (just now married or about to be married to Bernabo, whose wife Regina Scaliger had died a year before) shared the prison with their father and consort.

Together with this serious intelligence Hawkwood received entreaties to assist his father, mother, and brothers-in-law in this catastrophe. Among the brothers-in-law, Carlo especially wrote that he held the citadel of Crema in his own hands, as well as the fortress of Porta Romana at Milan, and was ready to pay him well, beseeching him to come in person as soon as possible, with as many men-at-arms as he could collect.

In this urgent case it is easy to conceive that Hawkwood's wife Donnina exerted herself warmly to send her husband to the succour of her relatives, but nothing prevailed, and Bernabo very soon died at Trezzo of rage or poison, while no one dared move a finger to help him.

In the first place Hawkwood, as we know, was in absolute discord with his father-in-law; next, although a brave soldier and a famous *condottiere*, he never could have held his own against the new Lord of Milan; and finally, we must allow, that besides resentment and caution, the very vulgar reasons of self-interest appeared to rule his mind.

Papers will speak! from the contracts stipulated (July 1st), at Villa di Cavazzo near Modena, in the house where Hawkwood was then residing, we find that he had before that time promised and sworn fidelity and homage to Gian Galeazzo for 1000 florins!

Now that shameful contract was to be improved upon, and Hawkwood *recognising his oath already sworn* and qualifying himself *as the most beloved kinsman of the illustrious lord Signor Galeazzo Visconti, with solemn oath on the holy Gospels, corporeally touching the holy scriptures with his hand* promised and agreed:

That if the count should request his personal service, he would hold himself obliged to go to him, excepting that he should be in the pay of any other Commune, lord or prince, to whom he were so bound that he could not with honour leave his service; but as soon as the time for this contract should be completed, he would feel himself bound to personally serve the count whensoever he pleased.

The count on his side should give him a salary of 300 florins a month, and the faculty of leading 30 lances, to which the count should give the same stipend as his other lances.

By order of the count, Hawkwood might also conduct a greater number of lances, who in that case would be paid, and bound like the others who were in the count's pay.

If Hawkwood—his service being required and he being free of other engagements—should not present himself for the count's active service within four months, the count shall not be obliged to pay the 1000 florins offered by his procurator in the preceding act of fidelity . . . .

The accessories in this contract are very interesting: for example, among the usual concluding formulae, the following is noteworthy: "the tenor of the clauses written herein has been read and vulgarised in the common tongue, to the full understanding of Sir John." He therefore knew no Latin, but could speak Italian perfectly. Besides this the act was not only written by Martino, *quondam* Giacomo de Robbis di Città di Castello, Hawkwood's notary and secretary, but also signed by the same notary at the request and order of Hawkwood, whose usual seal was appended to the deed a sign that Sir John Hawkwood did not know how to write.

But it is the subject of such a stipulation that most astonishes us. It seems impossible that Hawkwood, who was accustomed to put quite a different price on his sword, should needlessly and for mediocre gain sell himself to one who so seriously compromised his own interests, and even his family peace, since Gian Galeazzo, to justify his usurpation, made a kind of legal process *de vita et moribus*, (about life and morals), and sent out into the world a formal act of accusation. against Bernabo, alleging in it a curious species of *incesto concubinario*, pretending that the marriage of Bernabo and Donnina de' Porri was null and void:

Thus, the legitimacy of Hawkwood's wife, ensured by subsequent marriage, became impugned. It might be that Hawkwood, being a most astute man, wished in this surrender to lull the natural suspicions of Gian Galeazzo, reserving to himself to act as an enemy against him on a better occasion; and the fact remains that he never was in the effective service of Gian Galeazzo, and it was against him that he schemed so long and, as we shall see, conducted the last and most brilliant of all his campaigns.

CHAPTER 28

War Between the Carraras of Padua and the Scaligers of Verona

In the spring the Florentines, having ensured the acquisition of Arezzo, were undecided whether or not, to hire their favourite captain (so that in the summer he began negotiations with Siena); but in the autumn they adopted the more economical course of satisfying him with words and with some favours.

We know that he was exempted from the *estimo* (property tax) which was an ordinary tax, but he was not so from the extraordinary rates, and it is not to be wondered at, that he belonged to the category of backward payers, so that fines and penalties would have fallen to his share, had not the government exempted him from its usual rigorous rules, thus tempering it's fiscal refinement:

> Considering that Sir John Hawkwood is registered in the *prestanze* and *prestanzoni* (forced loans) of the city in the gonfalon of the Golden Lion (quarter of San Giovanni) and that, whatsoever the cause, he has not paid up to this date, but declares himself ready to pay, if the penalty shall be condoned; we hereby concede this, on condition that he pay within 15 days. (October 27.)

Following this, in Hawkwood's absence, (April 26, 1386), Donnina explained to the *Signoria* that her husband had made two loans, lending 400 florins to the Englishman William Boson, and 1000 to Wilhelm of Corbrich, and that now his property was charged with the payment of the duty relative to the said contracts and that he as a foreigner had nothing to do with such a tax, that neither to him, nor to others for him, was any notification given until the last few days; she supplicated therefore that without being required to prove her statement, it may be conceded to her to effect the payment within 15 days without the aggravation of a penalty. And this was graciously granted.

Whether Hawkwood were fighting, or where he stayed during the early months of 1386, is not clearly shown. According to Bonincontri (whom we have seen however that we cannot trust at all), he went as far as Hungary; according to the Paduan chroniclers he was in the service of the Pope.

We must look for him where there was fighting, and precisely at that time war broke out between the Carraras of Padua and the Scaligers of Verona, and numerous *condottieri* took part in it, on one side or the other, amongst whom there was in the Veronese camp a half-brother of the Black Prince, exiled from England for assassination.

★★★★★★

English adventurers continued to pass one by one into Italy, for many years after the first comers, up to the 15th century, but we need not believe that all those styled *Anglici* in documents of the time were really of English birth. The phrase means, merely, that they were in the rank of lances *all' Inglese* or organised on the English system. In fact, in 1397 Bologna had in her pay about 1100 men qualified as English, and yet not an English name is to be found amongst the constables and *caporali* of these troops at the general review held at Mantua.

★★★★★★

In fact, the anonymous and diligent Florentine diarist registers that Antonio Scaliger was defeated by the Carraras who had also Hawkwood in their camp. (May 11.) The latter could not have taken an important part in that campaign which was commanded for the Carraras by Giovanni degli Ubaldini, and decided by the Battle of Brentelle, (June 25), since at that time (May 28), the Commune of Florence was endeavouring as usual to conclude a general league—and equally as usual concluding nothing—against the mercenary companies; and hired Hawkwood as chief constable of eighty-two lances, who were paid at the rate of 18 florins each a month, with ten days *benvenuta* (meaning 'welcome' it was a kind of bounty money) on entering the service.

★★★★★★

To speak correctly, Galeazzo Gataro in his Paduan chronicles makes Hawkwood take part also in the Battle of Brentelle, but we must note that this chronicle, which is in Muratori, presents a great confusion of dates and of places, and an evidently erroneous repetition of facts. On the other hand, the chronicle of Andrea Gataro, who completed and rectified his father's work, does not mention Hawkwood in the campaign of 1386.

★★★★★★

Florence negotiated the league foreseeing that the war in Upper Italy would not last long, and that then the three thousand or more lances engaged in it would soon return to their usual brigandish proceedings. In fact, Hawkwood, leaving the honest Florentine pay, had again (September), moved to menace the Sienese, as before making the noble Antonio di Porcaria the bearer of his intentions. They first sent a certain Monaldi with soothing words, then a man named Coltini to see if Sir John would be content with 500 florins and the liquidation of his credit with Niccolo Piccolomini.

At the same time they hastily recalled an embassy from Cortona, perhaps fearing it might be taken in hostage, and demanded succours of troops from Florence, from Perugia, Pisa, and Lucca; but foreseeing too well the replies they were likely to get, they accorded at once 800 out of the 1000 florins demanded by the captain. Things being thus arranged, Hawkwood paid an amicable visit to Siena with an escort of 40 or 50 horsemen, thence he passed into Romagna, (December), but some of his men still remained to molest the Val d'Ambra, obliging the Sienese to apply for Florentine intervention.

However, before the year was over, the Lord of Verona engaged Lucius Landau; and the Lord of Padua on his side hastened to hire Hawkwood, with five hundred lances, and six hundred archers. We are inclined to believe that he had provided himself with this considerable brigade in the service of Queen Margherita of Naples, as we find that the *Signoria* had refused a loan of 4000 florins asked by the queen for Hawkwood. (July 16).

Carrara first wrote, and then sent Giovanni Ubaldini his captain-general in person, to stipulate the contract with Hawkwood, who was then in Faenza. The best relations existed between these two leaders: they had together beaten the Sienese, and Hawkwood looked on Ubaldini as the most experienced captain of the times; but yet he, who without doubt ranked first among the *condottieri* in Italy, would not easily have consented to serve under the orders of another; on the other hand he could not expect that after the recent brilliant victory of Brentelle, Ubaldini should cede him the command. We believe it was to regulate these difficulties that Ubaldini undertook the journey, and that he found a way to arrange it by attributing the honour of supreme command to the prince, *i.e.* Francesco Novello, the brave and youthful son of the Lord of Padua; and in reality reserving the effective direction of operations to Hawkwood and himself, he nominally holding the *bâton* as captain-general;—in fact they understood each other. Besides Hawkwood, Ubaldini hired in Romagna Giovanni di Pietramala with 1000 horse, hastening his march, because they wished to follow up the campaign vigorously during the winter.

Beginning of January, 1387, the body of the Paduan Army had already crossed the Adige, and taken up its position at Cerea; soon after, Pietramala and Hawkwood arrived, and posted their men at Montagnana; they, with the principal persons of the band, stayed at Padua, where they were honourably received, loaded with gifts, and lodged by the lord, Francesco the elder; between whom and Hawkwood many colloquies took place to concert the plan of the campaign.

All being arranged, Hawkwood and Pietramala returned to the camp, escorted by Messer Rigo Galletto; between Este and Monselice, Francesco Novello came to meet them, and taking up the troops at Montagnana, they all together directed their steps to Castelbaldo, where a chain bridge spanned the Adige. Finding the bridge broken, they crossed the river at another place, and concentrated themselves at the camp of Cerea.

A council of war was held immediately, in which Ubaldini (perhaps it had been already concerted) spontaneously ceded the *bâton* as captain to Hawkwood. The army was of a strength of 7500 horse, besides 1000 foot; they then resolved to march boldly into the Veronese territory and in fact pressed on to close under the city, spoiling everything without hindrance.

Antonio della Scala on his side, although he had lost Lucius Landau, who had been corrupted by the Carraras, had put together 9000 horse, 1000 foot, and 1600 between archers and crossbowmen, without counting a great mass of peasants—who in reality counted for nothing. He had also some artillery, that is to say, three machines which we might call *mitrailleuses*, composed of 402 *bombarde* (small mortars) disposed at different levels on each car, and which threw "great stones as large as hen's eggs." The Scaligers' captain-general was Giovanni degli Ordelaffi, but the effective *condottieri* were Ugolino and Taddeo dal Verme.

While the Carrarese Army rashly pressed forwards, that of the Scaligers took a long round, and descending along the right bank of the Adige, ended by finding itself on the enemy's line of communication, thus threatening to cut them out, and without delay cutting off their means of provisioning.

Very soon the Carraras found themselves unprovided with bread and wine, and reduced to meat and turnips; finally, they had to eat their horses. This lasted some days, and then they retreated in good order of battle, towards the Adige, where they would have found abundance.

The situation was critical. Hawkwood however was expert enough to evade a disaster.

Antonio della Scala sent to him and Ubaldini a certain man named Pulliano, with the apparent office of inducing them to persuade Francesco Novello to propose that his father should make negotiations of peace. Hawkwood discovered the spy under the disguise of envoy, and therefore kept him closely shut up in his tent the whole day, not allowing him to speak with anyone, and when night came, he dismissed him with his answer, and sent him away.

Indeed, if we may believe the Paduan chroniclers, Hawkwood must literally have worked miracles in that retreat. Galeazzo Gataro says that when at length the army again reached Cerea, they found that all the wine had been poisoned, but Sir John Hawkwood *"with his ring* put it right again."Andrea Gataro even embellishes the fable recounting that the water of the wells was poisoned and many died of it.

> Hearing this, Hawkwood who had with him an *unicorn five feet long, which I saw and touched with my own hands*, had it let down into the wells, and cutting it in many portions, he gave it as a drink to those injured, and thus remedied the cursed scheme of the enemy.

★★★★★★

Note:—It is not to be wondered at that people in those days believed in the marvellous virtue of the unicorn, as a test and antidote for any kind of poison. Another *condottiere* less antique than Hawkwood, *i.e.* Bartolommeo Alviano, took as his device an unicorn in the act of bending his head and putting the horn in the water with the motto *Venena pello*. Two centuries after

Hawkwood's time, the unicorn still enjoyed the greatest credit; princes disputed for the rare specimens of it at their weight in gold. Pope Julius III paid 12,000 *scudi* for the headless body of one, hence it is credible that the unicorn used by Hawkwood belonged to the treasure of the Carraresi, and that Francesco Novello had carried it to the camp, for amongst its other virtues is attributed that of preserving its possessor, from mortal wounds.

(From *L'Alicorno*, a discourse by the excellent doctor and philosopher M. Andrea Bacci, in which he treats of the nature of the unicorn and of its most excellent virtues to the most serene Don Francesco de' Medici, grand-prince of Tuscany. Florence, 1573 and 1582.)

★★★★★★

Continuing to retreat, the Carraras found themselves, (March 11), at the longed-for banks of the Adige, before Castelbaldo, where by the care of the Lord of Padua a great quantity of provisions were amassed, and the bridge rebuilt.

But the Veronese Army also arrived still intact, and we may believe the chroniclers when they tell us, the force was four times that of the Paduans, if we choose to reckon as combatants the 16,000 peasants who formed a rear-guard of plunderers to the real army. They certainly had the advantage of arriving fresh to the attack of an enemy who were in the last straits after a long and difficult retreat, and they were moreover strongly entrenched in a good position.

To cross the Adige under such circumstances was a serious risk for the army of Carrara. Hawkwood perceived immediately that it would result in a disaster; it would be better to fight, but on the other hand, to attack the enemy within its strong entrenchments seemed a desperate measure.

However, it was necessary to decide; several brigades, having arrived in sight of the river and bridge, deserted their standards to hasten to the provisions prepared at Castelbaldo. Novello, not having succeeded in retaining them, crossed the river himself to try and get them to return to their posts, and to bring provisions back to the camp. Meanwhile Hawkwood and Ubaldini, badly seconded, remained steady round the standards, discussing with the other captains the best mode of acting.

Novello having returned, he found that the council of war had decided to come to an engagement, and in this he honourably wished to take part himself, although Hawkwood exhorted him to retire to a distance and not in his own person to risk the state.

CHAPTER 29

The Battle of Castagnaro

Having assumed the responsibility of giving the orders of combat, Hawkwood commanded that every man should first eat and drink; and then armed at all points, should go each to his respective standard. Then he arranged the men-at-arms in eight battalions, of different strength according to the number of the contingent which each *condottiere* had at his command. Some numbered as many as 1500 horse, some did not exceed 500. Hawkwood kept in the front lines with his 500 lances and 600 archers; then followed in succession: Ubaldini, Pietramala, Ugolotto Biancardo, Francesco Novello, Broglia and Brandolino, Biordo and Balestrazzo, and Filippo da Pisa.

The two last battalions remained mounted, forming a reserve of 1600 horse, placed at a distance and commanded to guard the *carroccio*, (species of war chariot with the bell on it), the Carrarese ensign of the *Car*, the other standards, and the council of the camp. The other six dismounted, forming two lines of about 3000 men each, distant about two arrows' flight the one from the other; the pages were sent under cover with the horses, at a considerable distance.

Hawkwood also placed in reserve the thousand native foot soldiers (*provvisionati*) commanded by Cermisone of Parma, extending them in two long squadrons along a bank from which a moat was dug out, and over the bank he had improvised a *pavesata* which could oppose a solid resistance, and was garrisoned by 600 cross-bowmen.

★★★★★★

Pavesata, a temporary palisade formed of the large shields or *pavese* used by foot soldiers in the 14th century. They were of a square form with the upper corners cut off and so high as to almost entirely cover the soldiers who used them.

★★★★★★

Mounting a Thessalian charger (*destriero tessalico*) he did not fail to invoke St. Prosdocimus, St. Anthony, St. Justina, and St. Daniel, the protectors of Padua; and to incite every man to his duty, he gave the golden spurs to five Paduans whom Francesco Novello then created cavaliers, and on his own side he knighted some Englishmen.

All this was quite easy; the difficulty lay in making the Veronese Army abandon its excellent position, and in this he succeeded by sending to the attack the *saccomanni* and other light militia, mounted on horseback for the occasion: those, allowing themselves to be overcome and yielding their ground, drew the Veronese first outside, and then far away from the entrenchments, so that little by little their flank was exposed to the Carraras.

The manoeuvres commenced, Hawkwood with Ubaldini and Ugolotto Biancardo proceeded to survey the ground towards the enemy, and perceiving that this lent itself very well to the plan, with a rapid march moved the camp beyond the canal of Castagnaro, which is derived from the Adige, supporting his troops with its banks. He thus inverted the position, and the Carraras gained the advantage so lightly lost by the Scaligers. He had calculated so well, that the new position was scarcely taken when the Scaligers attacked them with the cry of *Scala! Scala!*

The enemy was already fatigued and disordered by chasing the *saccomanni*. It was still much superior in force, amounting in fact to twelve battalions of cavalry, besides a superiority of number, in archers and crossbowmen. The *mêlée* having begun, Hawkwood confided the lieutenancy of his own battalion to Pietramala, and followed by his page rode rapidly round the field to give another general glance and see how the affair was going.

The moment had come "to close the pincers:" he caused the band of Francesco Novello to change its position, for as this prince persisted in fighting, Hawkwood did not wish him to be too much exposed, he would at least leave a way of escape open to him. Then throwing his baton amongst the enemy, drawing his sword and crying to his men not the usual *Carro! Carro!* (Car), but the ferocious *Carne! Carne!* (Flesh), fell with his men-at-arms and infantry on the flank of the Scaligers, already engaged too far forward, whilst his clever archers showered their arrows from the bank, till it seemed to be raining. Ordelaffi and Ostasio da Polenta, who with 2500 horse constituted the reserve of the Veronese, made an effort to come to the rescue, but found the road already closed by Hawkwood's interposition.

The action was rapid in the extreme and the effect instantaneous; the enemy was driven back upon its standards which were thrown to the ground. Francesco Visconti, who guarded them, lost his own flag and was unhorsed. Ordelaffi captain-general, Ostasio da Polenta, the two Dal Verme, Facino Cane, many other captains, and about eighty cavaliers of rank, were nearly all taken prisoners. A thousand nine hundred of the cavalry took to flight, but being energetically followed up they were nearly all taken.

A corps of infantry and Veronese peasants commanded by Giovanni da Isola remained intact on the field. Hawkwood ordered them to yield, but they answered that they would, resist, and so they were cut to pieces.

Relatively to the success there was but little bloodshed in that battle (716 dead and 846 wounded), but the number of prisoners was extraordinary: in all there were 4620, of whom 2620 were soldiers forming part of mercenary companies, and 284 men-at-arms; besides the three famous *mitrailleuses* cars with their respective *bombarde* which had not had occasion to throw their *hen's eggs*.

We have a proof that the conflict was as short as it was decisive: in the dispatch sent to Treviso by Francesco Novello, and dated "from Castagnaro, in my fortunate army on March 11; an hour after sunset" (*a un' ora di notte*), which says that "the fight began an hour before sunset" (*alle ore 23*).

The Paduan chronicler says:

> Thus, by the skill of the knight Sir John Hawkwood was Messer Francesco da Carrara victorious over 14,000 men, horse and foot.

The victorious army returned triumphantly to Padua, (March 13); the old Lord Francesco da Carrara went to the gate of the city to embrace the captains, and re-entered with Hawkwood on one side, and Ubaldini on the other, their ensigns being very much applauded.

******

> The chronicler describes them in this manner: "a white and blue striped standard, in which is the device of cockle-shells (which pilgrims wear round their hats) and a blue flag with two white deer's horns with a golden star in the centre." He attributes both these to Hawkwood, but the latter notoriously belongs to the Ubaldini; we may then question the exacting of the colours in the standards which should have corresponded to the arms of the English *condottiere*, (see note, chapter 13.)

******

There was a great feasting of the people on the Prato della Valle, a great supper at Court, fires of joy and martial noises all night. It had indeed been a great victory, all the more valuable as it remedied a very critical military situation. Hawkwood had shown the finest qualities of a first-rate captain:—constancy in peril, rapidity in conceiving a good solution to a problem, and in modifying the plan chosen according to circumstances, resolution in action, a judicious use of the different arms, an exact valuation of the opposing forces, above all things a conscientious study of the ground, and knowing how to make use of it to attain his object, together with the personal courage to lead his men-at-arms at the decisive moment.

Hawkwood was at that time nearly seventy years of age, and yet he thought and acted with the vigour of the most splendid youth.

Having rendered such signal service to the Lord of Padua, he had a perfect right to expect some recognition, but things turned out differently. In his own interest Francesco da Carrara did not fail to ask Hawkwood's best advice how to carry on the campaign, and by following his instructions the Veronese territory again passed into the power of the Paduans; while Francesco Novello who would insist, contrary to his opinion, in passing the fortified moat of San Bonifacio, suffered considerable losses.

There were however serious dissentions between Carrara and his captain. The *Chronicle of Treviso* goes so far as to assert that if the Florentines had not intervened, Hawkwood would have been beheaded by Carrara—an incredible statement.

According to Ricotti, the disgust of Hawkwood was occasioned by an alliance of Carrara with Visconti, towards whom, Sir John maintained rancour—a doubtful statement.

★★★★★★

In fact, in consequence of the alliance the captains Ubaldini and Ugolotto Biancardo must have come to the aid of Carrara, but we know that they were in his service from 1386. Hawkwood had already left Padua when the alliance took place, by means of which the Conte di Virtù was enabled to cheat the Carrara family out of the state, and wrest their power from them.

★★★★★★

The Paduan chroniclers, instead, simply say, that the contract of Hawkwood terminated at the end of April and that he was obliged to return to Florence where he was made captain-general, an incomplete statement.

During that campaign the Florentines had not forgotten their favourite captain: they endeavoured to show in many ways that they preserved their faith in him and cultivated his friendship, having a care for his private interests besides punctually handing him the pay contracted for. They wrote to him not to make another contract with the

Carraras without first giving them notice, (January 10), so that they might take the necessary measures, and at the expiration of the term he did not fail to place himself at their disposal.

Then some would have preferred to dismiss him with thanks, promising to give him the first choice whenever they should need a captain: but as the necessity might unexpectedly arise, the decision to elect him for six months prevailed. (May 1st, 1387.)

This was pleasing to Hawkwood, for he was disgusted with the Carraras. That he was not duly paid his salary we cannot believe: in such a case he was not the man to go away without obtaining it by force. It was more probable that he was displeased about the ransoms of the numerous prisoners of rank made at Castagnaro; for three days after the battle Carrara had published an edict that the mercenaries were to give the names of all the prisoners, and not to dispose of them without his permission; then Carrara wanted them all at his own disposal, paying the ransoms it is true, but perhaps not so high as those demanded by the captor to whom they belonged.

It is certain that Hawkwood left the service of Carrara, feeling himself in some manner defrauded of his right. In fact, (June 16), the "Ten" of the Florentine *balia* wrote to the Lord of Padua recommending, with trust in his justice, the rights of Hawkwood, whom they had always found an upright and faithful man.

On its own account the Commune of Florence lent itself very willingly to favour the interests of Hawkwood, by facilitating the sale of his possessions, (January10), after having however verified that his title as proprietor was a just one; but the relative proceedings are too interesting not to be made the subject of a special chapter.

CHAPTER 30

Liquidation of Property

During so many years of war, between stipends, fees, annuities, profits on the pay of the soldiers, tithes on spoil, and direct plunder, ransoms of prisoners, with every kind of means (some of which would not be edifying, and besides it would be useless to discuss their legitimacy), Hawkwood must have made a fortune more than sufficient for the needs of his family. (We do not know for what especial merit a certain Guglielmo di Andrea of Avignon left Hawkwood a legacy of 20 gold florins in his will dated August 16 138-) He had thus been able to invest considerable sums in landed property, without counting Montecchio and other fortresses taken and held by him on the territory of Arezzo.

But if we may believe the declarations made before the Priors of Florence in an authentic document, he found himself hampered by a considerable debt. (February 5 1387.) Nor do we wonder at his pecuniary embarrassments: for a man of his stamp it was easier to make much money, than to keep that which had been gained, whether it were ill gained or well. We know that adventurers after having made extortions, from city and country, generally fell easily into the net of the usurer. Now there were in Florence usurers with a capacity to spirit away from Hawkwood those glittering florins which Spinello the treasurer had so often counted out to him on the part of the Commune.

We will sum up the tenor of the document according to the text preserved amongst the *Provvigioni* of the Florentine Commune:

John Hawkwood and his wife Donnina Visconti represent to the Priors, that John being in debt for a very large sum of money to several Florentine citizens, whom he desires to pay according to honour and duty, but is unable to do so without selling the undermentioned property, which they cannot sell because they can find no one who will guarantee the sale, by standing bail for them (as strangers); they therefore supplicate that the officers of the diminution of debts on the *monti* of the Commune (communal debt like our national debt, of which the capital was not paid back, but interest paid to the shareholders), shall be retained in the quality of syndics of the Commune for selling and alienating;—that the said official syndics—or even two parts of them whenever the others shall be absent or not forthcoming—may proceed to the sale in the manner and form which seems best to them, and receive the price, or cause it to be received; and that they shall charge John, his wife, and heirs, and the respective possessions, for the expenses of evictions and defence;—that with the price received they may be able to pay the creditors of the said John (with his consent however), and those shall be considered creditors and to the amount which shall be declared by the aforesaid officials, and the residue, if any, shall be given to the said John;—that if the latter should not consent to the payment of the creditors declared as such by the syndics, these shall keep the money in hand until they shall agree together;—that the sales so effected shall enjoy all the privileges and advantages of other sales hitherto made by the officials or syndics deputed by the Commune to superintend the affairs of absent and fugitive persons;—that thus the property sold shall not on any plea be taken away from the purchasers nor shall they be evicted or their right be in any manner contested, and that they shall not be molested in the proprietorship or possession of the said property;—that the magistrates shall not admit or lend ear to anyone who dares to act contrary to this, but shall absolutely repulse the action under penalty of 500 *lire* of small florins, besides the nullification of the act.

Excepting that anyone who considers himself wronged by the said sales may have recourse to, and get redress at the office of the Mercanzia, provided that he make the appeal within 15 days from the sale publicly announced by the herald of the Commune. The counsellors of the Mercanzia, within three days from the appeal shall elect and add to themselves two merchants, citizens and Guelphs at pleasure, for each of the five greater arts, under penalty of 50 *lire* of small florins.

The which counsellors and adjuncts, or even two parts of them, together in concert, shall under penalty of 1000 *lire* of small florins, examine and decide within one month from the appeal. And that the decision shall not be delayed by their absence, the official Judge of the Mercanzia, on the petition of the appellants, shall assemble in his own house the counsellors and their adjuncts until the decision be made, under penalty of 100 *lire* of small florins. But the aforesaid 15 days having elapsed, all appeal shall be inadmissible."

Here follows the description of the property:

A *podere* (farm) with houses both high and low, courtyards, *loggia*, dove-cot, garden, and walled stables for the master, with two separate houses for the workmen; together with arable land, vineyards and cane plantation, with trees, fruit trees and others, in the parish of San Donato di Torre near Florence, in the place called *in Polverosa*, bounded by moats the first and second on the Via di Polverosa, the third on the high road.

A piece of arable land with a house facing the aforesaid *podere*, with the Via Polverosa between them—the *podere* and the bit of ground together is said to be of a hundred and fifteen *sestari* (an ancient Roman measure) or nearly so by line.

A *podere* with houses, tower, and arable land, vineyards, and plantations in the place called la Rocchetta, in the parish of Santa Maria Maddalena, in the Commune of Poggibonsi, near the river Elsa.

Two other *poderi* with houses and trees in the same parish and Commune, in the place called Castiglioni,

Another palace, with vineyards and other *poderi*, together with pieces of wooded land in the Piano di Campi, parish of San Lorenzo; these other *poderi* are seven in number; one with a house in the place called Migliarino, another in Petriccio, two near the River Elsa, and one in a place called Caselle or Maltraversi.

From this it appears that all these lots formed dependencies of the farm and residence of Rocchetta.

They were in fact two considerable possessions, that of San Donate near Florence (very near the locality on the right of the Mugnone which in 1880 forms the princely suburban residence of Demidoff), and that of Rocchetta in the Commune of Poggibonzi in the Val d' Elsa.

In conformity to the dispositions of the *Signoria* already affirmed, the Priors consented to the request, probably already agreed to with the procurators of Hawkwood and Donnina, adding only that the consent of the conjugal couple should precede, concur with, and succeed the sales.

From ulterior documents it results that the sale was not effectuated. Hawkwood must have made an arrangement, and have silenced the creditors with the considerable gains of successive campaigns, or perhaps he found it sufficient to realise the urban lordships he possessed at Naples, Capua and Aversa; for almost at this same time he demanded of the Crown there the license to sell some *beni burgensatici* to the Admiral Giacomo di Marzano, to be able to pay a debt of 2930 florins which he had borrowed from the admiral: this license was granted to him. (October 17.)

From this Florentine "deed" we gather that part of the property was in the name of Donnina Visconti, perhaps acquired with her wedding portion.

No house is cited within the walls of Florence; which would lead us to suppose that Hawkwood had no property in the city, and that he was inscribed in the *gonfalon* of the Golden Lion only for the payment of extraordinary personal taxes; of which we shall find a confirmation later.

After the victory on the Adige, Hawkwood returned to the banks of the Arno where he wielded his captain's *bâton* in peace; there was a thought of giving him something to do, to make use of him as it were, by sending him with Rinaldo Orsini and a few troops to conquer the city of Naples for their ally Queen Margherita of Durazzo, who asked for money, but nothing was done. (July 6)

He was instead (September 18), paid 1200 florins for the fourteenth year of his life annuity, and another 1200 for the new contracts of the present *condotta*, and it is noteworthy that in the analogous warrant he is designated *olim capitaneo compagniae anglicorum in Italia militantium*, (of those who fight in Italy, once the captain on the companies of the English.)

Thus, we have the official confirmation of a fact verified some time since, that from an English *condottiere* Hawkwood had become captain of war to the Florentines.

The veterans of the White Company were dispersed, and served in this field or that, either individually or in small brigades.

The Englishman Beltoft had gathered together several of his countrymen in the service of the Pope, and these were totally defeated by Rinaldo Orsini and Bertrand de la Sale, the Gascon (the former leader of the Bretons), so that the Englishmen John Guernock, Johnny Boutillier (Butler?), Johnny Trichil (?), John Liverpool, Richard Gus (Goss?) and others, abandoning Beltoft, passed for the consideration of 7800 florins into the service of Florence, and under the command of their glorious old countryman; and another Englishman Nicholas Payton followed them.(September 18.)

The Florentines now (October), began to discuss another arrangement in hiring Hawkwood; they would have liked to augment his salary, and only pay it when they needed his services, but once more prudence overcame parsimony, and he was engaged for another year, from October 20, as captain of war. Successive commissions established the monthly stipend at 500 florins, without prejudice to other higher sums which might be accorded to him, and without any obligation to find men or horses. (November 14-17.)

It was a wise course, for Bertrand de la Sale came plundering on the Pisan territory, (December), and Hawkwood had the charge of keeping him at bay and not allowing him to treat Florentine territory in the same way, which charge he fulfilled.

His personal brigade was small and not in good order: it only numbered eighty-two lances, and for defects and fines, resulting from the review (which was held periodically for the stipendiaries), 104 florins, 16 *soldi*, and 8 *danari* were confiscated from the pay. (March 14. 1388.) As captain of war however he had the disposal of sufficient forces, so that he was able to concede a hundred lances to the Pisans who were menaced by Beltoft.

With the new year the latter had put together a strong company in which Germans predominated, and having made a league with Bertrand de la Sale and the German Averard (Landau?) della Campana, they extorted 34,000 florins from Siena, Lucca, and Pisa: then encamping on Perugian ground, (May), they were making negotiations to enter the pay of Pope Urban VI, who had come through Genoa from Avignon, with a numerous escort in which the five hundred horse furnished by Beltoft soon figured.

This constituted a peril to the Florentines, who sent Hawkwood to encamp between Cortona and Perugia with orders to hold all the men-at-arms equipped and ready to march, and at the same time they dispatched Vieri di Pepo, ambassador at Perugia, to see if he could come to an understanding with Beltoft and take him into their pay. But by order of the Pope the Florentine ambassador was arrested and ill-treated.

The *Signoria* then sent the commissary Vanni Vecchietti to Hawkwood, (May 8), with instructions to beg him to write to Beltoft communicating the event, showing the blame which would be attributed to him, and urging him to seek satisfaction.

Then Vecchietti was to make Hawkwood give him an escort of thirty horse to Perugia, where he should seek Beltoft, and speak to him to the same effect, and thus fulfil the mission which Vieri di Pepo had been unable to execute.

The scheme had its effect; the Company of Beltoft was hired by the Pope, (June), who wanted to attempt that enterprise at Naples which for centuries was the cause of so many Italian wars and foreign invasions, but he held himself bound also to the Florentines in certain circumstances.

CHAPTER 31

Carlo Visconti and the Pope's Englishmen under Hawkwood's Orders

Whilst Hawkwood was in camp near Cortona, his brother-in-law

Carlo Visconti, the son of Bernabo, was advancing in that direction, on his return from Germany where he had attempted to get together some soldiers for an attack upon the usurper the Conte di Virtù.

At the time he only had sixty mounted soldiers with him and on his way he had stayed a few days in Florence in an hostelry where he acquired a character of being a stupid and low kind of man, and the Florentines with their usual prudence, not wishing to compromise themselves with the Lord of Milan, for the sake of a pretender who had not very high prospects in view, had not associated much with him: on the contrary they had given the commissaries instructions to draw him away.

At Cortona he doubtless tried to ingratiate himself with his brother-in-law, and to plan out the revenge which they shared in common, and it is probable that Uguccione de' Casali, Lord of Cortona, in entertaining him so kindly did so more in respect for the *condottiere*, than pity for the exile. Besides being a *condottiere*, Hawkwood was moreover a formidable neighbour, and owned the Castle of Montecchio near Cortona.

The Florentines themselves thought that Hawkwood would yield to Carlo's arguments; for at the end of May he asked for leave of absence, but although there was no longer danger from Beltoft's company, they would not grant it, because *it seemed he wanted to insult the Conte di Virtù, which would be dangerous.* In fact, the Count, might have held the Florentines responsible if they had granted him leave. On the other hand, not to offend Hawkwood, they determined not to inform the Count of what they were doing on his behalf, and to ask Hawkwood how long he wished to continue his engagement as captain at 500 florins a month, and what guarantee he desired. (May 30.)

Now where subtilty and subterfuge were concerned they were in their element; still they did not know precisely what the captain's ideas were, only they began to doubt whether he intended (June), to go into Apulia against the French Anjou party for Queen Margherita.

Some wished to dismiss him, because his troops were doing all kinds of damage, besides which it was very expensive.

★★★★★★

5600 florins were paid to Hawkwood for the month of June, and on the 1st of July he received 12.000 more for three months, as the pay of 400 lances and 500 between foot soldiers and cross-bowmen, without bringing into account 1200 florins paid him on July 9th, for the 15th year of his annuity.

★★★★★★

Others feared the enmity of the King of France if he should go into Apulia, and the hostility of the Count di Virtù, if he went into Lombardy. But the majority were inclined to let him go, provided that the Commune should make sure of having a captain in case of need.

Not being able to acquire this assurance in any other manner, he was for the time being refused leave of absence by the *Requisiti*.

Later on, this matter was again discussed, (July), and it was decided to let him go, but secretly, so that he should seem to be making use of his rights, as he had done before. (1382.)

Meanwhile a very numerous company was gathering around Hawkwood. August 2, 1388, Urban VI had started from Perugia towards Tivoli with Beltoft's stipendiaries, declaring his intention of marching upon Naples. There were a thousand lances, many of them veterans of the "White Company," and the Pope, in order to flatter them, rode with them, armed, in a white coat, with his *bâton* in his hand, just as if he were their real captain.

But scarcely had they reached Narni, when discord broke out amongst the Englishmen: either through a sentiment of loyalty for their engagements, or because they mistreated the Pope's promises of payment, all the *caporali* (commanders) refused to follow Beltoft and the Pope, alleging as their reason that the company had agreed to be at the service of the Florentines, under certain circumstances. Now if they passed into the Kingdom of Naples, they would not have been able to fulfil this eventual obligation, for this reason more than two thousand of them set out to Perugia: Beltoft and his brigade, consisting of two hundred men, alone remaining with the Pope.

From Perugia they passed on to Cortona, where they proclaimed as their captain Sir John Hawkwood, who was already captain of war to the Florentines. He however was not pleased at seeing his company increase in this way, for after he had accepted the *bâton* of command, many Italians and Germans had joined it.

Therefore, (August 18), the "Ten of war" commissioned Biliotto Biliotti to go and tell Hawkwood that the number of English brigades being excessive, they preferred to obtain permission from the *Signoria* and Councils for Hawkwood to go and perform the services already discussed with him. And if they should not be able to obtain permission, they would send another commissary with orders, which would satisfy the brigades.

Meanwhile Biliotti was to be sure and flatter the knights, "to keep them amiable with fair speaking," and to inform the *Signoria* how he found them disposed, and how many, and who they were. (August 21.) The Councils and *Signoria* were unanimous in wishing to grant the dismissal proposed by the "Ten"; the only condition they made was, that Hawkwood should promise not to injure the allies of Florence, and to obtain the same pledge from as many as he could of the highest officers.

The adventurers had no difficulty in making these promises, but as for keeping them, that was quite another thing.

In fact while the "Ten" were sending detailed instructions to Biliotti, (September 6), concerning the payment of 3000 florins to Hawkwood and his brigade, so that they could pass from the district of Cortona, and Città di Castello, suggesting to him minute precautions so that the *procure* (power of attorney) of the knights, or of whoever was to receive the pay for them, should be according to rule, they added:

> Reprove Hawkwood, because by means of letters and also personally, he had requested 4000 florins from Siena, thus breaking his word, and tell him that he may now do whatever he likes with his brigade as we can make no further use of it.

And in fact, whilst Hawkwood was passing Città di Castello, and was on Perugian territory, the Florentines prepared to dismiss him, (September 16), always however, doing it in such a manner as to evade the enmity of the King of France, and of the Count of Virtù. The latter was very suspicious of Carlo Visconti's doings at Cortona, and it seems he attempted to remove his cousin by one of his favourite practices—poison.

They relate that having promised and deposited 30,000 florins, Maestro Gioioso, the physician of Casali, Lord of Cortona, let himself be induced to put some poison into certain figs which were brought to Carlo for breakfast. At the moment when he was preparing to eat them, a letter was brought to him from Hawkwood which put him on his guard against poison for himself, and for the Lord of Cortona, without naming the traitor. (From this and other facts already known to the reader, it results that Hawkwood had a well organised police. From his castle at Montecchio he could easily superintend all that was going on at Cortona).

Maestro Gioioso being discovered and convicted, was put to the torture on a car all through Cortona and then quartered. (August 8.)

Carlo Visconti having put together a numerous brigade had united with Hawkwood, so that the latter had more than 4000 cavalry at his disposal, but the hour was not yet come for revenge on the Conte di Virtù, and those 4000 horsemen dispersed, damaging Tuscany, the Papal States, Umbria, and the Marches.

★★★★★★

Here, according to the learned Rawdon Brown, should be recorded the exploit of 800 Englishmen, between men-at-arms and archers, who calling themselves the "brigade of St. George" sent Sir Robert Felton (a nobleman in the suite of the reigning Queen of England) from the camp at Serra near Fabriano, to offer their services a long way off to John of Moravia patriarch of Aquileja, knowing that he had to fight with his rebels (in truth he too wanted to wrest something from the Carraras of Padua, already reduced to great straits by the hostile coalition of the Count of Virtù and the Venetians). Felton passing by Venice procured recommendations from Pietro Morosini. The letter of proposal is signed by Sir John Armsthorp, John Barry, Robert Lock, Roger Baker, and Richard Swinford; and Brown wonders that no mention is made of Hawkwood who had been lately elected captain general of the English.

But Brown seems to have mistaken the facts. There still exist in the Archives of the Chapter-house at Cividale the above-mentioned letter of August 28th, and that of Morosini dated September 17th, as usual with no indication of the year. It cannot however be 1388, because Morosini's letter refers to relations already established in several affairs with the patriarch, and he did not come to Italy till September 23rd of that year. With more foundation, the Abbé Bianchi, a well-known historian of Friuli, assigns the date 1393 to both letters; hence those 800 Englishmen had nothing to do with Hawkwood, but belonged to the great Company of St. George which was formed in April and dissolved in September 1392.

★★★★★★

In spite of reproofs the Florentines could not resolve to do without a man whom they judged to be most capable of defending them in any eventuality, and they were less disposed than ever since the proceedings of the Conte di Virtù, whose unbridled ambition it was easy to imagine, after his having caused the total ruin of the Carraras of Padua. On account of these fears and in accord with the Bolognese (to whom Hawkwood had given the good counsel not to come to fighting with Ubaldini's company, but rather to make a composition in money), they

169

paid 3764 florins, (October 30), for a month's stipend for 1800 horses and 10,000 florins for their pledge not to injure—in the form of a company—either the Commune or its allies for two years.

At the end of the month the danger of hostility on Visconti's part seemed to increase, and in the Florentine councils very few could now have preferred sending Hawkwood to Naples by giving him money. Most of them insisted warmly on the expedience of retaining him at their disposal; preferably at a low price, then a *fair stipend*, but finally *at any price*. Rinaldo Gianfigliazzi said: "Don't dismiss him or the Lord of Padua will be discouraged;" and Franceschino degli Albizi used evangelical language saying: "Be vigilant because ye know not the hour, and take care that ye have oil in your lamps;" in other terms the famous admonition of Oliver Cromwell.

Meanwhile Hawkwood moved slowly towards the Kingdom of Naples, where Queen Margherita, regent for her son Ladislao, offered him high terms. He was near Trevi, (November 10), and was making negotiations to take Beltoft under him, with two hundred lances of his brigade, for which he asked 5000 florins from the Florentines. They sent Boccaccio Alamanni to tell him that 1000 florins had already been paid to his procurators Johnny Trekell and Pierotto Fedini; and that the other 4000 were ready at Perugia and would be paid as soon as it was made clear to them that Beltoft was effectually under his orders.

Alamanni was also commissioned to make Hawkwood restore a load of skins and the mules seized by the English from certain Florentine muleteers.

He must have received oral instructions to search out the *condottiere's* intentions: and it is certain that Ghino di Ruberto was sent to Hawkwood's camp (early in December), with written instructions of great importance, besides the order for the restitution of a mule belonging to Donate Acciaioli which was taken by Carlo Visconti's soldiers now included in his brother-in-law's company with his brigade.

CHAPTER 32
The Neapolitan Enterprise

The instructions to Ghino di Ruberto were to the effect that he should with the opportune information:

Confirm Hawkwood in his good resolution not to pass into the Kingdom of Naples.

The *Signoria* had in truth reason to doubt him, but they dissimulated; in any case the orator had to touch a very delicate note in intimating to the *condottiere* that the events in Lombardy and Tuscany were entangling themselves in such a form that, *the event which he had long desired, would soon happen, and if he stayed in this country, good would accrue, to himself and to his friends.* They showed by this their knowledge of the profound hatred against Gian Galeazzo cherished by Hawkwood and that he now intended to make common cause with his brother-in-law Carlo, who had entered into his company and that his daydream was a great war against the Conte di Virtù.

Ghino di Ruberto was besides instructed to suggest to Hawkwood that instead of going into the Kingdom of Naples, he should send to Otho of Brunswick (who was already fighting there against the Anjou party) to withdraw him from thence and take him into his company: *they two together would do great things, considering the valour of Messer Otho and his enmity to the Conte di Virtù.*

And he was to inform him that without going elsewhere, he might winter in the March of Romagna, where *there was good living*, and that the Count of Urbino had promised to receive them amicably and find them provisions.

If Hawkwood displayed a wish to follow up the march towards Naples, he was to try and frustrate it, discouraging the English knights by alleging the famine and discords down there. On his return he was to bring news whether Beltoft had entered the company, and all kinds of information as to the state of the troops.

The impressions brought back by Ghino were that "the Englishman was inclined to go into the kingdom; indeed he made no mystery of it," saying "that in the affairs of Lombardy one must act and not merely make a show (in truth he spoke wisely) alleging that we might always have him back again, and that he would return stronger and with a better brigade."

Therefore, (December 17), the *Signoria* dispatched Giovanni Orlandi, who to distract Hawkwood from his projects was to give amongst other reasons that:

Little honour would accrue to him from it, and considering how much he had talked of going into Lombardy in past times, it would seem he was postponing it from cowardice or some other cause.

If Hawkwood demanded money in return for his consent he was

to politely decline the request, observing that in the preceding month the Commune had lent him 5000 florins merely to oblige him, and strengthen his troops; so, he must now be obliging in his turn.

But the mission of Orlandi was fruitless, so much so that Niccolo Ricoveri deplored that it had become difficult to retain Hawkwood, as everyone desired. (January 27, 1389.)

They made still another attempt: Pera Baldovinetti was sent, (February 6), with instructions minutely mercantile. If Hawkwood insisted on having money, Pera was to endeavour cautiously to find out how much he expected, and to reduce it to the lowest possible figure, rather lending than giving it, and thus to extract a promise from him not to act until he had received an answer. If he hold out, then promise him 5000 florins as a loan—and if he be not content with a loan, then offer 3000 florins as a gift; but oh Pera! take great care! "before you offer him money, hear from himself what he wants, and do not offer the said sum all at once." If in spite of all this he persists in wanting to go, stop him by asking time to hear from Florence, whether she wants to hire him for herself.

These were the instructions dictated at the Palazzo Vecchio, but thought out in Calimala, (street in Florence where the "*Arte*" of the Wool Staplers had its headquarters); there was however one added of a secret-police character:

> Shew him the letters which we give you, and which are written by an English person, so that no one may cause him to break up his brigade. And tell him that Beltoft was here, and wanted to be released from his obligations to us, saying he wished to go with the other Englishmen. And that then he went to the Conte di Virtù, offering to draw away from Hawkwood the greater part of the English troops now with him.

Which information was not best adapted to persuade Hawkwood to bring his men, where he ran a risk of seeing them bribed to leave him.

Any way with two thousand lances hired by Queen Margherita till May, he marched rapidly towards Naples to help Alberico da Barbiano, and Otho of Brunswick in conquering that capital.

He arrived at Capua with 1300 horse, Otho of Brunswick was at Aversa with another 3000. (Beginning of March, 1389.) By orders given, in the queen's letters they concentrated at Caivano and marched with 5000 combatants towards Naples.

The capital was held for Louis d'Anjou, (March 14), by the viceroy

Montjoye, a man resolute to defend himself, although the garrison (for the most part composed of the Gascons of Bernard de la Sale) did not exceed 1100 horse, and had to blockade Castel Capuano, where the flag of the Durazzo had been raised. The citizens however were well disposed to resist, so Montjoye was able to make a sally from Porta Nolana and menaced the flank of the enemy as they marched, having now reached as far as a place called Liburna; here they halted two or three hours, sending forward a recognition: when seeing the danger from Montjoye's offensive movement Brunswick sounded the retreat, and they drew back to encamp between Afragola and Aversa.

The identical advance and the identical retreat were repeated, (March 23), perhaps they calculated on a sally of the little garrison shut up in Castel Capuano.

Then the fleet of Durazzo (four galleys and five brigantines) conducted by Luigi di Capua appeared in the gulf, (March 31), and took up its position behind Posilipo: the following night it approached Ponte Guizzardo and was placed (April 2), in communication with the army. At the hour of *tierce* next morning, there were Otho and Hawkwood again at Liburna scouring the plain of Casanova up to Naples. Two hundred horse and as many foot came out of the city, and a glorious skirmish took place. The troops of Durazzo left two knights prisoners, and re-entered the camp at Afragola without honour.

The garrison at Castel Capuano meanwhile (April 8), was in great straits: they engaged to surrender if no succour arrived within five days. At dawn on the day before this time, (April 12), was fulfilled the Durazzo party attempted a general action, and the army menacingly approached; Otho and Hawkwood attacked the city at Casanova, at San Pietro ad Ara, and in Borgo Nuovo. About forty of the bravest men risked a sally from Castel Capuano, but some of them were killed, others taken prisoners, and the rest had the good fortune to be able to re-enter the fortress.

The infantry, crossbowmen, and *saccomanni*, came out of Naples against the assailing forces, and they came to blows in a skirmish, in which the troops of Otho and Hawkwood were repulsed with sensible loss on all the line, and constrained to make a fourth fruitless retreat to Afragola. The army on its side could do nothing, and the attack on the town having failed, they placed themselves further back at a distance of two arrows' flight from the city. To sum up, it was a decisive failure, so much so that Castel Capuano surrendered to the Anjou party next day.

Meanwhile the Florentines recommended "*Madame's* state" to Hawkwood, for they favoured Queen Margherita rather than the French Anjou branch. (February 25.) A certain Benedetto di Nicola, to whom this mission was confided, was told also to insist, in praying Hawkwood to come to an understanding and unite with Otho of Brunswick, saying clearly when he could come to Florence and with how large a brigade.

The rupture with the Conte di Virtù was felt now to be inevitable, so (March 6), the *Requisiti* recommended the "Ten" to recall Hawkwood by all means, sending him orders and money so that he could bring with him other troops besides his own. Donate Strada was sent to him, March 15), on the following embassy:

> For reasons which regard his honour, utility and state, he (Sir John Hawkwood) must come to this country without delay, *to do those things which he, has always desired.* As he has promised, sworn, and sealed (without doubt in answer to Benedetto di Nicola), we wish him to be in our service with a company, for four months, commencing from the day he arrives in the plain of Viterbo and Montefiascone (the Tuscan frontier), when the contract will be given, and sworn, and the review held. Let him be in the aforesaid place on the 1st of May with troops up to 1000 lances, with foot soldiers and cross-bowmen, in all amounting to 5000.

If Strada could not see him before the 11th of April, he was to give Hawkwood twenty days to arrive at the place assigned. The money would be brought by a commissary to Viterbo.

He was to recommend him to accept in the brigade Messer Piero della Corona, Ivon Giovanni Brigante, Pansart and some other knights "who are great friends of his, and have sent a confidential messenger from Naples to say they would willingly enter the service of Florence." Excepting Corona, all those who thus offered to pass into the service of the enemy were Bretons hired by the Anjou party for the defence of Naples.

Finally, Strada must agree with Hawkwood on the best method of hiring also Otho of Brunswick, trying meanwhile to procure from the latter the release of a Florentine named Iacopo di Zanobi, who had been taken by his brigade. He was not to speak of his commissions *to any person in the world,* and the paper of demands to Hawkwood must be drawn up by a notary. Taking into consideration that, owing to the distance and the war, the messenger might meet with misfortunes, an identical commission was given also to Ghino di Ruberto, (March 23), only he was authorised to name another meeting place instead of Viterbo.

Although the enterprise of the conquest of Naples might by this time be considered a failure, Hawkwood did not hurry to move at the request of the Florentines. He sent envoys to excuse himself, and as to Delia Corona and the Bretons from Naples, he proposed that Florence should treat directly with them, and hire them into her own service.

Then Guido Cavalcanti was dispatched, (April 21), to renew, by a legal act, the recall of Hawkwood within twenty days; and agree that the Bretons should be comprised in the thousand lances granted to him. In this he ought to find no difficulty as he had only five hundred at present; if he wanted money, he would find a month's pay at Rome (less if possible), but he must be made to start without delay.

In fact, after receiving 3000 florins he took leave of Queen Margherita, (May 16), and moving his brigade slowly and reluctantly to Aversa and Rome, he then took the Orvieto road, (June 1 and 3), not without promising Urban VI to respect the territory of the Church and especially that of the Perugians.

★★★★★★

The pontifical brief relating to this pledge was published by Ghizzi in his *Historical notes on the castle of Montecchio*; the last sentence is noteworthy: in these words, Urban VI seems to allude to Hawkwood's projects against Gian Galeazzo Visconti, and in a measure to approve of them. The address is also interesting.

★★★★★★

Cavalcanti was in a letter desired to complain to Hawkwood of his dilatoriness, which was not in conformity with his contracts, and by way of hastening the captain's movements he was told to say that the rest of the money would be paid after the review of the troops, because before that "they could not decide how many they would have to pay for," and that the review must be held in the plain of Trevi or at Borgo San Sepolcro. "And take great care how you have given, or will give the money."

An ample comment followed these recommendations (June 8), in minute instructions to the commissaries Vettori and Iacopi about the hiring and inspecting of the soldiers, above all insisting that the commissaries should in all these operations make a point of the personal presence of Sir John Hawkwood, Johnny Butler, Liverpool, and several

175

other worthy knights.

The inspection over, Hawkwood was requested to come to Florence and consult with the *Signoria*: and in fact he came, since it was to treat of hiring him, June 10, (for four months, in *form of a company*), or at least to detain him on Florentine territory in such a manner as not to provoke the enmity of other Tuscan cities, which otherwise his soldiers might have injured.

They soon came to an understanding, (June 15), and "provided" to take 10,000 florins of the imposts on the *Distrettuali* (*i.e.* the inhabitants of the Florentine district) and to put it into the fund of the *condotta* to satisfy the engagement made with Hawkwood.

The contract was the engagement of the company for six months, at the rate of 500 florins a month for the captain; 9 florins for each of the 400 lances; 3 florins for each of the 500 between foot soldiers and cross-bowmen. None of the company shall, during the term of contract and the month succeeding it, be in any way molested for debts contracted or misdemeanours committed before the term (civil and criminal privileges in fact). Each one shall have the faculty to obtain his dismissal within fifteen days, on condition that he swear to return to his native country or go beyond the seas. Hawkwood and his officers shall be obliged to inform the *Signoria* of all that might come to their knowledge, which is injurious to the Commune, and, at Hawkwood's requisition, those who are disobedient or do not serve dutifully, shall be expelled the ranks.

This concluded, the captain left Florence, (July 7), to join his troops between Cortona and Perugia.

CHAPTER 33

War in Time of Peace

Gian Galeazzo Visconti Count of Virtù could not have borne a title more inappropriate to his merits. Pretending an alliance with the Carraras and to aid them against the Scaligers, he had possessed himself of Verona and Vicenza, and had treasonably wrested from them their dominions, and the hereditary lordship of Padua. Old Francesco da Carrara, after having abdicated in favour of his son Francesco Novello, had become more the prisoner than the guest of Visconti; and Francesco Novello in his turn had been obliged to renounce in favour of Visconti the dominions usurped by him. He was thus able to save his life and by dissimulating prepare his revenge.

Francesco Novello experienced the most romantic vicissitudes in that hazardous journey from Lombardy to Florence, where he hoped to obtain valid support in attempting the recuperation of the State, but they do not enter into our subject; it is enough to say that he arrived safely in Florence, (end of April), with his wife, children and all his family, and with money and jewels to the amount of 140,000 *ducats*.

Here he was joined by his brother Conte Carrara and they remained a long time, fomenting in the Florentines their hostility to Gian Galeazzo; but although Florence was justly suspicious of the aggrandizement and ambition of the latter, they were not yet disposed to become open partisans of the Carraras—that is to say to wage a war with Visconti.

Francesco Novello comprehended that he must bide his time, and meanwhile he thought of passing into Croatia to secure the concurrence of his brother-in-law Stefano Count of Segna, but first of all he wished to take counsel with two famous enemies of the Conte di Virtù—Carlo Visconti, and John Hawkwood, the former of whom was at Cortona, and the latter in his camp near there, or at his neighbouring castle of Montecchio; so Carrara with his brothers Conte and Rodolfo. and twenty horsemen went to Cortona.

Carlo Casali lord of Cortona, and Carlo Visconti not only received him well, but they also invited him to enter Hawkwood's company with 200 lances. He excused himself on the score of wishing to travel to Croatia, and proposed instead that his brother Conte, also a good knight, should be engaged with 100 lances if Hawkwood were content. They were to give 50 *ducats* a lance, and he would find the remainder of their pay. Hawkwood, being called to Cortona, came at once from his castle at Montecchio, paying great respect to the Carraras; indeed, he promised to Conte the *bâton* of Marshal, not only of the company, but of all the field, when they should fight against the Conte di Virtù.

Thus, the insolent career of Gian Galeazzo was secretly being undermined by many who had suffered from him, and who were already preparing arms while waiting their opportunity. Francesco Novello, resuming his perilous wanderings, passed into Germany, and to his sister the Countess of Segna at Modrussa in Croatia; from there he wrote to his brother Conte, to Carlo Visconti, and Hawkwood, recounting the progress of his schemes against their common enemy.

Meanwhile it was necessary that Hawkwood's company should live at some one's expense. By means of 13,764 florins disbursed to him and Count Landau, the English captain was bound not to molest either Florence or Perugia nor any other commune, and they were earnestly reminded of this compact, (July), by the "Ten."

It was therefore inevitable that he should inflict himself on the Sienese, the more so as the soldiers of Count Conrad Landau were added to his own troops. The Florentines themselves had managed that this brigade should unite with Hawkwood, and the two proceed together, (July 25); they were in all 3000 horse and 1000 foot, and the Commune paid them 20,000 florins for six months.

But the Florentines wished, at least in appearance, to preserve good relations with Siena, and could not openly consent to allow their *condottieri* to injure the inhabitants; Simone Altoviti was therefore sent to Landau, (August 2), and Hawkwood with the embassy of preventing them from overriding the territory of the Sienese, "who might impute the action to Florence;" but they added:

At least spread the report that they were asked to do so by the Count of Soana (who was in open hostility with Siena) or else that the Sienese are collecting men-at-arms of the Conte di Virtù to do them injury, and that they will not tamely wait to be beaten.

Matteo Arrighi and Lorenzo Machiavelli were sent, (August 3), with analogous instructions.

The two *condottieri*, although *ultramontanes* and illiterate, easily comprehended the Machiavellian Italian, and without ado fell upon the people right up to the walls of Siena, replying to the *Signoria* that "they did not intend to oppose the Sienese, but to go *against the troops of the Conte di Virtù, who had offended them by their insolent vituperation.*" (They attempted, says Malevolti, to set fire to the gate of San Marco and to penetrate into the city.) It seems true that the Sienese, knowing the feeling of Florence and Hawkwood towards Gian Galeazzo, took as their war-cry in the skirmish "*Long live the Count of Virtù, Count of Siena!*" And Hawkwood's men responded, crying "*Long live the Count of Florence and Messer Carlo*" (Visconti!).

The Florentines, who always wished to keep up appearances with the Sienese, insisted on openly reproving Hawkwood and Landau for these cries, denying that their men had a right to call themselves Florentine "seeing that they do so with the bad object of making mischief between us and our neighbours." Then they asked them, "*since they had avenged their honour* against the said people to respect the territory of Siena, as well as to desist from menaces to gain money from Pisa

178

and Lucca." In short, Florence made a display of having nothing in common with the enterprise of those bands against Siena, and even blamed them publicly; *i.e.* in the official instructions which passed through Siena to inform the Priors, (August 14.)

With extreme duplicity they gave Ormanno Foraboschi that same day the following secret commission:

> When you are with Sir John Hawkwood and the Count (Landau), say to them alone and in secret, that as they are on Sienese ground and the people are so ill-disposed, we beg them to stay on the territory for a month, doing as much damage as possible.

For this they offered a *backsheesh* of 1000 florins, reinforcements, provisions, and precise information respecting the Sienese forces, from whom the companies should gain some towns and not come to terms without first giving notice. Only they were to respect Pisa and Lucca.

To the commissary Francesco Rucellai they added (August 18), that:

> The company might by payment have provisions on the Florentine territory, although he must make a show of only conceding this by force, and if it should come to a fight and Hawkwood's army should get beaten, *which God forbid!* then he (the commissary) was to aid and assist them, by hastening the work of an hydraulic engineer (*maestro*), who had gone to Hawkwood to *cut off the water from the city of Siena*, where corn and bread were already wanting.

That was how Italian communes treated each other in time of peace!

Beginning of September, the difficulty was in making the troops respect the Florentine territory while devastating the Sienese. Complaints, either mild or severe, were of no use, nor were the efforts of the commissaries Matteo Arrighi, Guido di Tommaso, Biliotto Biliotti, and Lorenzo Machiavelli, to keep them at least six or eight miles from the confines of Florence; some of the adventurers seemed disposed to pass into the Maremma, but the English knights would not hear of it, and it finished by consenting, (September 26), that the troops might approach Florentine land when they needed provisions, as long as they kept the camp on that of the Sienese.

The truth is that between Florence and Siena the marauders stole so much that they were able to sell 1500 oxen by auction.

The two *condottieri* had commenced some mysterious and delicate affair with the Florentine *Signoria*, a business concerning which Guido di Tommaso and Lorenzo Machiavelli had secret instructions, both oral and written, for Hawkwood and Landau had asked for a *citizen to whom they wished to confide certain things*; we only know that Machiavelli was sent to hear them, endeavouring to extract the truth and sometimes holding separate interviews with each in turn.

We know on the other hand that those famous brigands were not all good fighting soldiers, and it required great caution in those who hired them (October 1st 1389), to get them equipped according to their compacts.

While the Val d'Elsa was thus being devastated, another company of English, Germans, and Italians led by Beltoft, after having damaged the territory of Pisa for thirty thousand florins, extorted thirteen thousand more to retire; then Gambacorti Lord of Pisa proposed the usual useless remedy—a general league against the companies. To this the Conte di Virtù, the Florentines, Sienese, and Bolognese adhered, and amongst the compacts it was decided to dissolve the great company which was then under the orders of Hawkwood and Landau. The Bolognese took 500 lances at their expense, and the Florentines 300 with Count Landau and other knights.

As to Hawkwood, the following proposal was made, (October 17), in the Florentine councils, by Alessio Franceschi in the name of the "Ten of war," and the other ambassadors from the congress of Pisa:

Considering the fame of Sir John Hawkwood, the *Signoria* will tomorrow convoke the councils (*collegi*) to deliberate on his *condotta*, and if the *Signoria* deem it well, they will also call some citizens into council, and the "Ten" will also assist.

His presence was not judged to be necessary—on the contrary they officially proclaimed the league against the companies, so that he again went towards Apulia to re-enter the service of the house of Durazzo. (October19.)

But 'ere long the relations of Florence with the Conte di Virtù became so strained that no objection was made to the proposal of Alessandro Niccolai, (December 9):

Let us provide ourselves a captain, and let him be one in whom the Commune can trust, and the Commune has faith in Sir John Hawkwood.

He was at Gaeta when the Florentine proposal reached him; the moment he had so long desired had come: the war with Gian Galeazzo now seemed inevitable, and the Florentines turned to him to conduct their army, knowing him to be the greatest leader of the times, and besides a special enemy of the Count, and they entreated him to bring with him his brother-in-law Carlo Visconti, hoping that he would be of service in exciting rebellion among the subjects of Gian Galeazzo.

CHAPTER 34

First Operations against Gian Galeazzo

The Count of Virtù had Carlo Malatesta in his pay, (1390), as captain general, with Iacopo dal Verme, Facino Cane, Biancardo and Ubaldini, almost all the most noted *condottieri*: Hawkwood only was wanting, who in his own person was capable of outweighing all the party and this made him not a little anxious.

Hawkwood on his part, having reached Rome, (April), without opposition, was with reason doubtful whether the Sienese or some other partisans of Visconti might not hinder him from arriving in Florence; he escaped the difficulty with his usual foresight, and sent men to several places to ask for safe conducts, while he with long marches and great fatigue took the unusual road through the Maremma instead. He lost a good many horses by the way, but arrived safe and sound at Volterra and then at Florence, (April 30), where he was received with great joy by the citizens.

He was engaged for a year with two hundred lances, and on the compact that if the request were made before the last thirty days of the agreement, he should be obliged to serve also the following year. Among the other obligations he assumed, he was bound to supply sentinels and guards, for night or day, as should be commanded. For the two years succeeding his engagement, he pledged himself not to act against the Commune, "*come compagnia*" i.e. as the captain of a company, and for six months not even as a stipendiary or as holding any commission.

For the rest they made the same conditions as on May 3rd 1387, with the addition of fifes and trumpets, for we have already seen that Hawkwood with good reason held to these accessories of military pomp.

Altogether we perceive that the Florentines were taking precautions, as though foreseeing a long and great war, and ere long they sent Hawkwood with his brigade and 500 cross-bowmen to the aid of

Bologna and Romagna, where the arms of Visconti were beginning to make themselves felt, and the "battle was imminent."

These reinforcements were followed by another English brigade which was at Volterra, and the men-at-arms were called up from Sienese—the defence of the territory and its towns being entrusted to native infantry. They reserved a more convenient time to hire Beltoft and send him against Siena. (May 9.)

Hawkwood however insisted that they should keep a strict guard on that side, because Giovanni Ubaldini was there, a *condottiere* of whom Hawkwood had a great opinion, deeming him to be worth a thousand of the best lances in his own person, and he did not leave until he had planned a very wide strategic moat from Montopoli to the Arno for the defence of the lower valley of the Arno. (They had in those days great faith in this kind of defensive obstacle.)

******

Giovanni Cavalcanti, an almost contemporaneous writer, mentions the advice of Hawkwood among the anecdotes published in the Appendix of his Florentine history, in the "Documents of Italian history" saying: "This excellent man went most mornings to consult with the 'Ten of war,' and more often than not it fell out that the said captain gave advice to the Ten instead of the Ten giving orders to him. His attending the meetings shewed that he especially desired the good of the city." Cavalcanti besides confirms the fact that the English *condottiere* had organised a diligent service of military spies.

******

He arrived at Bologna, (May 14), with only an escort of 15 lances and forthwith betook himself to San Giovanni in Persiceto, where under Giovanni da Barbiano 1200 lances and 3000 infantry were assembled at the expense of the Florentines and Bolognese. The rumour of his arrival was enough to make the Visconti Army abandon Crevalcuore, where they were really very well fortified. He profited by this to ravage the Modenese and Reggio lands, making raids for prisoners and cattle, and when Iacopo dal Verme, taking courage, had pressed on the Visconti Army, (June 20), as far as Samoggia a few miles from Bologna, he was soon on the defensive and encamped at the bridge of the Reno on the Via Emilia.

There, still in accord with Barbiano, he did not neglect to guard himself on all points, taking the best position, and garrisoning Casalecchio, occupying the bridge and pebbly bed of the Reno:—the enemy on his side fortifying himself with banks and deep moats.

Having obtained the consent of the Bolognese senate, Hawkwood sent Zuzzo the trumpeter to Dal Verme with a blood-stained glove, challenging him to come out to battle. Dal Verme declined the challenge twice with fierce abuse; the third time he kept the trumpeter prisoner for a night, but not feeling very safe, or from want of provisions, he removed from his position. (The fox would not meet him, and at night on 24th he slyly went away. Letter of June 27th from the "Ten of war" to Donato Acciaioli commissary in Val d'Elsa; Laurentian Library, Ashburnham MSS.)

Hawkwood quickly followed, and overtook him, constraining him to fight, while Barbiano attacked him on the flank; so that within two hours Dal Verme was beaten and put to flight, leaving as prisoners Facino Cane, Anghelino da Padule, fifty men-at-arms, and two hundred and twenty horses.

Not long after this a very important and pleasing piece of news arrived at the camp (June 21)—*i.e.* that Francesco Novello had victoriously entered into Padua, thus regaining his city; a notice which was celebrated by large bonfires, blowing of trumpets, and other signs of rejoicing. There was indeed a great desire to meet the enemy again and give him battle, to which Bologna would have consented, but Florence prudently opposed it, holding that one should only fight when one is compelled to do so, or is perfectly sure of victory.

The Florentines instead deliberated, (July 29), how they could diminish useless expenses, discharge those stipendiaries who did not serve as well as they ought to do, and reinforce Hawkwood with troops and money, so that he could hold the field as far as the Po, or even cross it. On the other hand the progress of Carrara's army towards Vicenza and Verona had constrained the Conte di Virtù to recall his troops from beyond the Po; so that with 1000 lances, and 500 foot soldiers, Hawkwood could freely override Lombardy (Cispadana), and he pressed on as far as Parma, regularly furnishing himself with provisions and respecting the inhabitants of the country, because he hoped by this means to induce them to shake off the tyranny of Gian Galeazzo.

Two pennons waved in Hawkwood's brigade—the arms of the King of France, and those of the Duke of Bavaria.

The King of France was always considered as the head of the Guelph party, and had received and favoured Francesco Novello da Carrara when he passed the Alps to initiate a general movement against the

Visconti, who were entirely Ghibellines. Besides this the Florentines were already negotiating for the French Army to enter Italy and decide the war which had commenced.

The Duke Stephan of Bavaria, who had married Taddea daughter of Bernabo Visconti, and was therefore the natural enemy of Gian Galeazzo, being solicited and well paid by the Florentines, had come with a considerable force to Italy aiding Carrara to besiege the fortress of Padua, and regain his other possessions.

August 6, the Florentines wrote informing the Duke of Hawkwood's march and praying him to unite with him; but instead of doing so, the duke sent ambassadors to the Florentines, to ask that Hawkwood might come to join him; meanwhile autumn set in, and the rivers swelled to such an extent that the operation was difficult and the Duke of Bavaria, having pocketed the Florentine pay for the fourth month, returned back across the mountains, not without a suspicion of an understanding with the Conte di Virtù.

Having returned from the incursion on the territory of Parma, (September), Hawkwood together with Barbiano sustained a most cruel fight with 300 of Carlo Malatesta's infantry. Contrary to the custom of war among the mercenaries, they, this time, fought "like barbarians, and each side made a miserable slaughter of the other." The victory was at length gained by the two captains of the League, who doubtless having superior forces at command were able to take the fierce but numerically few enemies on the flank.

Then having crossed the Po, Hawkwood gave assistance to Francesco Novello, who was fighting vigorously in Polesine, where he constrained the Marquis of Ferrara to leave the Visconti party, (October 3), and enter into the League. On this the bells were with good reason merrily rung at Bologna and Florence: for Gian Galeazzo, who at the commencement of hostilities was master of all the subalpine territory as far as Friuli and also menaced Bologna, was now reduced to defending himself on the banks of the Adige.

Florence was especially able to boast of her captain, and in fact she treated him with every loving-kindness.

The *Signoria* confided to him their good reasons for not wishing that Carlo Visconti should figure in the Staff, indeed they begged Hawkwood to keep him at a distance from the camp. They assigned to Sir John the lances they had denied to that Visconti, and excused themselves for not being able to take into their service all the knights he had recommended; besides which they made him a gift of a hundred good Lucca bows to arm his archers, and remitted his imposts.

In a letter, (November 11), from the "*Dieci di balia*" to Donate Acciaioli and Niccolo da Uzzano, ambassadors at Bologna, we read:

As to Giovanni Balcano, we are content that he shall have 30 florins a month for five months between us and the Bolognese, but in regard to John Guernock we do not want to give him anything at all. And tell Sir John not to give us so many worries on other people's account, for his own are enough for us. We are content to give Sir John those hundred bows which he had, and will take them off his account. We will send to Lucca for the best kind of bows, for they are not good here, then we will send them at once to Padua. Respecting Messer Carlo, we must beg you to urge Sir John to try by all means not to let Messer Carlo go to him there, for within the last few days certain persons from Milan have come to us secretly, telling us plainly that if Messer Luchino goes with the brigade the Milanese will let him enter, but if Messer Carlo goes, they will not turn, but will keep steadfast to the Count. (Luchino Visconti junior, called also Luchino Novello or Luchinetto, believed to be son of Luchino former Lord of Milan.) They assign their reasons for this, which are perfectly true. On this account we are content to give Messer Carlo a salary of 150 florins a month for four months, between ourselves and the Bolognese. Those twelve lances of Messer Carlo can go to serve Sir John unless Messer Carlo wishes to keep some of them with him, in which case you can cancel them. This "*provvisione*" is made only in case he does not go with Sir John, otherwise it is void. Sir John's forced loans and imposts shall be taken off; we have already seen the *Signoria*—you can tell Sir John so.

And in fact, (November 16), the Commune:

Out of regard to the brave knight, John Hawkwood, so prudent in affairs of war as to be superior to almost all those of his time in Italy, so devoted a friend and captain-general of war to the Commune—wishing to treat him with liberality, holds him free from every fine, impost or residue, and also from the great dues which are called *prestanze di libertà* or vulgarly *prestanzoni*, which he should have paid, and also from all the penalties for payments omitted.

Equal privileges were accorded to his wife, his sons, and daughters.

Fearing lest Alberico da Barbiano should eventually accept Gian Galeazzo's offers, the Florentines were disposed to engage also that *condottiere*, and commissioned Donate Acciaioli to go and meet him at Ravenna and enter into negotiations, but in this they wanted to secure the concurrence of Hawkwood. These were his orders:

> In conclusion request Barbiano that it may please him to be our captain-general together with Sir John Hawkwood, not because we wish to keep them together, but in different camps, each with an honourable brigade of Bolognese and our own troops, saying that we will give him such *provvisione* (salary) and men-at-arms as shall be requisite, and contrive to draw out his intentions and inform us of them. If he wants to have a decisive reply, tell him at last that we are content to take him for six months, and six more at the pleasure of the Bolognese and ourselves, giving him the same pay as that to Sir John Hawkwood, *i.e.* 500 florins a month for himself and two hundred lances. If he be not content, and wants greater things, do not break off with him, but give him good hopes without binding yourself, signifying his last intentions to us. (The "Ten of war" to Donato Acciaioli and Niccolo da Uzzano, October 6th 1390, the third hour of night.)

They could have managed without Barbiano, but in fact the Florentines had engaged in the war with exemplary energy, and were preparing a grand *coup*, *i.e.* while Hawkwood with all the army then fighting for them, and for the Bolognese, Carraras, and other allies, should attack the States of Gian Galeazzo from the east; the Comte d'Armagnac, who had been persuaded by his brother-in-law Carlo Visconti, and convinced by the good pay of the Florentines, was to descend from the Alps with 2000 lances, and 3000 infantry, and attack him on the west. Gian Galeazzo on his side had arranged to oppose d'Armagnac with the troops under Iacopo dal Verme, while Ugolotto Biancardo was sent against Hawkwood.

The latter was on his arrival at Padua (November 24), lodged with all honour in the court of Francesco Novello, his men being quartered some at San Martino and the rest at Montagnana. Here, (December), the captain was met by the treasurers Messer Lotto, and Messer Niccolo, who, as we gather from the following letter to Acciaioli, (December 15), is brought him the money for the pay, and a handsome

Christmas present.

> We wish you to say to those lords of Bologna that they must recognise how useful Sir John is to us, and how much good or ill it lies in his power to do us, seeing that he carries in his hands our State and theirs too, and that moreover it appears expedient to us, that we should jointly make the aforesaid Sir John a Christmas gift of a thousand florins, they paying a third of it, and we two thirds. In case they consent to do so, cause their share to be sent to Padua, and write by our commission to Messers Lotto and Niccolo, that they may pay our share of it. But if the Bolognese will not agree, then write to the said Messers Lotto and Niccolo, that they give the said Sir John five hundred florins on our own part.

During the month, at Padua the Count Giovanni da Barbiano joined them with two hundred lances, Count Conrad Landau with another two hundred, and Astorre Manfredi with fifty. (The arrival of Manfredi could not have been very welcome to Hawkwood after the interminable disputes of which we have spoken.) Add to these the troops of Carrara, and it made a fine and strong army for those times, so fine that the celebrated Pier Paolo Vergerio, Carrara's secretary, wrote with great magniloquence to his friend Doctor Giovanni da Bologna after he had seen them reviewed in a field outside Padua, (January 22, 1391), and had witnessed them manoeuvring with flying banners, and executing a mock battle. As to their number, he estimated it at nine thousand horse, and five thousand foot, without counting the multitude of *saccomanni*. No one could say precisely how many they were, but the expert Galeotto Malatesta suggested this method for an approximate calculation:

> Take the mean between the maximum given by exaggerators, and the minimum by detractors, and deduct a third.

This is more eloquent than any discourse, to make us understand that if the very captains who led them could not calculate the number of their forces from one day to another, they must have been even less able to depend on discipline and on the obedience of the mercenaries.

As to leaders, Vergerio particularly mentions Francesco. Novello lord of Padua as *generalissimo*, Conte da Carrara as commandant of the Paduan contingent, Astorre Manfredi and Giovanni Barbiano, while the Florentine troops are led by:

Signor Giovanni Aucud—who is so celebrated for the remembrance of his worthy achievements, and with this victory about to give the last and greatest elevation to his fame.

And in truth Hawkwood, now nearly octogenarian, prepared to undertake what was indeed the last and most splendid of all his campaigns. For more than fifty years he had been a soldier, a *condottiere*, and a captain, but he never displayed such energy, such promptness, such constancy, and such courage as we shall now see him do, in most difficult circumstances. One might say that before sheathing his sword for ever, he had called up at one time all his military virtues. And as in the sorry trade of a mercenary he had in comparison with others been almost an honest man, we may be allowed to contemplate him with almost reverent admiration in these his last feats of arms.

CHAPTER 35
The March to the Banks of the Adda

In 1387 the Carraras began a war with the Scaligers, and to complete their ruin they allied themselves with Gian Galeazzo Visconti, who, after having taken away Verona and its state from *the men of the Ladder (quei della Scala)*, wrested Padua and that state from *those of the Car (quei del Carro)*: it was indeed with good reason that he himself bore the ensign of the voracious serpent. (The Ladder or *Scala* was the ensign of the Scaligers, the Car or *Carro*, that of the Carrara family.) Now the old enemies were leagued together against the usurper: Samaritana della Scala, as mother and guardian of her son, invoked and obtained the aid of Carrara, that he, having regained Padua, should assist her to recover Verona.

After many councils with Hawkwood and the other captains it was decided to encamp on the Veronese territory without delay: and all preparations with regard to provisions and other necessaries being completed, the army made its exit from Padua, (January 11), two hours before sunrise, according to the advice of the astrologers. The numbers were soon multiplied—we will not venture to say reinforced—by a great many troops, Paduan, Vicentine, Veronese, citizens and countrymen, dwellers in the plains, hills, and mountains, who altogether brought up the number of foot soldiers to 15,000.

A part of the army marched along the lower Adige, (January 15, 1391), to cross it at the usual bridge of Castelbaldo, which they accomplished, the lady Samaritana riding amongst them in knight's at-

188

tire: thence they ascended the river banks towards Verona: and the body of the army, with Francesco Novello in the van-guard, took the Vicenza road, of which movement Donate Acciaioli, then Florentine ambassador at Padua, was informed by a note from Francesco himself.

They occupied the open borough of Illasi, and having found the fortress to be impregnable, unless under a regular siege, they left in the borough only a weak garrison (which a little while after was cut to pieces by the inhabitants in concert with the garrison of the fortress), and descended towards Verona taking a hundred and fifty prisoners and killing several of the Viscontese, who shut themselves up in the city and in their fortresses.

Beneath Verona the two invading armies united, pitching their camps on the two banks of the Adige, in sight of the city, while they scoured the valleys and plains for forage (they were bound under pain of the gallows to abstain from taking anything except hay and straw from the peasants), and trying to excite tumults by the cry of *Scala! Scala! Long live Can Francesco!* the young Scaliger.

But Ugolotto Biancardo had a few months back fiercely repressed an attempted rebellion and had wisely provided every defence: so that there was no probability of a favourable result. Therefore, the Lord of Padua, Francesco Novello, at the instance of Hawkwood, left the supreme and honourary command to Conte da Carrara, and returned to Padua with an escort of three hundred horse. The old captain was unwilling to have reigning or hereditary princes in the army, for he considered them as hindrances to the operations and battles; and would joyfully have sent to the devil even the lady Samaritana, who kept the army at making fruitless attempts on Verona and her fortresses, and who had hired his mortal enemy Astorre Manfredi.

The news of such a slow war could not be very welcome to the Florentines, who were spending so much on it. They would have liked a rapid march towards Milan, where it seems they had an understanding. (February 10.)

The "Ten" wrote to Donato Acciaioli and Francesco Allegri ambassadors at the court of Carrara, wondering that:

Our troops. . . . linger over such trifles, and leave the great deeds and good fortune which are prepared for them towards Milan, for he who will not when he may, cannot when he will. . . . Hasten the captain, our commissaries and the others, that they go to Milan without delay.

The same day duplicating the letter they said:

> Hasten the brigade, and send it towards Milan, and not remain wasting time about little castles, for the expense is great, and the hopes of success will become less if we do not act quickly.

And again, February 13:

> Work day and night that the troops cross the Adige.

Hawkwood was of the same sentiment, and had forestalled the exhortations: he made his army cross the Adige, and encamp at Santa Lucia, (February 9); which rejoiced the Florentines, who wrote to Acciaioli, (February 23):

> We are content with the news, provided the troops follow up the march towards Milan, where from certain things of which we have had secret intelligence, we have great hopes. . . .

But the extraordinary rigor of the winter rendered provisioning and marching very difficult: many volunteers were already disbanding, and instead of crossing the Mincio, the camp approached to within a few miles of Mantua, plundering the farms of cattle, and intimating to Gonzaga that he must either adhere to the League, or suffer the penalty of a general sack.

The Marquis of Mantua asked for time to decide. These new delays rendered the Florentines very impatient; they wrote again to Acciaioli (February 24):

> Let the Lord of Padua proceed boldly, and hold no parleying either with Agostino Cane, or any other enemy. . . . We have written to the camp by two of our couriers, urging that no discussions shall be held, and that they start at once, we have scolded and abused them well, and have made the Bolognese do the same.

Meanwhile Hawkwood discovered that Astorre Manfredi had held a midnight interview with certain peasants, and suspecting treachery, he raised the camp and returned to between Verona and Vicenza, thence on the Paduan land. Therefore, the following orders from Florence to Acciaioli, (March 1st), were useless:

> Exert yourself and see that the troops do not on any account leave the enemies' country, and that they hold themselves prepared and ready to turn back towards Milan, which we intend

them to do at all costs. And we have arranged to send money immediately, so that the troops have no cause for any excuses.

Hawkwood maintained that Astorre was plotting to murder both him and Francesco Novello, and said so much that Astorre was obliged to return to Faenza.

It is but too true that treachery was at that time so common a thing that it created no astonishment. The Count of Virtù by means of deceit induced Gonzaga of Mantua to order that his wife (Agnes daughter of Bernabo and thus a natural sister-in-law to Hawkwood) should be beheaded, as being implicated in the plot of Carlo Visconti, against the life of her husband.

But it might be that Hawkwood was ill-advised by reason of his old hatred. Vergerio, alluding to these reports, writes thus to his friend Giovanni da Bologna, (July 19):

In this retreat some were, as I believe, falsely accused of infamous felony; it often happens that in great things if the result does not correspond with one's hopes, that is lightly called a crime which is really only incapacity, and one attributes to the few that which is a general fault.

From these words we can comprehend that at Padua the want of success of that ill-attempted winter campaign was very displeasing.

As to Florence, the chancellor Ser Benedetto Fortini wrote to Acciaioli, (March 15):

All the good people and others here, think very ill of the way in which the troops have turned back from their object, for we had hopes of great doings. I know from certain signs in many ways, that if the army had neared Milan, the city would have revolted. Great things are expected from the coming of the Count d'Armignac.

News had been heard that d'Armagnac was to come down into Piedmont towards the end of May. All that was necessary then was that Hawkwood should make a move in time to attempt a conjunction, which would have been most fatal to Gian Galeazzo.

The end of that winter was employed in reinforcing the army and preparing it for the coming campaign. To keep it in exercise Hawkwood made frequent incursions into the Vicentine and Veronese provinces, inspiring the inhabitants with such respect that many of them took the trouble to buy provisions to supply his soldiers.

May 10, seeing the time was propitious, because the corn and oats were already high, and some, being already in ear, gave abundant forage, he issued from Padua with the army in marching order. Well provided with pay and food, he was content with the preparations, for which he gave Carrara great credit. This time he had the command-in-chief himself, Conte da Carrara, Lodovico Visconti, and Count Conrad Landau being under his orders; 1400 Florentine lances, 600 from Bologna, 200 from Padua, 1200 cross-bowmen and a great many infantry constituted a considerable force. These numbers are given by Minerbetti. Vergerio says 5000 chosen cavalry, and 2000 foot soldiers, adding that the red lily of the Florentine preceded all the other standards; then came the "Car" of the Carraras, the red cross and lily of Bologna, and then the ensign of the captain and the other *condottieri*.

The Adige being shallow was crossed, (May 15), without any other delay than that of putting to flight an exploring party of the enemy, consisting of 300 lances and some infantry. Another obstacle was presented by a wide and deep moat excavated by Antonio della Scala in 1386. Hawkwood made his men fill up a space large enough for the passage of the troops and rapidly marched on towards the Mincio.

If we may believe Vergerio, the captain on that occasion made an eloquent speech to exhort his soldiers to great deeds, which capricious invention we will leave to the fantastic rhetoric of the humanist. For we think it more likely that he bid them abstain from incendiarism, and from taking the peasants prisoners, because it was to the interest of the League to win the friendship of the population subject to the enemy.

The Mincio was also crossed without hindrance, and Vergerio relates that on Brescian territory Taddeo dal Verme opposed them with 9000 horse and 3000 foot, all hired soldiers, with a large number of peasant troops, and countrymen, besides a great many carts and mules. This time Vergerio has probably neglected to follow the golden rule of Galeotto Malatesta, for Leonardo Aretino's account is much more probable; which is, that the greater part of Visconti's forces had been sent towards Piedmont to oppose the now much talked descent of d'Armagnac, and that no troops were left in Lombardy except the garrisons alone, leaving the country freely open to the invaders.

Taddeo dal Verme, coming out of Brescia with seven hundred horse, placed himself on the bank, watching his opportunity to attack Hawkwood, who accelerated his march. The best moment seemed to be when he had crossed the Oglio at Rudiano, and a great part of the allied army was already on the left bank. Hawkwood had however calculated on this, and prepared his trap by placing Conrad Landau in ambush with 300 lances.

Taddeo found himself caught in the midst, and had great fortune in being able to flee, leaving about a hundred prisoners, and three hundred between killed and drowned. He returned with the mass of his army, but by that time the allies were established on the other bank, and recommenced their rapid march towards the Adda.

Hawkwood halted at Trescorre without molestation. At Colognola, under Bergamo, a fruitless attack was made on him by five hundred chosen cavalry from that garrison; but they were easily made an end of by an energetic counter-attack of Conte da Carrara, who was slightly wounded, and the Count of Anguillara, who was knighted as though to seal the victory.

Then they dispersed in the valley of San Martino, always having due regard to the inhabitants, and amicably buying provisions, so that a knight of that country joined the League bringing with him a thousand men-at-arms.

Thus they safely reached the Adda, and descended for three days along the left bank vainly seeking a ford, and having arrived at Pandino and the woods of Bofalora (Bernabo Visconti's hunting ground, and refuge from the plague) they pitched their camp, intending to decide on their forward march, as soon as they had notice from d'Armagnac, with whom they were to effect a conjunction on the Po, either at Pavia or Piacenza. Taddeo dal Verme was near them, having followed slowly behind, and Hawkwood did not hesitate to challenge him to a battle. After an exchange of cartels and messages, it was agreed that each army should choose four captains of note, and sixty men who were to fight in an enclosed field.

This was a remnant of chivalric military customs, which the mercenary soldiers cherished by tradition, but rarely used. The champions were already chosen, the first on the part of the League was Michele da Rabatta, but Vergerio does not give the names of the others.

Hawkwood moved his camp a little for better convenience of forage and provision; and the Viscontese made this a pretext for declining the combat, unless the allied army would return to their first position. Hawkwood however was not so short-sighted as to renounce a positive advantage; and hence, instead of the challenge, frequent indeed almost daily skirmishes took place: and when the Viscontese made prisoners, instead of agreeing as usual on a ransom, they deprived them of arms and horses so that they could not take the field again. In this way they tried to weaken the enemy, on which the allies took to fighting with extreme resolution, and as usual became victors freeing themselves at the same time of useless arms and mouths.

So, they steadily kept their favourable position on the Adda, and on the *fête* of St. John (the patron of Florence) they triumphantly ran the *palio* according to Florentine usage, with festive shouts to the great shame of the enemy who were constrained to take the most extreme precautions.

★★★★★★

It was an ancient Florentine and Tuscan custom to have races on the occurrence of civic solemnities and as an insult on the territory and under the walls of the enemy; such races were run by horses or foot soldiers or the courtesans of the army.

★★★★★★

Gian Galeazzo ordered that 300 Milanese citizens should go to reinforce the garrison of Lodi; being very devout, he ordered public processions for three days, and being timid and anxious to provide for his personal security, he armed another 1200 citizens, chosen among the most able men, as a bodyguard.

CHAPTER 36

The Retreat across the Adige

Hawkwood had carried out his part in the general plan of campaign excellently: he had reached the Adda, and there had for several days awaited the right moment to bring about a juncture with d'Armagnac, who was leisurely coming from France, and was still a long way off. In vain did Hawkwood urge him on by means of letters and embassies, and advising and begging him to accelerate his march. Gian Galeazzo was therefore able to bring nearly all his forces against Hawkwood, recalling Iacopo dal Verme from Piedmont, with 1800 lances and 10,000 infantry: together with Taddeo's troops they then were nearly 26,000 men, of whom 10,000 were trained soldiers.

The French *condottiere's* delay rescued Visconti from the danger of a simultaneous attack on both sides, and allowed him to fight the two hostile armies in turn, at his own convenience. For these reasons, and owing to the difficulty of procuring provisions, Hawkwood was positively compelled to beat a retreat. But even a retreat was a difficult matter to accomplish, in the face of an enemy much stronger than themselves, and with several large rivers to cross.

Iacopo dal Verme was so confident of turning it into a disaster, that he wrote thus to his master:

Write and tell me how you wish me to settle them.

And here Hawkwood proved himself a great captain, knowing in the first place that if he wished to procure relative liberty of action for himself, he ought to instil respect into his enemy, and give him a lesson: he therefore marched in an oblique direction between the Adda and the lower Oglio, but stopped at the castle of Paterno Fasolaro, where he strongly entrenched himself, and forbade his men to leave the trenches. Visconti's army encamped a mile off, and for four consecutive days advanced beyond a small stream running between the two camps, and offered battle. Hawkwood remained ensconced in his camp, leaving them to vent their anger in making provoking demonstrations.

By way of a practical joke Dal Verme sent him a fox in a cage. Hawkwood answered the enemy's envoy who brought the cage: I see that the animal is not dull, which means that he will discover a way out," and breaking one of the bars of the cage, he set the fox at liberty.

On the fifth day, when Visconti's soldiers were at their usual game, and thought they would follow it out, Hawkwood and all his men suddenly left their entrenchments, and fell vigorously upon the enemy whom they chased to their very camp; twelve hundred of Visconti's men were made prisoners, and there were fifteen hundred between killed and wounded.

In his turn Hawkwood offered battle by sending to Dal Verme a bloodstained gauntlet, a challenge which was accepted for the following day, but in the evening Sir John abandoned the camp leaving the banners tied to the tops of trees, and telling the trumpeters to sound the reveille till daylight, and then to forsake the banners and to go about their own business, moreover he managed to leave several beasts of burden along the way.

In this manner, by means of victory, deceit, and with the temptation of booty, he hindered the enemy, and having procured the necessary rest, he hastened to the River Oglio, which he reached at Soncino, with the intention of ascending its right bank as far as the known ford of Rudiano.

Visconti's soldiers prudently kept them back, making entrenchments, and skirmishing in such a manner, that for two days, (July 2 to 4), and for two nights there was a continual marching and sharpshooting, during which days by means of an ambuscade Count Conrad

Landau again distinguished himself, and Facino Cane, one of Visconti's knights, was severely wounded.

After all, if Hawkwood suffered fatigue in this most difficult retreat, it is very wearisome for us to search out the most probable details, amongst the incomplete and often contradictory narrations of the chroniclers, which offer serious discrepancies; so that it is not to be wondered at if Ricotti fell into the error of placing this retreat after the defeat of d'Armagnac, and to explain it as being the result of that rout, which took place on the 25th of July, when Hawkwood was already in safety on the left bank of the Adige.

For example, if we are to believe the story of Ghirardacci, it would seem that Count of Virtù in person, leaving the territory of Bologna, came to fight the allies on the Oglio; that Hawkwood, on account of inferiority of forces, was unwilling to risk a battle, but accepted it as a point of honour; that, after a couple of hours' fierce fighting, Visconti, seeing that his men were in disorder, took to flight with a few horses and much anxiety: and when he had found and reorganised a few cavalry and infantry troops, he attempted a rescue, lying in ambush at the pass of Rudiano.

So that when Hawkwood and his soldiers reached that place they were attacked by Iacopo dal Verme, Ugolotto Biancardo, Carmignuola, and Guglielmo Pusterla, and that having met hand to hand, they put to the sword almost all the assailants, naming especially Carmignuola and Pusterla; that the victorious Englishman made twenty of his bravest men *cavalieri aurati* (knights of the golden spurs) on the very field of battle: they were Francesco and Ettore Visconti, Count Hugh (of Montfort, a German), Filiberto and Febo della Torre (who would only wear a single gold spur), Ugo Guazzalotti, Conrad Prospergh, Count Bolsomino, Fritz, a German, Donino, an Italian, Rapp, a German, Berlinghiero (Beringer?), an Englishman, Count Micatinio, Guernock, an Englishman, and Martin, a German. . . . These particulars of dates and names cannot be imaginary.

Still neither Bracciolini, nor the chronicles of Este, nor those of Gubbio, or Gataro's Paduan ones, nor Corio, nor Ammirati say anything of all this; only Minerbetti remarks that Hawkwood, after having challenged Dal Verme to battle, knighted ten warriors.

Pier Paolo Vergerio, in a letter, written a short while after these events, proposing to relate them in full, merely says that, being attacked in the midst by Conrad Landau, a hundred of Visconti's most imprudent soldiers were slain; that, after two days' fighting, the army of the League having found a ford—difficult indeed but practicable—near a mill *on the lower Oglio* (and therefore not at Rudiano), they prepared to cross.

★★★★★★

It is a great pity that Pier Paolo Vergerio, who left us some particulars of this campaign referring to the uncertain rumours which were being circulated at Padua, did not put into effect the plan of writing a history of it, after finding out the facts from reliable sources. If he sometimes gives way in his letters to the temptation of rhetoric, a moderate judgment, and the analytical spirit, which are the guarantees of truth, are generally to be observed.

★★★★★★

When a part of them had crossed, Visconti's soldiers made their attack, but Hawkwood, always on the alert, had sent forward the archers, and bowmen, with the baggage, and had placed them in a lofty position on the bank, with orders to shoot fiercely at the enemy whenever they came within range; these orders were carried out, and thus a crossing was effected without much harm being done.

There is no doubt, that the Oglio was successfully passed, (July 4); and that Hawkwood must have maintained absolute superiority over Dal Verme in the battles fought with him, seeing that he was able to cross even the Mincio without molestation, and reach Castagnaro and Castelbaldo on the Adige, places where in 1387 he had gained the most brilliant of all his victories, on the borders of the Paduan territory, and thence to the gates of his home. Moreover, d'Armagnac had crossed the Alps and was although somewhat tardily approaching Alexandria. Gian Galeazzo was for this reason compelled to turn his best forces against him, as well as Iacopo dal Verme.

But at the very moment when he was reaching safety, Hawkwood saw himself threatened by a most serious and unexpected danger. He and his whole army were very nearly drowned, for the Visconti's Army had taken the precaution to break the embankments of the Adige, so as to submerge for several miles the plain in which the leagued armies had pitched their camp. It was night time, and the men were resting, and getting ready for their last march.

Being awakened by the noise of the waters, they would probably have been seized by a panic, if Hawkwood had not kept his presence of mind; he immediately made the cavalry mount on horseback, and the foot soldiers climb up behind them, and knowing the ground, and trying to find out the fords by the tops of trees emerging from the water, he lost not a few of his men, but saved the greater part, and succeeded in reaching a point where the water was not deeper than the horses' bellies, and in this manner having advanced ten miles, he reached the banks of the Adige below the rupture, where he did not find it difficult to cross. In this almost miraculous manner, he placed his troops in security at Castelbaldo near Padua, (July 12), and then at Montaguana.

The retreat was accomplished, and to this day it is greatly praised by the historians of the art of war.

Count of Virtù while sending to the Pope the copy of a letter from Iacopo dal Verme, announcing his own signal victory over d'Armagnac, spoke casually of the retreat, in the following words:

> Swift and precipitous flight of Signor Giovanni Acuto, and of the forces of the League from my territory, which was of such a kind, and brought about such a massacre of people and horses, and such a loss of baggage, that it might more fitly be termed a rout than a retreat.

And truly a great part of the infantry and many of the horses were lost; but Vergerio, the Carrara's secretary, judged more accurately that a retreat carried to the end, under the conditions which we have seen, was to be considered as a victory. If the splendour of a battle won on the field were lacking, it is plain that Hawkwood, owing to the great inferiority of his forces, was not in a position to attempt it without risk; on the contrary, we cannot even blame Dal Verme for not having attempted it, although he was much stronger, because he had to re-serve himself for his encounter with d'Armagnac, and content himself with getting Hawkwood's army out of the way.

In conclusion, we have here the strange case of each of the hostile parties contemporaneously attaining their own object:—Dal Verme of causing the retreat; Hawkwood of accomplishing it; and his success deserves more praise, because great difficulties were placed in his way.

And the fact that Hawkwood made twenty cavaliers, from amongst those who had greatly distinguished themselves in this glorious cam-paign, was no vain ostentation.

Hawkwood stopped several days at the court of Francesco Novello, where he was received with the applause due to the captain, who had carried out his part nobly, and had saved the army; and Ugolotto Bian-cardo, who had become captain of Visconti's soldiers on the Adige, although reinforced by Antonio Porro and Balestrazzo, did not even dare to attack the states of the Carrara as long as Hawkwood defended them.

The Florentines, before their captain undertook the expedition to the Adda (as we shall see when the account of the war is finished), besides re-electing him for a year, (May 2), with 220 lances and the same pay, had been munificent in their kindness to him and to his family; he had solemnly promised to fight bravely (like a man); now the Florentines themselves, judging that he had kept his word, discussed about writing him a letter of praise, (July 27), and sending him the 5000 florins he had asked for.

Meanwhile d'Armagnac had been utterly routed and mortally wounded in the predestined plain of Marengo: this fact raised the fortunes of Gian Galeazzo Visconti, and permitted him to make preparations for transporting the war into Tuscany. But only vague rumours of this were heard in Florence, (August 2), as it was there being determined:

> To take care that Hawkwood should be able to keep the field beyond the Po, and at the same time lend a helping hand to d'Armagnac's troops, to warn him not to tempt fortune, but to proceed cautiously and safely moreover to send him reinforcements in case d'Armagnac should be already beaten.

When a true statement of the case was heard, (August 13), they sent him the reinforcements. And a short while after, when they saw that Iacopo dal Verme was passing into Lunigiana, they recalled him in great haste.

Hawkwood set out from Padua (September 12), accompanied as far as the gates by Francesco Novello, who after many embraces took leave of him outside them. Now we shall see him again at arms with Dal Verme, conducting himself with the same prudent firmness in the Val d'Arno which he had displayed in the Valley of the Po.

CHAPTER 37
The War in Tuscany

With 1200 lances and 1000 bowmen, Hawkwood hurried on by forced marches, crossed the Apennines by the hill of Sambuca, and thence he hastened to San Miniato al Tedesco by way of Pistoia. There Count Giovanni da Barbiano joined him with 600 lances and 700 cross-bowmen from Bologna, and then came 1500 lances and 2000 between foot soldiers and archers, who under Luigi da Capua were fighting for the Florentines against Siena and Perugia, the allies of Visconti. Thus, Hawkwood had 3300 lances and 3300 infantry, while Dal Verme reinforced with Sienese and Pisans by the Visconti had 3000 lances, and 5000 infantry; the forces were nearly equal, so it was easy to foresee that neither of the two captains would lightly risk a great battle.

They faced each other, Dal Verme at Cascina, and Hawkwood at Montopoli; the former passed by a march at the flank to Casoli, the latter distributed his men in the strongholds of Poggibonsi, Colle, and Staggia with the understanding that a single march was to bring them all to him, as soon as the enemy appeared.

Dal Verme ventured to the foot of the fortress of Poggibonsi; Hawkwood, who had 1000 lances there, let him pass, only molesting him with skirmishes, without hindering his sacking, and incendiarism, nor the pitching of his camp on the Elsa. Then quickly gathering all his troops in the plain of Poggibonsi, Hawkwood encamped in a strong position three miles in the rear of the enemy.

The Visconti Army raised their camp by night, and the next evening, after a very fatiguing day (being much molested in their march, and that not without loss), they pitched their tents on the confluence of the Elsa and Arno. And Hawkwood, aiming to cover Florence, took an opposite position between Empoli and Montelupo.

Between September 20 and 21, Dal Verme passed the Arno at Fucecchio, crossed the hills of Pietramarina and halted at Poggio a Caiano.

Hawkwood in his turn traversed the Arno at Signa, and rounding the plain placed his camp at Tizzana. It was a game of chess played by two brave champions, but this procrastination served Hawkwood's purpose, as it gave him a better chance of being reinforced. There was naturally great anxiety in Florence, but they knew how to keep down their impatience. Filippo Corsini said in the *Consulte e pratiche*, September 21:

> Let us take measures to save our towns and people. We must press closely on the enemy while reinforcing the camp with foot soldiers, and not oblige the captain to give battle.

And Filippo Cionetti advised:

> Let us make a last effort to reinforce the camp, and end the affair honourably. We should collect all the *distrettuali*, (country militia, called out from all the district of Florence in time of

war), and for this they should send one from each house.

Ranieri di Luigi Peruzzi was of the opinion that:

We should reinforce the camp with citizens, peasants and *distrettuali*, and also exhort Hawkwood by reminding him of his own words, that with 500 lances, 2000 infantry, and 1000 crossbowmen. . . .

Here the document is mutilated, but it certainly means to say that those forces would have sufficed for the undertaking.

During the two succeeding days the Florentines sent no less than 10,000 men to reinforce the camp. They were nearly all peasants, but we shall see them behave like spirited and brave soldiers.

In the night, news was brought to Hawkwood that the enemy was making a move. (September 23 and 24.) He thought their march was directed towards Pistoia, and took up his position accordingly, disposing his men in three battalions in the best order, and under their respective ensigns. Daylight proved that the enemy had taken the road up Monte Albano, to pass into the Val di Nievole; so he immediately detached 1000 lances to follow and attack them in the rear; and sent all his infantry by a side route of mountain paths to get in front of them, while he followed more slowly with the main body of lances and archers, in order of battle: and as he was doubtful of some ambuscade he made the troops keep a vigilant look-out.

Taddeo dal Verme, who commanded the rear-guard of the Visconti army, was obliged to face about and give battle; and in a very short time was routed and defeated: 2000 foot, almost all Sienese and Pisans, remained dead on the field; and 1000 were taken prisoners. Of the men-at-arms about 400 were killed, and 200 taken captive, amongst whom were Taddeo himself, Gentile Varano da Camerino, and Vanni d'Appiano.

Meanwhile the Florentine infantry reached the mass of the Visconti army at the foot of Monte Vettolini, and endeavoured to hinder them by skirmishes, but nightfall overtook them sooner than Hawkwood did;—his troops being very tired, and destitute of provisions and forage.

Dal Verme on the other hand spurred on by danger, after having repulsed a last attack of the too spirited infantry at Pieve a Nievole, hastened through the valley at the foot of Montecarlo, where he arrived four hours after sunset. There he halted a short time, and at midnight again marched on. After refreshing his troops at Lucca, he did not pitch his camp till he could fortify himself in the already strong position of Ripafratta.

As soon as day broke Hawkwood presented himself in order of battle at Montecarlo; he found some lame and hamstrung horses, a great deal of baggage, several *bombarde* and tents, but no enemy! They had to stay two days on the Pescian territory to recover themselves, and when they reached Lucca, they found that the enemy was impregnable at Ripafratta. Then having returned into Val d'Arno, Hawkwood thought to guard against any eventuality by encamping under San Miniato, and in fact Dal Verme re-appeared, and fortified himself at Cascina.

At Florence many fires of rejoicing were lit on the palace of the *Signoria* and all the other prominent places, to celebrate the victory of Tizzana, and a jubilant letter was written to Pope Boniface IX; but as "appetite comes with eating," they now wanted the total destruction of the Visconti Army or nearly so.

They did not reflect that Hawkwood might with reason fear an ambush at Tizzana, and even with his extreme daring irreparably lose the day.

As to Dal Verme, after the experience of his marches and counter-marches following the defeat, he must by this time have been convinced that he could not succeed in getting the upper hand, and still wished to attempt a *coup-de-main* by surprising the town of Santa Maria a Monte. He hoped thus to mislead the adversary, and induce him to withdraw his garrison from that place; October 11, he left Cascina, and moved towards Fabbrica. Hawkwood changed to Castel Florentine, but took care that a good guard should be kept on all points.

October 14, Dal Verme abandoned Fabbrica by a quick march, crossed the Arno, and vigorously attacked Santa Maria where the garrison held firm; the enemy maintained the siege for four hours, but having suffered serious losses without gaining anything, and fearing lest Hawkwood should come on them from the rear, they left their scaling ladders on the walls, and recrossed the Arno in haste, encamping between Cascina and Pisa. Hawkwood had in fact returned to San Miniato.

The chronicle of Gubbio says that Hawkwood had treated with the Bretons who were in Visconti's army, and agreed on a betrayal, that this treaty was discovered, and all the Bretons put to death; but when we remember that the chronicler estimates the Bretons at five thousand, it is time to ask whether Dal Verme had enough faithful soldiers to kill the traitors!

Dal Verme, it is true, could do very little good, and the autumn being now far advanced, he retreated into Liguria; while Sir John Hawkwood took up his quarters in the fortress of Val di Nievole.

Hostilities however did not entirely cease: for not being able to do anything better, Gian Galeazzo Visconti tried to interrupt and injure the Florentine commerce, knowing that would strike them on their most vulnerable part. This he did by means of the Genoese galleys, which cruised before Leghorn and the port of Pisa; and as the Florentines opposed to them, with good success, the galleys of a certain Gargiolli, a Florentine pirate, he by favour of the Pisans and Iacopo d' Appiano was allowed to place his troops in the valley of Calci, in Monte Pisano, whence he could easily intercept the road through Val d' Arno between Florence and the sea.

It was therefore Hawkwood's business to guard the road and protect the merchants, and in fact as a large convoy of five hundred packhorses laden with grain and other merchandise was to go from Pisa to Florence (December 16), John Beltoft was sent to escort it with two hundred lances and five hundred foot soldiers, together with Hugh Montfort and about a hundred horsemen.

The convoy and its escort followed the road which to this day, (1880), runs along the left of the Arno; the river was very full, however Iacopo d'Appiano informed the Visconti's Army, which was ensconced beyond, of all that was going on, and indicated to them a ford which though difficult was quite practicable.

The convoy having nearly reached the country-town of Cascina, lo! two thousand of Visconti's cavalry plunged in the stream, and swimming across with great difficulty threatened an attack; and behold! Beltoft without waiting for them, shamefully took to flight with his two hundred English lances, leaving the convoy, infantry and Count Hugh's hundred, horsemen in the clutches of the enemy! Montfort opposed a desperate resistance, but was at last taken and his soldiers nearly all killed or captured. Some five hundred loads, and two hundred mules were lost, worth altogether 15,000 florins.

This event was very displeasing to Florence, especially because the Sienese and Pisans rejoiced over it. The brave Count Hugh was ransomed by the Florentines, and received with great honours on his return, while Beltoft, blamed and driven away by them, passed into the service of the Pope, and soon after, being taken by the Orsini, he was beheaded.

Hawkwood too had his share of responsibility in the affair, either for not caring to inform himself of the forces of the Viscontese, or for having sent an insufficient escort. It seems he excused himself to the *Signoria* by letter, and proposed to vindicate that injury by attacking the Viscontese.

December 18, in the *Consulte* Filippo Corsini proposed:

> Let us reprove Hawkwood for the error he has committed, but incite him to the enterprise of which he has written, which will recuperate both his honour and that of the Commune; reinforcing him as well as we can. Let him encamp near Cascina.

But Donate Acciaioli more calmly counselled:

> Let us incite and even commend Hawkwood for what he has written, but moderate him, so that he proceed with caution and prudence, not to put the State of the Commune in peril.

A general peace was soon after concluded at Genoa, (January 20, 1392), and solemnised in Florence, (February 18), with fires of joy and illuminations, with a *Mass for peace* in Santa Maria del Fiore (the Duomo), and notice was given of a great tournament which was to come off on the calends of May.

The captains of war gave up their ensigns, and measures were taken to relieve the Florentine tax payers, now almost exhausted by the heavy weight of the 2400 lances and the 3500 infantry then in their pay. By compositions according to the time for which they were hired, the lances were reduced to less than 1000, and the infantry to about the same number. (End of February.)

However, before Hawkwood could take his final rest, he had still to make a last expedition.

The peace left many adventurers unoccupied, and they immediately gave themselves up to brigandage. March, Azzo da Castello had already formed the nucleus of a company on the territory of Urbino. Broglia, Brandolini, Biordo dei Michelotti, and a great many others being dismissed by Gian Galeazzo, wished to join Azzo as he passed by Bologna from Lombardy, and they commenced their march in that direction. The Bolognese demanded help from the Florentines, who soon sent 500 lances under Hawkwood and Count Hugh. April, the adventurers took the road by Sarzana and the Maremma, but they hurried so much for fear Hawkwood should overtake them, that they left a great number of their horses by the way.

Thus, the military fatigues of Sir John Hawkwood ended with a modest expedition on behalf of public security, and he retired to quiet life in Florence.

CHAPTER 38

Marriages of Janet and Catherine Hawkwood

We have said that Florence showered signal favours on Hawkwood during the campaign.

Before undertaking the dangerous expedition from Padua towards the Adda, he, with due reflection on his advanced age, obtained from the Florentines a certain and sufficient provision for the latter years of his life, together with ample wedding portions for his daughters, and a pension to his wife after his death.

These facts result from the *Capitoli* (pacts or conventions made between two States or two belligerent armies; the word is also used for Statutes of Companies or Confraternities), agreed between Giacomo di Borgo della Collina. Hawkwood's procurator, and the Signoria of Florence, (April 8, 1391), of which the following is a summary:

> The 'Ten of *balia*,' considering the great war of Florence and her allies against Gian Galeazzo and the Sienese, and judging that the worthy and in deeds of arms most approved and valorous knight John Hawkwood, who has fought for a long time with extreme probity, prudence and good fortune, and has long been a devoted friend to the Commune of Florence, whose wars he has faithfully conducted—recognising also the offers made on his part in negotiating for the said war against the enemies of the Commune, and chiefly considering his brave deeds in the said war, and above all diligently taking heed to the felicity and prudence with which for so long he has kept, con-ducted, and governed the men-at-arms, and to what happy and prosperous results all the warlike affairs have proceeded under his hands—and though he be already remunerated as captain of war, they (The Ten) recognise the expediency of encouraging him still more with the under mentioned benefits, pensions, favours and privileges.
>
> That prudent man Giacomo di Piero di Borgo della Collina, having entered the presence of the 'Ten' to say in the name and stead of Sir John Hawkwood, that the said Sir John always intends to be a devoted friend of the Commune, and that in

the said war, as he has done before, he will give himself in the best manner for the defence of the Commune, and the offence of her enemies, overriding in a hostile manner the territories of the Conte di Virtù, and manfully combating against him and his adherents.

Having taken the votes of the *Signoria*, the *Gonfalonieri* and the twelve *Buonornini*, they deliberate:

That Hawkwood together with his wife and family shall be received as a perpetual friend of the Commune, and deputed its captain of war;

That besides the pension of 1200 gold florins conceded since 1375, he shall, during his life, receive a new annual pension of 2000 gold florins, without any deduction, and the first year of this new annuity shall begin with May 1st 1392;

That the annuity shall be paid every three months, without the necessity of ulterior formalities;

That to the first three daughters, whom Sir John at present acknowledges, and whose names are given below, shall be given as portions, when they marry, or shall be of a marriageable age (*i.e.* at least 14 years old), 6000 florins of gold—that is to say 2000 for each;—the chamberlains shall pay these portions to their respective husbands, or their procurators, on presentation of the matrimonial contract, and providing it be made with the consent of Sir John, if he be alive, or his procurator;

And as it is asserted that one of the said daughters, that is to say Janet, has at present completed the age of 14 years, from this time hence, whenever it shall please her father that her marriage shall be contracted, the payment of the portion shall be immediately made.—Janet is the first of the daughters, Catherine the second, Anna the third;

Moreover after the death of the said Sir John—which God grant may be a peaceful and happy one after a long life, and meanwhile may he give him good fortune, and direct his steps happily—that the noble Lady Donnina, wife of Sir John as long as she is a widow, and remains in the city, country or district of Florence, with the son or daughters of herself, and the said Sir John, shall have every year of her widowhood the pension and gift of 1000 gold florins, in honour of the memory of that noble and brave man her husband;

Whenever however she lives away from her son or daughters,

or out of the city and county, the pension shall be deducted *pro rata* of the time;

And that the said Sir John, with his sons and descendants in the male line, born, or yet to be born, shall enjoy the privilege of Florentine citizenship, and shall only be excluded from the power and ability of holding office in the commune or city.

The war ended, these *Capitoli* were accepted, (March 14), and ratified by Hawkwood in a public deed.

Then he gave his attention to marrying his daughters honourably; Janet was fifteen years of age, and Catherine scarcely fourteen.

He found a husband for the eldest in the very noble family of the Counts of Porcia in Friuli. This was the young Brezaglia son of Count Lodovico, formerly *proetor* and captain of the people at Bologna, next *podestà* of Ferrara, (1391) and then captain of the people at Florence. (1393.)

★★★★★★

In the Italian republics the offices of *podestà* (civil governor) and captain of the people were always held by strangers from other cities who had no kinship with the city they ruled—the offices were held yearly.

★★★★★★

The marriage was celebrated (September 7, 1392), by the following deed drawn up by Ser Giovanni di Simone:

Performed in the house inhabited by sir John Hawkwood (Sig. Giovanni Haucut) situated in the district of Florence in the *popolo* (parish) of San Donate a Torre, the witnesses present being the noble gentlemen Guido son of the late signor Tomaso knight, Andrea di Neri Capponi, and Ser Benedetto di Ser Lando notary of Florence, together with the citizens and others especially bidden and invited.

The noble gentleman Brezaglia son of the magnificent lord signor Lodovico Count de' Puziliis (of Porciglia or Porcia) on the one part; and the noble lady Janet—daughter of the magnificent and potent knight Sir John Hawkwood of England—Florentine citizeness, on the other; who with the consent of the said Sir John her father, here present, consents to be the said wife.

The required questions and answers by word of mouth (*verba de presenti*) having been spoken, and the ring given and received,

legal matrimony is contracted between them. The said Brezaglia with the said lady Janet as his spouse and legitimate wife,
and the said lady Janet consenting to take the said Brezaglia as
her husband and legitimate spouse.

The receipt for the 2000 florins, which was paid by Hawkwood
as Janet's wedding portion, was given in a deed drawn up, (November 19), by Ser Lorenzo, the procurator of the Porcias, (*i.e.* Count
Lodovico, with Iacopo and Brezaglia, his sons).

A note of this is also to be found in the books of "customs on contracts" for the taxes which we should call "registration fees."

For his second daughter Catherine, Hawkwood chose a man of his
own profession, the German Conrad Prospergh, a brave young soldier
of fortune. The documents do not prove him to have been of noble
family, although some chroniclers call him Count. Florence had hired
him for the League with two hundred lances, (1391), and Hawkwood
himself had given him his spurs, during the retreat on the Oglio the
year before.

While Hawkwood was campaigning in Tuscany, (December), Prospergh being detained in the pay of Bologna, commanded six hundred
lances on the territory of Reggio, and showed himself a good disciple
of his future father-in-law; for he was able to draw the Visconti into an
ambuscade, and to capture sixty men-at-arms, a hundred *saccomanni*,
and two hundred horses.

When the war was over, a tournament was held on the public
square of Bologna, on February 28th 1392, to enliven the citizens and
soldiers.

After dinner in the presence of all the people, *the famous captain*
Conrad Prospergh appeared with a band of thirty-four Italian
soldiers, equipped in white armour with his grand white ensigns. The opposite band was of thirty-three German horsemen
with red doublets, who were commanded by Prendiparte della
Mirandola. They tourneyed worthily with lance and sword. The
senate distributed money to the soldiers, and a cap entirely covered with the finest pearls to each of the captains.

And in Piazza Santa Croce at Florence, (May 12), when a tournament to celebrate the peace was held in May, Prospergh again won
the highest honours. Eighty knights divided into two brigades, were
armed for the joust; the red commanded by Prospergh, the white by
Count Antonio Guidi. The victor in each brigade was to receive as

a prize a little lion covered with pearls: Conrad Prospergh won the prize for the "red" side.

We may suppose that Hawkwood and his ladies assisted at this tournament, and a romancer might without too much boldness imagine that the young Catherine's heart palpitated in sympathy for the victorious knight.

The fact remains that, by a legal document, (November 5), Hawkwood promised Catherine in marriage to Conrad Prospergh, German knight and captain, and to assign her such a portion and in the manner, which shall be determined by the arbiters, which are the Signoria of Florence, and that of Bologna.

The intervention of these sovereign arbiters is a proof of the high consideration in which Hawkwood was held, and of the great honour shown him in the marriage of his daughter. The rank of the witnesses contributed not a little to this, one was Milano de' Rastrelli of Asti, formerly a Florentine stipendiary in 1376, then marshal, and who in due time was honourably interred in Santa Croce, in the south aisle of which might once have been seen his banners, targets, shields, his tunic with his emblematical arms, and a memorial tablet with some funereal verses.

★★★★★★

We take these particulars from the monograph by D. Maria Manni. The numerous ensigns and memorials of the soldiers of the Commune in ancient times were removed from Santa Croce in our days.

★★★★★★

The second was also a marshal, named Bartolomeo dei Gherardacci di Geri of Prato, surnamed Boccanera (black mouth), formerly exiled, and then in 1382 pardoned by the Florentines, after which he became their captain-general; the third was no less a personage than Messer Ugolino de' Preti da Montechiaro of Bologna, at that time captain of the people in Florence.

The marriage was celebrated some weeks after the betrothal; in fact a public act signed at Hawkwood's residence at San Donato in Polverosa, January 20, 1393, (witnesses amongst others Ser Francesco da Milano, Hawkwood's chancellor, and Ermanno of Acqui his usher) declares that Hawkwood had on that day married his daughter to Conrad Prospergh; who on his side acknowledged the receipt of the wedding portion of 2000 florins disbursed for Hawkwood by the chamberlains of the Commune. The chamberlains on behalf of the bride Catherine, acknowledged the receipt from Prospergh of 50 *lire* of *Morgengab*, (a present from the bridegroom to the bride the morning after the wedding) according to the custom of German weddings. The civil laws were less strict and more easily satisfied in those days.

Nor is the relative note lacking in the book of "customs on contracts." An entry under the date of *Duomo 1392* (by the Florentine style the year 1392 ended on March 24th 1393) is thus worded:

> To the noble and worthy soldier Conrad Prospero German, captain and stipendiary of the Commune of Bologna, 2000 florins for the *dote* of the generous lady Catherine— daughter of the magnificent and potent knight Sir John Hawkwood, captain-general of the Commune of Florence—and now wife of the said *signer* Conrad.

Hawkwood however did not intend to expend his own wealth in marrying his daughters. He might perhaps have provided the necessary *trousseau*, but gorgeous dresses and other accessories to celebrate the wedding festivities were considered by him as superfluous. The mother had to provide them, and she was obliged to turn to her son-in-law. Strange as it may appear, we have a proof of it in the following letter of the bridegroom Prospergh to Donato Acciaioli.

> Magnificent and powerful cavalier, with due recommendations I pray you for the love of myself and the good fame of Sir John Hawkwood that you will use your influence with the honourable Signoria of Florence that I may have 1000 florins which are owing of my pension, either in money or in note of hand, that Madonna Donnina may dress my wife for the wedding on the 24th of this month. Madonna Donnina writes that nothing is wanting except the money to dress her. I have ordered them to make great *fêtes*, but they have put off so long the purchase of gowns for the maiden, who from what Madonna Donnina writes is more to you than your own child, and she tells me that for her there is no one like you, for she owes you more than her own father. I am always prepared to obey your every command.
>
> Bologna, January 9th.   Conrad de Prospergh
>   knight and captain."

★★★★★★

Donato Acciaioli, one of the most illustrious Florentines of his age (he translated Leonardo Bruni's history of Florence from the Latin, held high magisterial offices, and fulfilled important embassies), was on good terms with several of the English knights and especially with Sir John Hawkwood.

Manni (1770) speaks of several letters from Hawkwood to Acciaioli preserved in the Archives of the Certosa (near Florence—and founded, as all know, by the Acciaioli). At the time of the French suppression the Archives of the Certosa passed to the State, and in 1853 to the State Archives of Florence. The indices of these Archives register some letters and other Acciaioli papers; but posterior annotations say "missing" or "other things." There are also two imposing parchment envelopes with the words: *Letters addressed to the magnificent knight Donato Acciaioli,* in a fine border in the style of the 16th century, illuminated in colours on the back. One contains some insignificant monastic papers of the 17th and 18th centuries; the other is connected with the Acciaioli, but contains only certain accounts relative to the feuds in the Neapolitan states; the rest of the papers being copies of papal bulls, privileges, etc., entirely extraneous to the Acciaioli.

The letters were therefore abstracted, before the Certosa documents were transferred to the State Archives, and it is very likely that they ended in the celebrated collection of *Sig. Libri,* and then in the not less celebrated Ashburnham collection, of which the greater part of the Italian element returned to Italy on their purchase by the government, and was deposited in the Laurentian Library. Here there really exist fifteen large envelopes containing papers and letters of the Acciaioli; on one of the envelopes is written on the front and back with pencil the indication "Sir John Hawkwood" and on the other envelopes is marked "Letters and papers concerning Giovanni Acuto—relating to G. Acuto" extracted in the date 1878-74 etc.

Had there been perhaps a special pile formed of all that related to our *condottiere?* We cannot assert this, none of the fifteen envelopes contain the letters, seen by Manni himself; but we have found, instead, some documents relative to him, and a note from the Englishman John Beltoft, which recommends his comrade John Liverpool to Donato Acciaioli. Therefore, without absolutely excluding the hypothesis that the Ashburnham collection has been sifted on behalf of English libraries or archives, and Hawkwood's letters kept in England, we may with more probability hold that Manni was mistaken about the above-mentioned papers "relative to Acuto."

★★★★★★

This document in good truth makes us doubt whether Hawkwood, now an aged man, had not given way to the sordid passion of avarice, which when it becomes habitual is often apt to increase in the old age of men who have gained and accumulated much in life. On the other hand, we know that if Hawkwood had gained much, he had saved little, for his patrimonial condition is noted and documented. Facts are not wanting to prove that he knew how to be liberal with his money; Cavalcanti recounts that in one of the frequent occasions in which Hawkwood had to treat with Spinello Alberti, when the compact was concluded he made a present of 6000 florins to Spinello, who religiously passed it into the treasury of the Commune; but even if we choose to imagine the anecdote inexact, and that the 6000 florins had been saved by the ability of Alberti in making negotiations, there is nothing in the life of Hawkwood which authorises us to see in him the avarice of a Harpagon.

★★★★★★

It is certain that the honesty of the treasurer Alberti was exemplary: in the *Chronicle* of Giovanni Morelli we read: "He was loyal and faithful to our Commune, and after his death his portrait was placed in the Chamber of the Commune to do him honour. He died so poor that his family could not give him the honourable funeral that he well deserved."

★★★★★★

Prospergh's letter might rather contribute to prove that which we have already seen, and shall find Hawkwood himself asserting, that his financial position was not at all a brilliant one.

CHAPTER 39

Monument to the Living Hawkwood

1393, the old *condottiere* was now drawing near the end of his life, and the Florentines, though they could not expect any more signal services from him, were yet generous in shewing him honour and conferring favours.

Let a proper provision be made to reward Hawkwood's services, in a manner which will display the gratitude we owe him; we will give him 25 lances, and observe all the compacts stipulated with him; and let the *Signoria* make this provision as soon as possible, (March.)

In fact, he was immediately hired, (April 2), with twenty-five lances including archers.

There was a general feeling, that not only ought all the agreements made with him, (April 6), to be observed, but that it would be right to procure him some prerogative besides.

Meanwhile he gave his attention to regulating the affairs of his patrimony in the best manner, as one who feels death approaching is anxious to leave his family without embarrassments. He had a settling of accounts, (June 2), with his former secretary Ser Francesco da Milano, and on the same day, at San Donate in Polverosa, his wife Donnina Visconti with her husband's order and consent signed an act of notary nominating Donna Agatina, daughter of Messer Cuccolo da Giussano, as the agent for her affairs at Milan; a choice which Hawkwood ratified in his own name.

These interests at Milan—whether referring to her marriage portion, or hereditary or other possessions—must have been very unsafe under Gian Galeazzo Visconti. Hawkwood also gave a power of attorney to Antonio di Porcaria, (December 2), to receive certain sums not yet paid him by the Commune of Bologna. Nor were property taxes and financial difficulties lacking to Hawkwood in Florence.

He represents to the Priors, (July 11), that on the 10th of September 1392 the extraordinary accountants of the Commune had declared him to be debtor to the Commune for the sum of 1834 florins, on the original sum of 3000, of which he had paid the rest with the money received during his stay in the Kingdom of Naples, and they had intimated to him that:

> The 1834 florins must be paid within three months and fifteen days under penalty of a quarter of the sum in addition.

He added that he had not been able to pay, because the Commune had not disbursed to him the annuity of 2000 gold florins. He therefore asked that the debt against him should be annulled, that the cancelling thereof should be free of charge. He also explained that he had in pledge at Venice and Bologna some worked silver and jewels of no slight value, for which he paid very heavy usury, but from want of money was unable to redeem them; that considering the innumerable daily expenses his income was not sufficient for the support of his family. He was therefore obliged to sell his property, and having no bail for the sales he prayed that Guide Lippi, Davanzato Davanzati, Andrea Vettori, Niccolo da Uzzano and Ser Benedetto di Lando might be made syndics for the purpose.

We remember that in 1387 Hawkwood had made an analogous request to the Commune, but he could not in the meantime have effectuated any sale in Tuscany, as the description of the property alleged in this petition of 1393 is identical with that of 1387, the only difference in the more recent catalogue being that some of these possessions are placed in the name of John, son of Hawkwood, or in that of Donnina his wife.

★★★★★★

Neither is there in this second appeal any sign that Hawkwood possessed any house or habitation within the walls of Florence, and this is confirmed by what Giovanni Cavalcanti says: "This esteemed man stayed in Santo Antonio inside the Porta di Faenza." That is to say that when he visited the city from his suburban residence of San Donate, he lodged at Sant'Antonio, which was a vast convent, belonging to the regular *"canons hospitaller"* of Sant'Antonio of Vienne in France. The prior of Sant'Antonio had the title of *commendatore*.; the fraternity possessed a large block of houses with gardens and fields and every convenience just within the Faenza gate.

Both church and house were magnificent and noble buildings: among others Buffalmacco and Lippi painted frescoes in them. A bull of Calixtus III (1455) distinguished the monastery, the hospital, the mansion and the annexes. We understand then that it served as a free hospital for the poor, and as an hostelry for those who were able to give alms as an equivalent. The Commune of Florence had taken Sant'Antonio under its protection; Cardinal Giovanni de' Medici, afterwards Leo X, was its *commendatore*. But it was completely destroyed in 1534 by Duke Alessandro to build there that fortress *da basso* which still (1880), remains as a monument of Medicean tyranny.

★★★★★★

It is not strange that the alienation should be difficult, if we reflect that the continuous and costly wars had impoverished the citizens, either on account of the imposts or the suspension of commercial transactions.

From these documents it would appear that at the end of a career, apparently lucrative, Hawkwood had only a limited and compromised patrimony: that Tuscany and Italy had given him means to live in good style with his numerous family and to marry his daughters well, but his military habits had not allowed him to save much capital. Or he might also have sent some of his savings to invest in his own country.

However this may be, the Florentines, before he died, displayed an affection, gratitude and honour, so solemn and extraordinary, that the most sordid of mercenaries must have been touched;—how much more then must it have been appreciated by him, who, on the scales of conscience, had always given good weight of fidelity and honour compatible with his calling.

In the Council of the *Podestà* and Commune, (August 22), the following deliberation was carried by a majority of 177 votes, against a minority of 8—almost unanimously in fact:

The magnificent and potent Lords, the Signori Priors of the Arts, and *Gonfaloniere* of justice of the people and Commune of Florence, being desirous that the magnificent and faithful achievements of the here-written Sir John, his fidelity to the honour and grandeur of the Florentine Republic, should not only be rewarded by remuneration during his life, as was done in his pension, but perpetually shown to his glory after death; and above all that brave men may know that the Commune of Florence recompenses true service with her recognition and beneficent gratitude. . . . deliberate that the members of the *Opera* (Board of works) of Santa Reparata, *i.e.* the greatest of the Florentine churches—or even two parts of them if the other should be absent, or not forthcoming, or dissentient, or unwilling— shall as soon as possible, beginning at the coming year, cause to be constructed and made in the said church, and in a conspicuous place, high and honourable, as shall appear best to them, a worthy and handsome tomb for the ashes of the great and brave knight Sir John Hawkwood, English captain-general of war to the said Commune, and who has more than once in the wars of the said Commune been captain-general. And the said sepulchre, in which the body of the said Sir John and no other body may be placed, shall be adorned with such stone and marble figures and armorial ensigns as shall seem convenient, either to the magnificence of the Commune of Florence, or to the honour and lasting fame of the said Sir John. And they may and ought to spend. . . . as much, how and whensoever they will.

Here Gregorovius exclaims with indignation, that "Florence who denied Dante a resting place, should erect an honourable monument in her Duomo to that robber of a Hawkwood!"

But though this action may at first sight seem monstrous, there is nothing in it which should excite our wonder. The exiled Alighieri was not to his fellow-citizens and contemporaries that Dante who in years to come was to subdue the universe by admiration of his "divine Comedy;" he was a man of great genius, much culture, bold character and above all a man who, implicated in the political contests of his Commune, was left among the vanquished and exiled ones, who in exile continued to agitate for the restoration of the *ghibellines* in his city where the great majority were *guelphs*.

As to Hawkwood, we may judge his trade of a mercenary to be dishonest, but in those times, it was a necessity created by circumstances: the Italian states were not accustomed to provide for their political needs by any other means. Hawkwood had several times efficaciously defended the Florentine Republic against external enemies, and more than once had he secured internal order; he had done his duty almost conscientiously, and certainly to the satisfaction of the Florentines who hired him. It would be an exaggeration to say that the Florentines considered him as a patriotic hero, but it would be unjust to pretend that they ought to consider him as a brigand.

It is also certain that sensible people knew how much better it would be for the Italian princes and communes not to be subjected to the forced services of *condottieri*. Franco Sacchetti thus concludes his 181st Novella, which we have already referred to, and which speaks of Hawkwood by name:

> Woe to those men and people who trust too much in men of this kind. In them there is neither love nor faith. They often do more harm to those who pay them, than to their adversaries' soldiers; and this because, although they make a show of wishing to fight and combat one against the other, they love each other, better than they like the people who hire them, and they seem to say: You rob on that side, I will rob well on this.

But this same Sacchetti, in his 36th Novella, must needs ridicule the stupidity of the Priors of Florence in the war of 1363, when Hawkwood fought for the Pisans, recognising that:

> Those who are used to commerce can never know what war is, and therefore the Communes who do not live in peace are

undone.

Now, municipalities did not know how to keep the peace, and being composed of merchants knew not how to make war; they were therefore constrained to submit to the mercenary and untrustworthy arms of adventurers.

Hawkwood's general reputation as captain of war in Italy is easily gathered from the exaggerations of chroniclers and contemporaneous rhetoricians. The *Chronicles of Treviso* say that:

Hawkwood had fought in Italy twenty-three times in regular battles as a leader of men-at-arms, and had always been victor except once when he was vanquished.

Vergerio proclaims him "a man of generous spirit and long experience," and does not hesitate to compare him "for valour and glory almost equal to the ancient Imperators."

CHAPTER 40
The Castle of Montecchio

It is for a curious reason that Pier Paolo Vergerio hesitates to rank John Hawkwood *quite*, on an equality with the great captains of classical antiquity. Being, as all the humanists were, a fanatic on the subject of Latin, he cannot forgive Hawkwood's being born elsewhere than in Italy.

However he adds:

From all that is indicated in his actions and customs, he has no longer a remnant of foreign blood, for after having exhausted it in many wars, he has become regenerated more strong and more sound in fibre, and has reconstituted a new body under the more genial skies of Italy.

In writing thus, Vergerio yields a little to the love of ingenious conceits and graceful phraseology, but he doubtless writes on a foundation of truthful observation. Being Carrara's secretary, he had occasion to be near Hawkwood during the winter of 1391, and after the campaign of that year: and we need not marvel that the Englishman, after thirty years unbroken residence in Italy, and after having founded a family and established his personal interests there, should appear almost more Italian than English.

For the rest, the mild climate of Italy could not render him immortal, neither could his interests, kinships and Italian habits cause

THE CASTLE OF MONTECCHIO–VESPONI

him to entirely forget his native country.

In 1394 Hawkwood must have been nearly an octogenarian, and one might say he had lived in continual wars.

Now he only thought of providing for his children, and arranging his affairs, so that he could return to England and finish his days in peace there.

He augmented his daughter Janet's wedding portion, (February 7), and in case of restitution, (when the wife dies without children, the wedding portion is returned to her family), her father-in-law Lodovico Porcia promised to renounce the "*benefizio del foro*" as had been agreed. The augmentation was of 1000 florins. (This appears in a marginal reference to a note relative to the *dote* in the *Books of Customs on contracts, Duomo*.)

To return home it was necessary to liquidate his landed property in Italy: from documents which we shall see later it would appear that he himself effected the sale of the suburban possessions at Florence and near Poggibonsi, which had been projected from the year 1387, perhaps reserving his house at San Donate in Polverosa during the remainder of his stay.

But besides these he possessed a group of buildings which formed a little *military dominion* in the territory of Arezzo, *i.e.,* the castle of Montecchio, the strongholds of Badia al Pino and those of Migliari. These small forts could not have been very important, they were simple bastions or temporary fortifications, constructed by Hawkwood, or which he had used in his frequent sojourns with his brigade between Arezzo and Cortona, or in his campaigns against the Sienese. They might also have served for outposts, for the better security of Montecchio towards the territory of Siena. There are no existing remains of fortifications either at Migliari or at Pino, and we only have these slight mentions of the places; that Migliari in Val d'Ambra was a village dependent on the neighbouring Abbey of Agnano till 1384, in which year the Abbey (under the date of May 9th) placed itself under the Florentine Republic which soon after become master of Arezzo.

The Abbey of Pino was a more important possession. In the 10th century it was a dependency of the Abbot of Santa Fiora, was raised to a *Commenda* (land belonging to the Church, the income of which was given to a priest or a knight), in the 15th century; after that it passed to the nuns of St. Bridget (1734), in the Pian di Ripoli and finally to the Florentine hospital of Bonifazio.

We have already seen that Hawkwood, on returning from the

Kingdom of Naples (1384), into central Italy, and fighting against Siena, had taken "certain places," regarding which he had made some proposals to the Florentines which they at the time excused themselves from answering.

It is very likely he had proposed to sell them, and that the places treated of were Migliari, del Pino, and Montecchio. The latter is in our own days a most remarkable and well-preserved monument of ancient fortification, and as Hawkwood liked to stay there, as we see in Franco Sacchetti's 181st Novella, it merits a short description.

The castle of Montecchio-Vesponi rises above a hill on the northern boundary of the Val di Chiana, between the town of Castiglion Fiorentino and the city of Cortona.

★★★★★★

The traveller who goes by rail from Florence towards Perugia and Rome cannot fail to see, on his left hand, between the stations of Castiglion Fiorentino and Cortona, the beautiful view of Montecchio with its picturesque battlemented towers

★★★★★★

It was already existing in the beginning of the 11th century, and during the 13th was enlarged, so that the "ancient" and "modern" parts were distinguishable one from the other, and it enclosed within its walls as many as fifty six habitations which were rented by tenants, the little church of San Biagio and a communal palace with the relative courts; it had, in its dependencies, moats and *carbonaie* (dry ditches), suburbs and outskirts, fields and woods, land and vines, and belonged to the Commune of Arezzo. Towards the middle of the 14th century it was, like Castiglione, held by the Perugians, and it is probable that having been damaged in the preceding wars, it was at that time, (1351), transformed and fortified so as to take the distinct character of a fortress which it still preserves, for it sustained a long siege by the Tarlati of Arezzo, the Casali of Cortona, and the troops of archbishop Visconti, after which it returned into the power of Arezzo.

Pignotti evidently errs when he states that the Florentines became masters of it in 1360 and confided the government to Hawkwood—who had not then crossed the Alps. We are on the contrary confirmed in the opinion that Hawkwood assumed the lordship on his own account, (1384), and with the consent of the Florentines, for the *Signoria* commanded the Podesta of Castiglione (1387) to allow three mule loads of armour and implements which Hawkwood intended to send to Montecchio to pass without toll. And when Florence, after Hawkwood's renunciation, (May, 1394), obtained possession of Montecchio, she absolved this Commune from the customs, taxes and fees which it should have paid to Arezzo, as well as from all denunciations, condemnations and reprisals before the month of December 1384.

From the *Capitoli* relating to it we also find that Hawkwood, as lord of Montecchio, received the introits of customs, imposts, contracts, duties, loans, taxes, and a nominal toll, which was however rather important, on cattle and sheep, for the receipts of three years were destined to make a moat and other enclosures in the neighbourhood of Arezzo; that the keep of Montecchio was kept well supplied with ammunition and provisions: that a syndic presided over the Commune and that the inhabitants made regular provision of salt and wine, and possessed large and small cattle of their own, and a *soccida* (contract for hiring out cattle on a similar principle to that adopted by our dairymen on English farms), with the people of Cortona.

Whether Hawkwood in the ten years of his dominion worked at the restoration and modification of the walls, towers and keep of Montecchio is not proved; in any case the fortress preserved a certain military importance almost to the end of the 17th century. At that time, owing to the changed conditions of strategy, it became too antiquated and useless to form a good weapon of war; so, the keep with its lofty tower, which some years before had been esteemed at 500 *lire*, was sold for 100 *lire* to a sergeant named Orazio Nocci. (1623.)

In 1641 Montecchio was raised to a marquisate by the Grand Duke Ferdinand II in favor of Tommaso Capponi; but his son the Marquis Lorenzo dying without offspring, Montecchio reverted to the State, and in the succession of governments in Tuscany it remained the property of the Crown until in our days it was purchased by the noted financier Giacomo Servadio together with vast *demesnial* estates in the neighbouring hills, and in the plain below, and it now belongs to his heirs.

A description written in 1575 mentions that the tower had several stories with vaulted ceilings and a good roof; it contained a dove-cot, and a bell; that it was a square tower, the sides of which were eight *braccia* (the *braccio* is about 23 inches) wide, and the height fifty *braccia*; it was well preserved, and in good condition. The keep, which was joined to the tower on one side, measured on the other sides, respectively twelve, twenty, and twenty-five *braccia*; the rooms which first existed there had been already demolished. The moats outside the walls surrounded the castle on all sides except the west, where the gate was situated. They were fifty *braccia* wide and occupied a superficies of twenty thousand square *braccia*.

Another description dates from 1640 and gives a circumference of four hundred and fifty *braccia* to the external walls and a diameter across of a hundred and forty-seven *braccia*. The fortress contained nineteen *fuochi* (hearths or family dwellings) and fifty-three souls, the greater part under the cure of a vicar—all being peasants except the sergeant Nocci who lived on a private income at the tower. The people went to work in the fields lying below, and exercised no industry, excepting that the women spun wool and flax; three of the inhabitants were inscribed in the infantry militia, but were more adapted to peace than to arms.

Inside the circuit were two churches, the *pieve* (vicarage) of San Biagio, and the "company" of the Holy Sacrament. For the rest there was much poverty, good air, abundant hunting and fishing in the plain.

> As to the habitations inside the fortress they are almost all huts, low, dark, and very ill kept, and in many places, they are in ruins. There is a small house for the officials, which serves also as a council chamber, and is very bad.

On this picture if we allow for the wear and tear of the elements, and the permanent neglect of men, for another two centuries, we may have an idea of what Montecchio has become in our day. Its last proprietor restored the great tower which had been split by a thunderbolt, and replaced the Ghibelline battlements of the boundary walls and seven towers which rise from them; thus from without, the fortress even now presents an imposing aspect, both military and picturesque, high on that hill covered with olives and pines, and thick underwood, in which the wild pomegranate predominates. But the moat is filled up, and within the enclosure the aspect of poverty disputes the space with the ruins. No more over the arched gateway are seen the figures of the protecting saints of Montecchio, St. Biagio, Martin and Egidio; they have completely disappeared.

The parish church, which served also as a cemetery, has been dismantled; nothing remains of the keep but its walls, and we can hardly find a trace of the projecting gallery with its *piombatoi* which anciently defended the gates.

★★★★★★

Piombatoi were a species of loop-holes made in the floor of a projecting gallery in the battlements of an ancient fortress for the purpose of throwing down stones or heavy missiles on the assailants.

★★★★★★

By a broken stairway we may with difficulty ascend to the only part of this gallery which remains on the boundary wall, towards the west, in which loop-holes had been pierced at the epoch when fire arms were first used. A very good wooden staircase entirely modern conducts us to the platform of the tower, from which the view is magnificent. It overlooks the Val di Chiana as far as Monte Amiata, across a branch of Lake Thrasymene, and the picturesque country town of Castiglione Florentine, but the bell no longer disturbs the rest of the pigeons, falcons and swallows whose abode it is.

The few poor houses surrounding it are as miserable as possible; only two human families reside there, with some fowls and a donkey, who may chose his meals among the chestnut burrs, acorns, poppies and nettles in the shadow of the wild *ailanthus*. Some vines, figs, and olive trees seem to vegetate there only to emphasize, by reminding one of fruitful culture, the almost sepulchral loneliness of that place, where, between one campaign and another, the old English *condottiere* repaired for brief repose and to refurbish his arms, and where charity was denied to the monks who dared to ask it in the name of peace.

CHAPTER 41

Death and Funeral Obsequies

The Commune of Florence had favourably received the proposal of Hawkwood as to the alienation of Montecchio, and of his other fortresses in the province of Arezzo, (1394), but the negotiations were complicated, as he wanted at the same time to liquidate his annuity for a fixed sum.

After many discussions the affair was concluded by the *provvisione*, approved by the Council of the Commune with 181 votes against 24;—here is the substance of it:

> Considering that Hawkwood, weary by reason of his great age, and, as he asserts, weighed down by infirmity, wishes to return to his old country, and to dispose of his pension, as well as the under mentioned among others of his possessions, and hence to make an exchange or composition (*staglum*); taking into account the negotiations which for some months we have been making, both on the part of the Commune and on that of Sir

John; and wishing to dispose of them as seems most advantageous to the Commune, the council of the *Gonfalonieri* together with that of the twelve *Buonomini* after serious deliberation ordain,

That the recipient Commune shall by public act be liberated and absolved from the here written pensions and sums due to Sir John, in such a manner that they shall not last longer than the present month of March, (1394), and from thenceforward shall no longer be due, but from that moment the Commune shall be free of them;

The chamberlains of the Commune shall pay to Sir John or his procurator six thousand golden florins without any deduction, and without other formalities except the present provision, the payment of which sum shall be made as will be declared below;

With the addition, however, that the herein mentioned fortresses, strongholds and possessions shall be held by the Commune, and to this end that all the rights appertaining to them shall be conceded by Sir John or his procurator, placing the Commune in their possession and custody.

Pensions and sums owing, above mentioned.

1st of 1200 gold florins annually for the duration of his life, granted in 1375;

2nd of 2000 gold florins yearly for his life, conceded on April 1st 1391;

3rd of 1000 gold florins granted to the Lady Donnina wife of Sir John, as long as she lives with her children in the city, country or district of Florence (April *ditto*);

4th sum of 2000 gold florins assigned as *dote* to the third daughter of Sir John (April *ditto*).

Fortresses and Places.

Castle of Montecchio;

Stronghold or Castle of the Abbey of the Pino;

Stronghold of Migliaris;

with the rights, jurisdictions, appurtenances, tribunals, men and persons etc.

Of the said sum of six thousand gold florins two thousand to be paid immediately, the other four thousand in three rates, the first within four months, the second within eight months, the third and last within a year.

Moreover, as it is said that Sir John wishes to leave us, and with his family to go to England whence he had his origin that the *Signoria* shall appropriate a thousand gold florins to purchase the objects with which they think well to honour Sir John and his son, according to the credit and magnificence of the Commune.

That the sums to be paid as above cannot in any manner or for any claim be sequestered under penalty of a thousand small florins.

All questions which might arise, concerning the execution of that which is above mentioned, shall be settled by the *Signoria* and their decision shall have absolute force.

That the *Signoria* shall dispose as to the custody, government and administration of the three castles which are ceded.

Finally, that the contracts or acts which are stipulated in order as above shall be free from all and every tax.

Man proposes and God disposes: five days after this *provvisione*, Hawkwood, who had for some time been reduced to pass his time between the bed and the couch, instead of setting out for his fatherland, departed for that journey which has no return.

How Messer Giovanni Acuto captain of war of the Commune of Florence died, and how the Commune paid him the greatest honours and he was interred in Santa Maria del Fiore.

Thus, runs the title of a chapter in the chronicle of Piero Minerbetti, which assigns the date of March 16th as the day of his death, while the 17th results from documents. It may have been during the night between the 16th and 17th. It says that Hawkwood was ill at his place outside the city (without doubt it was San Donato), but that he died from a stroke of apoplexy.

The Priors elected a commission of citizens to order and provide splendid obsequies, without regard to expense, and they proved really grand.

All the priests of the city attended, meeting in Santa Maria del Fiore; the *catafalque* was gorgeous; the choir, and other convenient places of the church were full of lighted torches.

The *Signoria* provided handsome black dresses for his son, wife and daughters, and all the numerous household.

The bier, adorned with very rich drapery of crimson velvet and gold, was first placed on the Piazza della Signoria, where the funeral procession formed, and to which all the magistrates contributed; *i.e.*

the *Signoria* sent a hundred large wax torches, a banner with the arms of the Commune, another with the arms of the people, a standard with the arms of the Commune, and the shields pertaining thereto, a helmet with a golden lion with a lily in his claw as a crest. This was a Florentine ensign, and would seem to symbolise the valour of the *condottiere* who was so faithful to the Commune.

The captains of the Guelph faction sent twenty wax torches, a pennon with the Guelph arms, and a helmet with the same design as a crest.

The "Six of the Mercanzia" sent twenty wax torches, and moreover they personally attended, together with the consuls of the Arts.

The soldiers of Hawkwood's lances with fourteen caparisoned horses carried several flags and pennons with his arms, his helmet with its crest, and the pennon with the Harpy (an ensign almost too eloquent), his sword and his shield.

The bier was raised by the cavaliers of Florence, none of whom were missing, as it was to do honour to such an illustrious comrade, and was carried to fetch the corpse where it lay (probably from San Donate it had been placed in some church in the city). It was laid on the open bier robed in cloth, of gold, and the cavaliers carried it to San Giovanni (the Baptistery) and placed it on the holy baptismal font covered with cloth of gold. Here Hawkwood was wept for by the women in the presence of a great crowd, for all the shops of Florence were closed.

★★★★★★

Manni observed how Dante desired similar solemn funeral rites in the Baptistery.

He noted the error of those who arbitrarily amplified the women weeping (*donne piangenti*) over Hawkwood's bier into noble matrons (*nobili matrone*); these were nothing more than a derivation from the Roman *preficie*,(mourning women), and the custom is still kept up in many places on the Mediterranean.

★★★★★★

He was then carried into the Duomo, and placed under the *catafalque*, where the clergy recited the office, and a funeral oration was pronounced.

Finally, he was interred in the place temporarily ordained, and the *Signoria* and people returned to their houses. (The diarist Simone della Tosa observed that the *Signoria* were accustomed never to go out of the palace unless on occasions of the greatest solemnity.)

226

The place chosen was in the choir, and here Manni observes: "This was not the present choir but the first and more ancient wooden one," and supposes every vestige of the sepulchre was lost, either when the new choir was made, or when the pavement was re-covered with marble (1519-1524).

But it is also likely that the temporary place of sepulture in the choir had no especial mark, the definite tomb having been decreed seven months before. It was not built however, as the remains were sent to King Richard II in England.

Minerbetti's description in prose is precisely analogous to that of a contemporaneous *Cantare* in *rima ottava*.

If the *Obsequies and honours made for Messer Giovanni Aguto our captain of war* furnished the argument for popular poesy, and inspired a poem of ingenuous but decidedly elegiac character, it shows that the man was sincerely loved and esteemed in Florence. There was nothing now to hope or to fear from the dead man: the sumptuous official observances decreed by the magistrates might have been the fruit of political prudence, to shew to future *condottieri*, that the Commune knew how to value and recompense their fidelity; but the verses correspond to a heartfelt sentiment, to the sincere opinion of the citizens.

This is the more valuable in that the verses retained their popularity for many years afterwards. Benedetto Dei, who wrote his chronicle late in the 15th century, remarked that he knew them by heart. The poet is not known, but this matters little: he was the interpreter of all the people.

To the details described by Minerbetti the *Cantare* adds his own, from which we learn that the ensigns, flags, and helmets with crests were carried on large war chargers, draped with housings and breast plates; it is specified that the flags offered by the wife and family of Hawkwood were six in number; that the general closing of shops was ordered under penalty, and many men dressed in black by the Commune followed the bier with their heads covered with hoods, as a sign of great grief; and that a multitude of priests walked behind bearing torches and candles and singing psalms. There were the minor friars, the Servite monks, those of San Marco, Ognissanti, Monte Uliveto, the Dominicans, the monks of the Angioli, the Carmine, San Miniato and "all the rest" (*tutti quanti*), and all the bells rang out a death peal.

At the holy font of the Baptistery, the corpse was exposed on the bier, which was surrounded by thirty wax torches; a drawn sword was laid on the breast, and the *bâton* of command in the hand.

The obsequies in the Duomo being finished, the priests carried the body into the sacristy.

The *Cantare* ends by invoking from the Lord and the Madonna eternal life and supernal glory for him who had lived under the wings of victory.

CHAPTER 42

The Monument in Santa Maria Del Fiore

The state ceremonials of Hawkwood's funeral (April 14), were costly in proportion to their grandeur: the account was made up, with a result of 410 gold florins, 1 *lira*, 11 *soldi*. There still remained to provide the monumental tomb, in conformity to the deliberations taken during Hawkwood's life, and as in those days no public work of any importance was admitted in the city unless it fulfilled the exigencies of art, the following "provision" was taken, which is mentioned, (1395), by C. I. Cavallucci:

> Being desirous of renewing in a more decent manner the tomb of Piero Farnese and satisfying the provision of the Commune respecting the monument—the *operai*, (members of the "Opera" of the Duomo, a large society of influential citizens, artists and architects, who superintended the works of the Duomo), wishing to place the said tombs in the *façade* which is between the two doors towards Via dei Cassettai, (on the north side of the cathedral), will cause to be made: and they commission Agnolo di Taddeo Gaddi and Giuliano d'Arrigo, painters, to design and paint them for the price of thirty florins.

★★★★★★

Note:—Piero Farnese, a worthy captain, died, in the service of Florence against the Pisans, in 1362 the year before the English came into Tuscany. He also was honoured by the Florentines with a sepulchral monument in Santa Maria del Fiore: there is still seen his marble *sarcophagous* over the first lateral door to the right, adorned with the lily and the cross of Florence, the arms of the Guelph party and the Farnese lilies, formerly the *sarcophagous* supported a canopy over the statue of Piero Farnese mounted on a mule, to record that in the day of his victory over the Pisans his horse had been killed and he had continued to fight mounted on a mule; but both statue and canopy, which were of wood painted and gilt, tumbled to pieces in 1842 when they were removed to clean the inner walls of the cathedral.

★★★★★★

But then a request came to the Commune of Florence, which truly honoured the memory of John Hawkwood: the King of England demanded that the body of the warrior should be restored to his native country; and the Commune did not refuse it, perhaps remembering that a little time before his death Hawkwood was arranging everything for his return home. The consent of the *Signoria* was given in the following letter dated June 3rd 1395, (the text has been published by Manni):

> Most serene and invincible prince, most reverend lord and our especial benefactor.
> Our devotion can deny nothing to the eminence of your highness. We will leave nothing undone that it is possible to do, that we may fulfil your good pleasure. And therefore, although we hold that it reflected glory on us and on our people to keep the ashes and the bones of the late brave soldier, and most remarkable leader Sir John Hawkwood (*Haukkodue*) who, as commandant of our army, fought most gloriously for us, and whom at the public expense we interred honourably in the principal church of our city, nevertheless, according to the tenor of your request, we freely concede permission that his remains shall return to his native land, so that it shall not be said that your sublimity has uselessly and in vain demanded anything from the reverence of our humility. . . .

The ashes of Hawkwood having been transported to England, it no longer appeared urgent to erect his tomb and that his memory would be sufficiently honoured by the fresco which had been painted to serve as a model on the wall of the Duomo. Time went on to 1436, when they were setting the Duomo in order for the solemn consecration which was to be given by Pope Eugene IV who was in Florence for the famous council. Either because the picture had suffered or they wanted it to be a little more decorous, the *"operai"* deliberated (May 18, 1436), "to repaint the figure of Sir John Hawkwood in the same manner and form as it was before painted." A few days afterwards (May 26), the idea prevailed of erecting the monument:

> Let us make the tomb of Signor Giovanni Hanto according to the decisions of the councils of the People and the Commune of Florence, and hasten them in the work for the honour of the

229

Commune and the Opera.

But this proposal only lasted a few hours; for reasons it is allowable to suppose of economy, they returned to the idea of the *fresco* (May 30): and Paolo Uccello was commissioned to paint the figure of Hawkwood in *terra verde* (a colour that imitated bronze) where it was at first, and with the salary which shall be determined.

Neither ability nor reputation were wanting in Paolo Uccello; he was however unfortunate, as we read of him in Vasari: he executed the commission rapidly it is true, but with little success. In fact, it was deliberated in council, (June 28):

> That the head master of the works of the Duomo should cause the horse and figure of Sir John Hawkwood done by Paolo Uccello to be destroyed, because it is not painted as it should be.

We must admit that some kind of merit was acknowledged even in that first work, for the commission was renewed to the same artist. (July 6.)

> Paolo Uccello shall again paint and portray in *terra verde* the figure of Signer Giovanni Hauto and of the horse of the said Sir John, for the salary and price which shall be established.

This time Uccello employed an extra fortnight and no objection was raised: the "*operai*" commissioned, (August 31), two of their number, Francesco di Benedetto di Caroccio Strozzi and Simone di Noferi Bonaccorsi, "to put a price on the picture of the horse and person of Sir John Hawkwood, painted in the principal Florentine church."

Vasari says:

> This work, was then thought, and is still considered, one of great beauty of its kind; and if Paolo had not made the horse move his legs on one side only, which horses do not naturally do, since they would fall if they did (which happened, perhaps, because the artist was not accustomed to ride, or to see so much of horses as of other animals), the work would have been perfect. The proportions of the horse, which, as has been observed, is of immense size, are extremely beautiful. On the basement are inscribed the following letters: *Pauli Uccelli opus*.

For the rest the criticism of Vasari on the horse does not hold, as Fossombroni and several other competent observers cited by Cicognara have shown: Hawkwood's horse has the pace of the *ambio* (amble).

The *fresco* was transferred to canvas about 1845 and moved from the northern to the western wall of the Duomo over the lesser door on the left, while above the right door is, also in *fresco*, the equestrian figure of another *condottiere* much esteemed in Florence—Niccolo Tolentino.

Paolo Uccello's grand picture of Hawkwood, with a stone cornice in the style of the decorations of the Duomo, occupies almost all the wall; the cornice rests on two half capitals with rich foliage of acanthus leaves. The equestrian statue stands out from the reddish-purple back-ground, framed in a wide and elegant frieze of "grotesques," and other renaissance mouldings painted in grey "chiaroscuro" on gold colour. Hawkwood has a cap on his head, and a short doublet over the armour; he holds in his right hand the *bâton* of captain of war. A *sarcophagous*, resting on a fine architectural base of two grades, serves as a pedestal for the statue. The whole is in a monotone bronze green, except the arms, the housings and harness of the horse which are of a scarlet colour with large silver bosses.

So, this picture gives no authority for the assertion that Hawkwood was of a ruddy complexion, with brown hair and eyes: we can only see that he was of more than medium height, with broad shoulders, powerful client, and the very build of a warrior. His face seems to have been entirely shaved (a custom taken probably from the Bretons in Lombardy, where the word *britonare* long remained, meaning "to shave," but the usage was general in Tuscany a long while before the English came there).

We may admire the regular and sculpturesque features, in which the English may recognise not only the type of their own race, but see that in character they especially resemble the hereditary physiognomy of the Stanley family.

The epigraph, composed by Bartolommeo di Ser Filippo Fortini, says:

JOANNES ACUTUS EQUES BRITANNICUS
DUX AETATIS SUAE CAUTISSIMUS ET REI
MIL1TARIS PERITISSIMUS HABITUS EST.

It is a modest and reserved epigraph, whose truthfulness we cannot doubt, and to which we, who have studied the life of the *condottiere*, may even find something to add. It is decidedly preferable in every way to the bombastic epigram with which Giulio Feroldo pretended to celebrate the imaginary portrait of Hawkwood, published among the "Illustrious warriors" by Paolo Giovio.

The short biography compiled by the famous bishop of Como is merely fantastic, but it proves that the fame of the English adventurer survived for several generations in Italy.

Nor was the memory of his achievements soon extinguished in the popular tradition: for several years after his death his name was not only still extolled, but the details of his feats of arms were generally known.

★★★★★★

We have already noticed and the reader of this story will have verified the multitude of variations with which the documents and the contemporaneous chroniclers wrote the name of Hawkwood.—Some chroniclers even mistook his nationality: the *Chronicle of Rimini* called him "a great German commander."—And even learned men of modern times had a difficulty in finding the orthography of the esotic surname: Michele Luigi Malpeli, publishing in 1806 the *Dissertations on the ancient history of Bugnacavallao* speaking of Acuto, observes in a note: "This English surname was Karcond."

★★★★★★

I like a man who is subtile and long sighted. Perhaps that is what my friend does when he quotes to me the ruse of Sir John Hawkwood when he wanted to flee.

. . . . You who give out that I like to live in disorder, do you not remember that story of Sir John Hawkwood!

. . . . . Is it not true. . . . that John Hawkwood was not worth 500 lances.

These allusions are found here and there in the interesting *Familiar letters of Ser Lapo Mazzei* written at the beginning of the 15th century.

In fact, the best Italian *condottieri* who bore arms in Italy after Hawkwood, *i.e.* Alberico da Barbiano, Attendolo Sforza, Braccio da Montone, not less than Carlo Malatesta, Paolo Orsini, and Mostarda, may be considered as his disciples in the art of war, for if not wholly pupils they fought with or against him. As Ricotti justly observes:

I do not know if Giovanni Acuto were the last of the foreign *condottieri* or the first of the Italian ones, that is the first who designed and perfected those military factions with a certain science. Next in rank came Braccio and Sforza with their two schools, (the *Braccesque* and the *Sforzesque.*)

Hereditary Liquidation

The illustrious *condottiere* being honourably interred, the Florentine Commune gave its attention to the execution of the compacts made with him almost in *articulo mortis.* The mercantile spirit of the citizens suggested the expedience of procuring some advantage, some prerogative, while giving effect to those stipulations, seeing that *chi muore giace* (he who dies lies still), they thought it urgent beyond everything to go directly and take possession of the Castle of Montecchio. (April 6, 1394.)

They easily induced the widow Donnina to write to the castellan that he should consign the fortress to them, and accompanied the letter with the following message which we translate:

To Richard Kell, castellan of Montecchio.
Our well beloved! According to the agreement which we made not long ago with the magnificent Sir John 'Haucud' when he was in this life, his noble consort the lady Donnina writes that you may concede to us the fortress of Montecchio, with its guard and garrison. We require therefore that you consign the same, with all the munitions of war which it contains, to Antonio Materio, our well-beloved familiar, whom we send for this purpose, and who will receive it in the name of our Commune by public act of notary. Then, as soon as may be without inconvenience to yourself, we beg you to come into the presence of our *Signoria,* to the effect that we may know what is due to you for stipend and *provvigione,* which we shall pay integrally, and send you without delay. (April 25.)

We see that if Florence demanded her dues, she did not refuse to give the same to others. The last contract was to the effect that the engagement of the twenty-five lances, and the stipend of 1200 florins, and the pension of 2000 florins would not cease till the end of March.

It was therefore requested of the *Signoria* on behalf of his children that the payment might be effected for the whole month, although Hawkwood died on the 17th, subtracting only the payment of the fifteen lances, who were serving the Commune at Mantua, and were there directly paid by it; and that the required payments should be made to any procurator of the late Sir John, who should have permanent power of attorney since his death. The petition was made "so that the said children may pay the expenses of the funeral and the domestics who had served Hawkwood during his life." On the whole it was a claim founded on justice, (April 27), and was accepted with 188 votes against 28. (*Provvisione* published by Antonio Modin.)

Had Hawkwood made a will? It was asserted that he had, and it was even added (for example in the *Dictionary of the 19th Century*) that he left a legacy to found in Rome a hospital for English pilgrims, as though in expiation for the rapacity of his career, and for not having taken the cross against the *infidels* as he had promised. It is certain that this problematic foundation had not a canonical institution. If he ever made a last testament, he did not make it in Florence; the archives of Florentine notaries exist in a complete and well-arranged condition, classified by quarters; the indices of the testator's name drawn up in Florence after 1350, were taken from the *Opera of the Duomo*, which exacted a small tax for each will. We have found a mention of the will of John Berwick (Giovanni Berichie) in 1385, but no sign of that of John Hawkwood.

Nor does his name figure in the registers of the hospital of St. Maria Nuova, to which it was the custom in those days to leave some alms in every will.

But although he intended to return to England, he feared his end was drawing nigh; a deed executed on January 10th 1395, of which we shall soon see the substance, commenced by recalling the transaction of March 1394, with these particulars, that:

> Hawkwood, weighed down by old age and a certain singular infirmity (?) which almost continually keeps him in bed or in the house, not being able to fulfil his military or other duties, *but rather fearing a speedy death*, is prudently induced etc.

Nor did Hawkwood die without leaving a general power of attorney in the interest of his children, to Giovanni di Iacopo Orlandini: and his faith was fully justified, for Orlandini executed the trust with much zeal.

The final compact with Hawkwood reserved to the *Signoria* the resolution of eventual questions, and these were not long in rising up.

By force of that contract the Commune was to pay 1000 florins to honour the departure of Hawkwood, who intended to go to England: death prevented the journey—ought those 1000 florins to be paid notwithstanding?

And how could they pay the 2000 florins of wedding portion to Anna third daughter of the deceased? as she was under age, and had no guardian or possibility of having one, and being a minor, she was not empowered to give a receipt? In every way the *Signoria* and the Councils, acknowledging the propriety of faithfully observing the agreement, deliberated (December 15), to consider Orlandini as procurator of Anna the minor, and to pay to him her portion and the donation of 1000 florins.

Through Orlandini's zeal and the goodwill of the *Signoria*, the liquidation of accounts between Hawkwood's heirs and the Commune proceeded expeditiously. The Commune decided, (December 22), that:

> The nobleman John *fils*, and the daughters of the deceased John Hawkwood, and therefore his inheritance and estates, and the estates of the said John his son, shall not at any time nor by any claim be summoned, taxed or molested either in the city, country or district of Florence, by anyone who is not of Florentine birth or of Florentine parentage on the male side, for any obligation contracted in his life by the aforesaid *quondam* John Hawkwood.

This was according to international private right, as it then existed, but it might happen that some Florentine would buy the credits and in that case the benefit would all go to the usurers.

The widow Donnina, to obtain power of administration, declared (January 10, 1395), that she required a tutor (*mundualdus*) who could authorise her legal acts instead of her deceased consort, and begged that the notary would allow Orlandini to be this legal guardian. This being done and drawn up, she:

> With the consent, authority, and permission of the guardian, being certified by the notary of her rights, and of that which she was about to do, accepted the transaction of March 12th, inasmuch as regarded her annual pension of 1000 florins, and gave a receipt in full with a promise *in perpetuo* never to demand it again, under penalty of 2000 florins.

It is noteworthy that the deed was executed "in the house of habitation of the before mentioned lady in the parish of Santa Maria di Quarto, *pieve* di Santo Stefano in Pane." She lived then in the suburbs, but not at San Donato, which confirms that Hawkwood must have effected the sale of his possessions in preparation for his intended return home, only reserving the temporary use of San Donato.

Correlative to the above, Giacomo Orlandini as agent to the deceased Hawkwood gave on the following day, (January 11, 1395), a full receipt and promise never again to demand the annual pensions of 1200 and 2000 florins, nor the 2000 florins for Anna's wedding portion and the 1000 florins of yearly pension to the widow Donnina. He moreover ceded and transferred to the Commune the proprietorship and possession of the fortresses in the Arezzo territory.

The said Orlandini besides, of his own spontaneous will, moved thereto by affection for the son of Sir John for whom he had long conducted negotiations, and so that the 1000 gold florins might be paid by the Commune besides the 6000 (according to the contract of March 12th and the declaration of December 15th, 1394), engaged that Anna's wedding portion of 2000 florins should never be required of the Commune, he being himself the guarantee to hold the Commune indemnified for any pretension to the whole or a part of this claim.

A last difficulty arose, derived from a new law of December 1394, respecting the payment of stipends, which was resolved by abrogating this law for the occasion, (February 25); consequently, recognising that to the late (*olim*) John Hawkwood 7000 gold florins, in all, are due, of which his agent has as yet received 5000, the chamberlains are authorised to place on the side of expenditure the payment of the entire sum.

In fact, the registers of the Chamber show that the payments, begun October 1st 1394, were completed and regulated under the two dates of March 4th and 10th 1395, *i.e.*:

March 4th florins	2000		
	1333	*soldi* 6	*danari* 8
	1333	6	8
March 10th	1000		
	1333	13	4
	————	——	——
	6999	25	20

The 1000 florins, as we know, were those destined to compliment the departure of Hawkwood for England: but in the register of the chamberlains they are entered to *honour the son of Sir John*.

And in truth Hawkwood's son was flattered and favoured by the Commune in regard for the merits of his father. Whilst the suits relating to the liquidation of the paternal estate were pending, Giovanni Augud junior was engaged with two lances, comprising his own person and lance, from January 4th to the end of March 1395, with a stipend of 16 gold florins a month each lance. There is nothing to show that he was already a man of war, and this appears to be merely a mark of honorary courtesy.

Having terminated the arrangements of the patrimonial affairs in Italy, the widow Donnina decided to go to England with her children (*i e.* John and the young girl Anna), for her husband had also left possessions in his native land, which required the eye of a master in those times which were so hard for orphans and widows.

The Signoria of Florence did not fail to introduce the widow and her children to the King of England by the following letter of recommendation, which we here translate:

To the King of England.

Most serene and most glorious prince, and our lord and singular benefactor.

We cannot in any way neglect the posterity of your subject, the noble and brave knight Sir John Hawkwood, who for a long time has faithfully and with true honesty fought in our service, nor may we omit to render honour and service to him in every possible manner, the more so that the progeny of that man, whose glorious celebrity reflected honour on all the English nation, are left far away from their fatherland, and since the death of that worthy sire find themselves as strangers and pilgrims in Italy, although for the merits of the father, our city is disposed to embrace them, and welcome them as our own children.

★★★★★★

Note:—How much Hawkwood's achievements raised the reputation of the English in the Florentine minds, is seen in the negotiations about the hiring of Nicholas Clifton, recommended by the King of England, and who had before been in the Florentine service (see chapter 21).

★★★★★★

Therefore, it is that their mother—a consort truly worthy of such a husband—having decided, as soon as the age of her children will allow of it, to transfer herself with them to England; we with all possible devotion recommend the children and family of the aforesaid Sir John to your Highness, with every reverence, and with all the affection in our power, supplicating the clemency of your sublimity, that from the height of your exalted state you will deign to receive these wards with benevolence, and aid their undertakings with your royal favour. And verily the estates under wardship are those of the widow and orphans, whom divine laws ordain shall be taken care of by the princes of the world, and judges of the earth.

Therefore we add that it becomes your royal majesty to remember with grateful memory, even after death, the virtue of those subjects who shed honour on your country, so that the minds of others may be inspired to show themselves equally great, and the reward of their good works may be transferred to their heirs; so that they may hope to live in fame even after death, seeing that by the merits of their fathers the children of the brave receive especial favours and grace. As to us and our devotion, most benevolent prince, we cannot express how acceptable and pleasing anything which may be done for the family of the aforesaid Sir John will prove to us.

Given from Florence, March 29th. III indiction (1395).

Chapter 44
Hawkwood's Descendants

Notwithstanding the warm recommendation of the Florentines, it is not known precisely whether Donnina Visconti put into effect that removal into England which she had planned. The letter in which the Commune of Florence granted, (see chapter 42), to King Richard the remains of John Hawkwood for which he had asked; concludes with the following expressions, without mentioning the widow (June 30):

> The son and the posterity of the said Sir John, who rendered famous the name and glory of Englishmen in Italy, and also our merchants and citizens, we recommend to the benevolence of your highness with all due reverence and with all possible supplication.

★★★★★★

Just as the name *Francesco* in Italy increased after Italian intercourse with the French, so the military predominance of the English in the second half of the 14th century gave rise to the names *Inghilesco* and *Inghilese*; a daughter of Bernabo Visconti was also called *Inglesia*.

★★★★★★

Perhaps the widow remained in Italy, where her kinship and the high esteem inherited from her husband enabled her to marry her third daughter as well as the others. (It seems that Hawkwood asked Niccolo one of the illustrious and rich Sienese family of the Salimbeni to be godfather to one his children, and his friendship with Acciaioli is also well-known.)

The latter in fact (as we know from a book of *Riformngioni* of 1418 cited by Manni) married Ambroginolo di Piero della Torre, of the great Milanese family, a relative of Buonamico della Torre, who was captain of the people at Florence in 1420, and *podestà* in 1431; the marriage was not ill-assorted, as the Torriani had already fallen not only from the Signoria of Milan, but also from the successive patriarchal splendour of Friuli.

Manni supposes that from this same Anna was born another Donnina, who afterwards married the Milanese captain Giovanni Casati, and was the mother of the humanist Scipio Casati: but Manni was sometimes at fault in his suppositions, as for instance when he thought that Hawkwood was the son of a certain Anizzo because he had sometimes found the name Anisi united with that of John Hawkwood in matters of war; but we know that this was no other than the German Anisi di Ricten.

And were there not some romancing genealogists who wanted to trace the descent of the Lords of Montauto and Anghiari from Hawkwood?

It is not known whether Hawkwood's race was perpetuated in Italy through Catherine wife of the valiant German Conrad Prospergh. As to Janet who had married Brezaglia di Porcia, some documents in Friuli (which from her place of residence call her Zannetta di Castell' alto), state that in 1425 she was left a widow without children.

In the *Transactions of the archaeological society of Essex* we find named as the wife of Sir William de Coggeshall "Antiocha, daughter and heiress of the famous warrior Sir John Hawkwood, and of Aufricia his wife, the natural daughter of Bernabo Duke of Milan." Let us pass over the fact that Bernabo was not a duke, let us pass over the name of Aufricia given to the wife of Hawkwood, and merely note that the silence of the Florentine documents entirely excludes the existence of a fourth daughter from that marriage.

For the same reason we cannot admit a fifth, Fiorantina who, according to Corio, was married to Lancelot of the noble Milanese family del Mayno. Perhaps Fiorentina was the daughter of Hawkwood's first wife, whose name is entirely unknown, and who is not *documentally* proved to be his legitimate wife. That she was a legal wife rather than mistress is however confirmed by the memorial on the monument erected to Hawkwood in his native place.

At Sible Hedingham, near Hawkwood's Manor, in the parish church of St. Peter, may be still seen a part of a canopy under an arch, where there once rose a noble cenotaph; the arch bore the allusive heraldic decoration of a hawk flying amidst trees (Hawk-wood), and several figures of hawks are sculptured in other parts of the church. This suffices to make it clear that the monument belonged to a Hawkwood, and that the church, whose architecture answers to the epoch of Edward III, but whose foundations are much more ancient, was rebuilt or restored, at the expense, or by liberal contributions from one of the Hawkwood family, in the last half of the 14th century. There seems no doubt that the monument was precisely the tomb of our John Hawkwood.

It had been for some time destroyed for the substitution of benches in 1631, when John Weever wrote, but both he and Morant agree that with the abundant (?) money yielded by the heritage of Hawkwood, and sent to England, his friends erected the cenotaph: and Morant (who must have seen some old design) adds:

"From the effigies on this monument it would seem that he had two wives."

Weever even gives the names of these zealous friends, who were Robert Rokeden senior, Robert Rokeden junior and John Cook—perhaps the man whom Italian chroniclers called *Cocco* and who was amongst the leaders in Hawkwood's Company. And not content with perpetuating the memory and providing a tomb for the captain, they also took thought for his soul, by founding a chapelry in the same church, and another in the Priory of Hedingham castle "to pray for the souls of Sir John Hawkwood, and of Thomas Oliver (there are still Olivers in Essex, 1880), and John Newenton Esquires, two of his comrades who died in Italy."

The priest of the chapelry of Sible Hedingham lived in a house close by, called the Hostage (anciently Hostelage) because it formerly served as a hospice for pilgrims.

Thus, the man who in his life time had always renounced peace, had solemn repose after death with many prayers and *requiems*.

As to his son, the father's reputation and the recommendations of the Florentines, united to his patrimonial heritage, rendered him good service in his fatherland. He was created knight and naturalised in the eighth year of King Henry IV, as appears from the Record *Johannis filius Johannis Hawkewood, miles, natus in partibus Italiae, factus indigena anno 8 Henrici IV: mater ejus nata in partibus transmarinis.* (1407)

These favours, like the homage rendered by King Richard II to the memory of Hawkwood, in asking the Florentines for his remains, shew that if there had been circumstances in the fortunate life of the *condottiere* which caused him to fall into disgrace with his natural sovereign, the position achieved by him in Italy had entirely rehabilitated him.

We speak thus because in the English Parliament Rolls, in the 51st year of Edward III, is registered (1376-77), a "petition of Sir John Hawkwood to the king demanding a patent of pardon as the king has promised to Sir Robert Knolles," (Hawkwood's comrade, see chapter 2), for God and charity. We must however confess that there is no proof of the result of the petition, nor even whether it received an answer, and that we are not in a position to throw any light on the cause, or significance of the facts to which it refers, for at that time Hawkwood had been fighting fifteen years in Italy, where the King of England had no rights, nor interests, or disputes.

We can only risk a supposition: we already know that, (1368), when the Duke of Clarence, son of Edward III, died in Lombardy a short time after having married Violante Visconti, and her father Galeazzo lost no time in retaking possession of the places in Piedmont which had been given her as her portion, Hawkwood, without mixing himself in the contest, continued to serve the Visconti elsewhere. It might be that his conduct in this circumstance being considered by Edward III as incompatible with the loyalty of a subject, may have been declared to be criminal and punished as such, for example by banishing Hawkwood from the kingdom.

It is not probable that the petition was from John Hawkwood the elder brother of our *condottiere*, because he would have been distinguished as *senior*: there is in fact a document of the 45th year of Edward III, (1370-71), referring to a judicial sentence, respecting divers possessions, between Thomas de Vere Earl of Oxford and his wife Matilda on one part, and several persons qualified as usurpers on the other, John de Hawkwood senior being named among the usurpers.

To return to Hawkwood's son, who unlike his father had no history after his elevation to knighthood, we only learn from English papers that in the 10th year of Henry IV (1409), he had possessions to let at Padbury in Buckinghamshire, and that he married a certain Margaret with whom he lived to extreme old age. In 1464 the couple were still alive at Sible Hedingham, where they enjoyed the life-hold possession of eighty acres of land, probably under the high dominion of the Earls of Oxford.

At that epoch there were neither adventurers, *condottieri*, knights nor lances of English birth in Italy. The military forces were in the hands of Italian companies. France on her side had ended by repelling the invasions (perhaps legitimate but not national) of England, who was now wearying herself in the civil wars of the "two Roses."

Apropos of this, it was asserted that the emblems of the white and red Roses were brought back to England by the adventurers returning from Italy.

Catherine of Siena, writing to Queen Johanna of Naples, deploring the schism and war between the partisans of Pope Urban VI and the antipope Clement, added:

> Alas! how can you help your heart breaking when you think that they are divided on your account, and that one holds a white rose and the other a red?

And Niccolo Tommaseo. the saint's commentator, notes:

> They do not seem to be translated ensigns but real ones, there are no other mentions of them; and we only know that the arms of one of Urban's nephews were six red roses; perhaps Clement's French partisans had taken the white rose for opposition or in memory of the lily. Burlamacchi suspects that the English adventurers, dispersed from Count Alberico, carried those ill-omened ensigns to England after Hawkwood's death.

All these are mere fantasies: the lily of France was a golden one, not white: Count Alberico da Barbiano dispersed the Bretons and not the English: the Prignani, nephews of Urban VI, had not six roses for their arms. We do not know the origin of the symbols to which Catherine of Siena refers; and only find that white and red roses were taken as factional emblems in several of the southern Italian cities, for example at Benevento and Amalfi.

As to the origin of the two English roses, the history has been well told, and put on the stage with exquisite elegance by Shakespeare.

As we are quoting this universal poet, we may find in him a passage exactly applicable to John Hawkwood.

> Lucio. Thou concludest like the sanctimonious pirate, that put forth to sea with the ten commandements but scraped one of them out of the table.
>
> 2 GENT. Thou shalt not steal?
>
> Lucio. Aye! that he raz'd.
>
> 1 GENT. Why! 'twas a commandement, to command the Captaine and all the rest from their functions: they put forth to steal. There's not a souldier of us all, that in the thanksgiving before meate, do rallish the petition well, that praies for peace.

But Italy, who had received from England the curse of rapacious companies, and did not render "Measure for Measure," found her compensation some centuries later, when in the great enterprise of re-establishing her national unity, the English gave her a moral and political support which was truly valuable. And now the two people are the most sincere supporters, in Europe, of that peace whose very name John Hawkwood refused to hear invoked by mendicant friars.

243

LEONAUR

ALSO FROM LEONAUR
AVAILABLE IN SOFTCOVER OR HARDCOVER WITH DUST JACKET

THE FALL OF THE MOGHUL EMPIRE OF HINDUSTAN *by H. G. Keene*—By the beginning of the nineteenth century, as British and Indian armies under Lake and Wellesley dominated the scene, a little over half a century of conflict brought the Moghul Empire to its knees.

LADY SALE'S AFGHANISTAN *by Florentia Sale*—An Indomitable Victorian Lady's Account of the Retreat from Kabul During the First Afghan War.

THE CAMPAIGN OF MAGENTA AND SOLFERINO 1859 *by Harold Carmichael Wylly*—The Decisive Conflict for the Unification of Italy.

FRENCH'S CAVALRY CAMPAIGN *by J. G. Maydon*—A Special Correspondent's View of British Army Mounted Troops During the Boer War.

CAVALRY AT WATERLOO *by Sir Evelyn Wood*—British Mounted Troops During the Campaign of 1815.

THE SUBALTERN *by George Robert Gleig*—The Experiences of an Officer of the 85th Light Infantry During the Peninsular War.

NAPOLEON AT BAY, 1814 *by F. Loraine Petre*—The Campaigns to the Fall of the First Empire.

NAPOLEON AND THE CAMPAIGN OF 1806 *by Colonel Vachée*—The Napoleonic Method of Organisation and Command to the Battles of Jena & Auerstädt.

THE COMPLETE ADVENTURES IN THE CONNAUGHT RANGERS *by William Grattan*—The 88th Regiment during the Napoleonic Wars by a Serving Officer.

BUGLER AND OFFICER OF THE RIFLES *by William Green & Harry Smith*—With the 95th (Rifles) during the Peninsular & Waterloo Campaigns of the Napoleonic Wars.

NAPOLEONIC WAR STORIES *by Sir Arthur Quiller-Couch*—Tales of soldiers, spies, battles & sieges from the Peninsular & Waterloo campaingns.

CAPTAIN OF THE 95TH (RIFLES) *by Jonathan Leach*—An officer of Wellington's sharpshooters during the Peninsular, South of France and Waterloo campaigns of the Napoleonic wars.

RIFLEMAN COSTELLO *by Edward Costello*—The adventures of a soldier of the 95th (Rifles) in the Peninsular & Waterloo Campaigns of the Napoleonic wars.

LEONAUR

ALSO FROM LEONAUR
AVAILABLE IN SOFTCOVER OR HARDCOVER WITH DUST JACKET

OFFICERS & GENTLEMEN *by Peter Hawker & William Graham*—Two Accounts of British Officers During the Peninsula War: Officer of Light Dragoons by Peter Hawker & Campaign in Portugal and Spain by William Graham .

THE WALCHEREN EXPEDITION *by Anonymous*—The Experiences of a British Officer of the 81st Regt. During the Campaign in the Low Countries of 1809.

LADIES OF WATERLOO *by Charlotte A. Eaton, Magdalene de Lancey & Juana Smith*—The Experiences of Three Women During the Campaign of 1815: Waterloo Days by Charlotte A. Eaton, A Week at Waterloo by Magdalene de Lancey & Juana's Story by Juana Smith.

JOURNAL OF AN OFFICER IN THE KING'S GERMAN LEGION *by John Frederick Hering*—Recollections of Campaigning During the Napoleonic Wars.

JOURNAL OF AN ARMY SURGEON IN THE PENINSULAR WAR *by Charles Boutflower*—The Recollections of a British Army Medical Man on Campaign During the Napoleonic Wars.

ON CAMPAIGN WITH MOORE AND WELLINGTON *by Anthony Hamilton*—The Experiences of a Soldier of the 43rd Regiment During the Peninsular War.

THE ROAD TO AUSTERLITZ *by R. G. Burton*—Napoleon's Campaign of 1805.

SOLDIERS OF NAPOLEON *by A. J. Doisy De Villargennes & Arthur Chuquet*—The Experiences of the Men of the French First Empire: Under the Eagles by A. J. Doisy De Villargennes & Voices of 1812 by Arthur Chuquet .

INVASION OF FRANCE, 1814 *by F. W. O. Maycock*—The Final Battles of the Napoleonic First Empire.

LEIPZIG—A CONFLICT OF TITANS *by Frederic Shoberl*—A Personal Experience of the 'Battle of the Nations' During the Napoleonic Wars, October 14th-19th, 1813.

SLASHERS *by Charles Cadell*—The Campaigns of the 28th Regiment of Foot During the Napoleonic Wars by a Serving Officer.

BATTLE IMPERIAL *by Charles William Vane*—The Campaigns in Germany & France for the Defeat of Napoleon 1813-1814.

SWIFT & BOLD *by Gibbes Rigaud*—The 60th Rifles During the Peninsula War.

LEONAUR

ALSO FROM LEONAUR
AVAILABLE IN SOFTCOVER OR HARDCOVER WITH DUST JACKET

ESCAPE FROM THE FRENCH *by Edward Boys*—A Young Royal Navy Midshipman's Adventures During the Napoleonic War.

THE VOYAGE OF H.M.S. PANDORA *by Edward Edwards R. N. & George Hamilton, edited by Basil Thomson*—In Pursuit of the Mutineers of the Bounty in the South Seas—1790-1791.

MEDUSA *by J. B. Henry Savigny and Alexander Correard and Charlotte-Adélaïde Dard* —Narrative of a Voyage to Senegal in 1816 & The Sufferings of the Picard Family After the Shipwreck of the Medusa.

THE SEA WAR OF 1812 VOLUME 1 *by A. T. Mahan*—A History of the Maritime Conflict.

THE SEA WAR OF 1812 VOLUME 2 *by A. T. Mahan*—A History of the Maritime Conflict.

WETHERELL OF H. M. S. HUSSAR *by John Wetherell*—The Recollections of an Ordinary Seaman of the Royal Navy During the Napoleonic Wars.

THE NAVAL BRIGADE IN NATAL *by C. R. N. Burne*—With the Guns of H. M. S. Terrible & H. M. S. Tartar during the Boer War 1899-1900.

THE VOYAGE OF H. M. S. BOUNTY *by William Bligh*—The True Story of an 18th Century Voyage of Exploration and Mutiny.

SHIPWRECK! *by William Gilly*—The Royal Navy's Disasters at Sea 1793-1849.

KING'S CUTTERS AND SMUGGLERS: 1700-1855 *by E. Keble Chatterton*—A unique period of maritime history-from the beginning of the eighteenth to the middle of the nineteenth century when British seamen risked all to smuggle valuable goods from wool to tea and spirits from and to the Continent.

CONFEDERATE BLOCKADE RUNNER *by John Wilkinson*—The Personal Recollections of an Officer of the Confederate Navy.

NAVAL BATTLES OF THE NAPOLEONIC WARS *by W. H. Fitchett*—Cape St.Vincent, the Nile, Cadiz, Copenhagen, Trafalgar & Others.

PRISONERS OF THE RED DESERT *by R. S. Gwatkin-Williams*—The Adventures of the Crew of the Tara During the First World War.

U-BOAT WAR 1914-1918 *by James B. Connolly/Karl von Schenk*—Two Contrasting Accounts from Both Sides of the Conflict at Sea D uring the Great War.

Ingram Content Group UK Ltd.
Milton Keynes UK
UKHW041824240323
419083UK00013B/188/J